# REINHOLD NIEBUHR

# REINHOLD NIEBUHR

## A POLITICAL ACCOUNT

### PAUL MERKLEY

McGill-Queen's University Press
Montreal and London
1975

© McGill-Queen's University Press 1975
International Standard Book Number 07735 0216 5
Legal Deposit third quarter 1975
Bibliothèque nationale du Québec
Design by Hjordis P. Wills
Printed in Canada by T. H. Best Printing Co. Ltd.

This book has been published with the help of a grant
from the Social Science Research Council of Canada using
funds provided by the Canada Council.

# CONTENTS

# PREFACE

This book is meant as a contribution to political history, and it is as such that I would like it to be read. The events with which it deals did not take place at the center of political decision, nor even in the vestibules leading to the center, where one finds those who have the ear of the decision-makers. Many who have, at one time or another, held concessions at one or another corner in the vestibules—I am thinking, for instance, of Arthur Schlesinger, Jr.,[1] who was an assistant to President Kennedy; George F. Kennan,[2] who was Chief of the Policy Planning Staff under Secretary of State Marshall; McGeorge Bundy,[3] Kennedy's Special Assistant for National Security Affairs; and Vice-President Hubert Humphrey,[4] among others who have served Democratic presidents from Franklin Roosevelt through Lyndon Johnson—have left testimonials to the effect that Reinhold Niebuhr was their primary intellectual mentor. Even Niebuhr's severest critics are united in believing that he is the political philosopher *par excellence* of the passing generation of liberal intellectuals. To Christopher Lasch, for example, he is "the chief architect of the new liberalism," who is responsible for freezing political debate for two decades "in the polemical patterns of the late forties."[5] To Morton White, he is the villain whose "thunderous cannot" stultified political thinking for a generation.[6]

But in view of the low estate of theology among intellectuals generally, how did it happen that an American *preacher* came to be the intellectual mentor of that hard-nosed company of practical politicians which includes the Schlesingers, the Bundys, and the Humphreys? No one has stated this dilemma with greater clarity than Morton White—possibly because, as one who regrets Niebuhr's influence, he is not tempted to make things easier for Niebuhr's admirers:

> The contemporary liberal's fascination with Niebuhr, I suggest,
> comes less from Niebuhr's dark theory of human nature and more
> from his actual political pronouncements, from the fact that he
> is a shrewd, courageous, and right-minded man on many political

questions. Those who applaud his politics are too liable to turn
then to his so-called theory of human nature and praise it as the
philosophical instrument of Niebuhr's political agreement with
themselves. But very few of those whom I have elsewhere called
"atheists for Niebuhr" follow this inverted logic to its conclusion:
they don't move from praise of Niebuhr's theory of human
nature to praise of its theological ground. Therefore we may
admire them for drawing the line somewhere, but certainly not
for their consistency. . . . The fact is that once his unfaithful
admirers reject Niebuhr's theological doctrine of original sin
they have no way of justifying the implications of inevitability
and inexorability in that part of his doctrine which they do
accept.[7]

Exactly! It seems to me that those of Niebuhr's admirers who embrace
Niebuhr's political credo without embracing his theological presuppositions owe us some explanations. Niebuhr's own politics cannot at
any point be disengaged—even for purposes of passing discussion on
its "appropriateness" or its "relevance"—from his theology. It is the
entire argument of this book that Reinhold Niebuhr's *unmatched* influence upon the imagination of the liberal-intellectual generation of
the middle decades of this century is owing to the theological ground
of his work, and reflects the continuing dependence of political discussion upon ethics, and of ethics upon theology.
    The distinguished political philosopher Hans Morgenthau provides
us a broad hint in this direction:

I have always considered Reinhold Niebuhr the greatest living
political philosopher of America, perhaps the only creative
political philosopher since Calhoun. It is indicative of the
very nature of American politics and of our thinking about
matters political that it is not a statesman, not a practical
politician, let alone a professor of political science or of philosophy,
but a theologian who can claim this distinction of being the
greatest living political philosopher of America. For we have had
a tendency as a people—one that goes back to the eighteenth
century—to take our political institutions for granted, to regard
them as the best there could be, which need no philosophic
justification or intellectual elaboration.
. . . So it was unlikely, in view of the normal operations of the
American political system—the lack of sharp and stratified class
distinctions and of fundamental and permanent conflicts—that
there should arise [in our own time] a political philosophy from
within secular political society. It needed a man who could look

at American society, as it were, from the outside—*sub specie
aeternitatis*—to develop such a political philosophy; and that
man, I think, is Reinhold Niebuhr.[8]

To say that Reinhold Niebuhr was given to looking at American man
"*sub specie aeternitatis*" seems to me a needlessly coy way of saying
that he used the logic of theology. To say that this special gift of
Niebuhr's is the key to his success as "the greatest philosopher of
America" is to imply that a theological tradition is available to the
American intellectual as part of the complete inheritance of American
political debate.

I am aware that many of Niebuhr's most enthusiastic followers
(those whom Morton White has called "atheists for Niebuhr") believe
that his politics and his theology are readily separable. Niebuhr's
friend Sidney Hook insists that "logically not a single one of Reinhold Niebuhr's social, political and ethical views can be derived from
his theology."[9] It is no part of my purpose in this study to attempt
to prove Niebuhr's commanding influence upon this generation; if the
testimonies of the persons already cited do not suffice to demonstrate
this point, I know of no satisfactory way of doing it. I have written
these pages in order to demonstrate quite a different point: that in
Niebuhr's own intellectual pilgrimage theological commitment has
been the prime mover.

Quite apart from the inadvertent weaknesses in it, this book has
several intended gaps as well. I have deliberately avoided lengthy
treatment of those aspects of Niebuhr's work which have received
most attention in other books, and have given proportionately greater
attention to less publicized aspects of his work. Though I will have
much to say about the theological ground of Niebuhr's politics, this
is not a book about his theology—which is the subject of most of the
monographs. Several books, dissertations, and learned articles deal
with his contributions to political theory, and most of these dwell on
international affairs and upon the 1950s and 1960s. I have chosen to
emphasize the formative years (the 1920s, 1930s and 1940s), to give
more weight to domestic affairs, and to emphasize, as much as the
record permits, his practical political activities.

As a result, there is a warp in my work which the reader, if he
really cares to know all there is to know about Reinhold Niebuhr, will
have to correct by reading other works. Perhaps the best way of
discharging my obligation to the reader is to recommend to him that
to compensate for my neglect of systematic analysis of Niebuhr's
theology, he turn to the volume of essays edited by Charles W. Kegley
and Robert W. Bretall;* for political theory to Gordon Harland's

*Full titles are in the bibliography at the end of the book.

*The Thought of Reinhold Niebuhr*; and for analysis of his foreign policy writings of the 1950s and 1960s to Ronald Stone's *Reinhold Niebuhr: Prophet to Politicians.*

I have attempted to present Rienhold Niebuhr in a way that emphasizes the integrity of his life and work. He was a man of Pauline faith—which is to say, a man whose political behavior must be baffling to those who expect to find the key to a man's integrity either in philosophical consistency or in sociological situation. During a lifetime of active involvement in American political life, Reinhold Niebuhr did much good and a certain amount of mischief. Both the good and the mischief are traceable to the same source: his faith. For too long, Niebuhr has been misrepresented by the political theorists and the historians as a link in the pragmatic tradition. It is time we began to do Niebuhr the justice of taking him at his own evaluation —as a dogmatic Christian. The meaning of his own life, he believed, was in the keeping of God. And so, he believed, was the meaning of his nation's history. He believed that history was radically open to all possibilities of both good and evil until its end—and he could thus nonchalantly apply to America's collective destiny the dictum of St. Paul that he applied to his own: that, "whether we live, we live unto the Lord, and whether we die, we die unto the Lord; whether we live therefore or die we are the Lord's."

# ACKNOWLEDGEMENTS

So many generous and patient friends and colleagues have read and criticized parts of this work over several years that I am obliged to offer a blanket acknowledgement and beg all those who know that they belong to count themselves in. Gary Clarkson must be singled out, for he worked over the last draft for me and gave invaluable advice and moral assistance; and so must John Dourley, my favourite theologian, who emphatically disapproves of much that is in these pages.

Linda Alexander typed the final draft, and Barbara Dakin typed a mountain of correspondence: they are equally models of diligence and tolerance. I owe a very special debt to Lillian Bourke who for three years kept the secret of the Vice-Dean's research retreat (fourth floor, south wing, behind the door marked "Teaching Assistants: French"); and to Dean Derek W. Sida for his cooperation and encouragement. Grahame Hodgson worked with the manuscript over several weeks confirming citations for me. Ian Reesor did the bulk of the work on the Index, and with Joan Harcourt of McGill-Queen's University Press, worked very hard to tone things up in the last editorial stages.

For financial assistance of my research at the Library of Congress, I am indebted to the State University of California at Fresno, and to Carleton University. For their very special contribution to the success of this research I am deeply indebted to Werner and Anna Mattersdorff of Temple Hills, Maryland.

Some parts of the material in Chapters Fifteen and Sixteen appeared in articles published in the *Queen's Quarterly*, in the Autumn edition of 1964, and the Winter edition of 1971. For permission to quote from those of Reinhold Niebuhr's books which are published by Charles Scribner's Sons (see bibliography, page 273) and from June Bingham's *Courage to Change*, I express my gratitude to Charles Scribner, Jr., and Charles Scribner's Sons; and similarly for permission to quote from the book, *Leaves from the Notebooks of a Tamed Cynic*, and to make use of the Reinhold Niebuhr Papers, to Professor Ursula M. Niebuhr. (Mrs. Niebuhr's valuable anthology of certain of Reinhold Niebuhr's prayers and sermons, entitled *Justice and Mercy*, was published by Harper and Row as this book was in galleys, and thus does not appear in my bibliography).

PART

I

# BETHEL'S PASTOR

Chapter

# 1

# BEGINNINGS

This would be a duller world, and more dangerous besides, if everyone believed everything he was told merely because it had, for instance, the authority of the *Atlantic Monthly* behind it. Which is, no doubt, why Providence vouchsafes to us, from time to time, the likes of H. J. Behr—who threw down his copy of the July, 1916, edition of that magazine and fired off an angry letter to the editor:

> I have just read with interest in the July "Atlantic" an article by "Reinhold Neibuhr" [sic] on "The Failure of German Americanism."
>
> Who is "Reinhold Neibuhr?"
>
> He is not mentioned in a number of biographical references I have consulted, and it is quite posible that the foregoing is his pen name. If so is Mr. Neibuhr a German-American as you imply on the front cover? Or is this a Rooseveltian article insidiously dressed up to make sharper your thrust against Germans in America? It would be abhorrent to feel that British influence, and perhaps gold, have not only dominated the outgiving of our Press, but also added a touch of finesse to the usual integrity of the "Atlantic."[1]

A man with a name like Behr might, in the overheated atmosphere of 1916, be excused for doubting the genuineness of so incredibly Teutonic a name as Reinhold Niebuhr, attached as it was to an article castigating the German-Americans for their "indifference and hostility . . . to our ideals!"[2] But in truth Reinhold Niebuhr's Germanness was come by honestly. His father, Gustav, the son of a prosperous landowner of northwestern Germany, had come alone to America at the age of seventeen, in flight (as he later told his children) from the suffocating authoritarianism of his father, and of Prussian life in general. Gustav Niebuhr quickly made his way to one of those close-knit, and spiritually self-sufficient German-speaking communities of the nearer mid-west (in this case, near Freeport, Illinois) whose origins as settlement go back to the immediate post-Napoleonic wave of German-speaking immigration. By the time Gustav Niebuhr arrived on the scene, the heroic pioneer phase was well passed, and the current generation was enjoying a reasonably settled, comfortable-to-prosperous living. A quarter-century back, Carl Schurz, a political genius out of that company of larger-than-life refugees from the aborted German uprisings of 1848, had shepherded the Germans of mid-west America into the Republican party in time to be a possibly deciding factor in the nomination of Abraham Lincoln. Since then, the Germans of middle America had held a lien on a portion of the Republican party, and thus enjoyed a political security that other hyphenated-Americans could only envy. A sense of having partici-pated *en bloc* on the side of right in the Civil War was an essential part of the self-confidence of this community. For them, as for Carl Schurz, the great accomplishments of Lincoln's Republicans —the Homestead Act, the railroads, and of course Emancipation— were revolution enough. They fancied themselves the embodiment of America's character-building, class-levelling magic. The newer wave of social protesters (the Free Silver-ites, Farmers Alliance, Nation-alists, Single-Taxers, and the other radicals who would shake up politics in the 1890s in the movement we call Populism) would find little sympathy in this crowd. They were still as reliably Republican as their fathers and, if anything, even more deliberately German.

The success of mid-west Germans in maintaining their cultural identity owed much to their remarkably vital German-language press[3] —which in turn was owing to the inordinate proportion of intel-lectuals in the ranks of the class of 1848. It was also owing to the vigor of the German churches. In the mid-west, allegiance was divided between Lutherans (internally divided into rival Synods, which differed bitterly throughout the nineteenth century on matters of doctrine and polity) and the Evangelical Synod. The word "evan-gelical" (*Evangelische*) has a quite different burden in nineteenth-century German ecclesiastical history than it has in the British. In Germany, it signified the common Protestantism of Lutheran and Reformed (that is, Calvinist) traditions. In 1817, the Prussian King, Frederick William III, imposed an ecumenicism from above upon the Lutheran and Reformed Churches of his kingdom, under the name of the Evangelical Church of the Prussian Union. His example was followed by churches of the lesser German states; and from this point onward, the term "evangelical" applied to such united churches. German Lutherans already in America held back; and their leaders were in fact generally vehement against the watering-down of traditional distinctions of doctrine, polity and liturgy that these unions had brought about. But each new wave of German immigration, especially that from Prussia and the North generally, strengthened the Evangelicals. By stages, beginning with a conference of Reformed and Lutheran missionaries in Missouri in 1840, the Evangelical Union took distinct congregational shape in the American mid-west. By 1850, a theological seminary was established at Marthasville, Missouri (later called Webster Groves) under the name Eden Theological Seminary. In 1866 the denomination took the name German Evangelical Synod of the West, and in 1877, the name became the German Evangelical Synod of North America.

After some time as a farm laborer, Gustav Niebuhr entered theological studies at Eden Theological Seminary. During his first assignment as an assistant pastor in San Francisco, Gustav acquired a bride, Lydia Hosto, the daughter of the pastor. Then followed a series of calls of short duration to small Evangelical congregations throughout Missouri and Illinois. It was while they were serving the congregation at Wright City, Missouri, that Karl Paul Reinhold was born, in 1892. He was the fourth born, the third to survive infancy. Two years later, the family went to St. Charles, Missouri; and in 1902, when Reinhold was ten, to Lincoln, Illinois.[4] Reinhold Niebuhr remembered his father as a man of firm character and "vital personal piety"[5] with an irrepressible intellectual side to him, which he nourished by daily reading in Greek and Hebrew scriptures, in conscientious study of the newest theological wave out of Germany (Harnack, for example) and much secular reading, especially history. He was a complicated man, whose apparent serenity of spirit was hard-earned. As a Christian intellectual, he never permitted himself the indulgence of unexamined faith. His political liberalism was maintained only by constant wrestling against the internalized image of the Prussian ways he had voted against with his feet, at such a cost in social privilege and economic advantage. He was a vigorously committed progressive who doted on Theodore Roosevelt, in a community of self-righteous conservatives; he was a spiritual liberal among men who had, for the most part, long ago walled themselves off from the alien Anglo-American world with the strong defense of folk loyalties, compounded of not a little racial-nationalism, all under the protective coloration of religious faith.[6] Niebuhr recalled as well that his own decision for the Christian ministry was made in emulation of his father, and at the age of ten. He held to his decision apparently without faltering, despite the realization that he could not, in his father's denomination, expect to rise out of what he recalled as the "genteel poverty"[7] in which he was reared.

When he entered Eden Theological Seminary in 1912, Reinhold Niebuhr was not, by his own recollection (substantiated by the recollection of his contemporaries there) entering a very demanding intellectual company. When he graduated (in 1913), he was probably still more indebted to his father's scholarship than to his formal education. So far as the denomination was concerned, he was now a finished product; and so the wheels were set in motion to assign him to his first permanent pastorate.

But Reinhold Niebuhr didn't feel very finished. His petition for deferment of the obligation to undertake a permanent pastorate, for the sake of graduate training in some outside seminary, was received with some alarm by the elders of his denomination. It was not that Niebuhr planned to forsake the pastoral ministry for the ivory tower. Since his father's death in April of 1913 (during the last weeks of his graduating year at Eden), he had been serving the Lincoln congregation as a student pastor, and was making a good impression. (To have moved, with ·success, into the pulpit of a small congregation in a small and self-contained community that has watched you every step of the way since the age of ten, must surely test everything that needs testing in an apprentice preacher!) He was looking forward to a charge of his own. But the reading he had done under his father's aegis had raised questions in his mind that the complacent and conservative scholarship of his denominational college had not satisfied. The confidence that the denomination invested in Reinhold Niebuhr's sense of calling when they agreed to that deferment so that he might go off to Yale in the fall of 1913, was to be repaid many times over.

Yale it was, because by 1913 Yale's Divinity School had slipped out of the company of first-rank theological academies, its standards were "indifferent" (Niebuhr's word); and the most highly commended graduate out of the Evangelical Synod of North America could not expect to be taken as a prime candidate at a school of the first rank, such as Union Theological Seminary in New York. (So, at least, Reinhold Niebuhr recalled the situation.)[8] Even at Yale, Niebuhr had to contract with the Dean of the Graduate School to maintain straight A averages in return for the School's risk in accepting a student with such deficiencies as his education at Eden had, they said, left him with. It was a lesson in humility for Eden Theological's prize winner, as he wrote to S. D. Press, a former professor at Eden, and now a valued confidant: "The more I look at the thing the more I see that I have been cheated out of a college education. Elmhurst is little more than a high school. I thought once that I lacked only the B.A. but I have found since that I lack the things that make up a B.A.: philosophy, ethics, science and a real course in English. Everywhere around here they not only assume that you have a B.A. but they assume a fundamental knowledge of these college courses. I have bluffed my way through pretty well by industrious reading but I feel all the time like a mongrel among thoroughbreds and that's what I am."[9] But perhaps there is a lesson in humility for Yale, as well, to contemplate in retrospect, for there are few graduates of Yale of greater renown than this young man who felt "like a mongrel among thoroughbreds" in 1914. The correspondence between Niebuhr and Professor Press, which has been recovered through the industry of Mrs. Bingham, reveals that this matter of Niebuhr's deficient formal education preoccupied him to the extent that he ran scared through his two years at Yale (the first year for the B.D., the second for the M.A.)—and emerged with excellent marks.

The other great preoccupation of those two years—and for a long while to come—was money. Part-time assistance in a small congregation in Derby, Connecticut, brought in something, but not nearly enough. Writing on borrowed stationery bearing the letterhead "The Courier-Herald Co./Walter Niebuhr, Pres./Lincoln, Illinois," he unburdened himself about these matters to Professor Press: he felt duty-bound to discourage his older brother's officers of financial help, for Walter was already contributing to the support of their widowed mother, and was at the moment going heavily into debt to make his start in newspaper publishing[10]—"I feel therefore that any help he gives me is retarding his growth and independence which he needs for his life's calling."[11] Under these circumstances, Niebuhr concluded that he could not afford graduate work beyond the M.A.[12] In any case, Niebuhr had persuaded himself that he had had enough of the ivory tower, for the time being: "frankly, the other side of me came out: I desired relevance rather than scholarship."[13]

There is a time and place in life for everything, then. Niebuhr's craving for formal instruction had been satisfied by the two years at Yale. He had had the inspiration of at least two great teachers— Douglas Clyde Macintosh and Frank C. Porter, the first a systematic theologian and the second a New Testament scholar[14]—and what more can one reasonably ask? His own religious viewpoint had shifted a good few degrees in the liberal direction, so that he was moved to wonder out loud whether his more modern views might not "jeopardize any influence which I might in time have won in our church."[15] There is a calculating, or prudential tone to that remark, which, taken together with his references to his brother Walter's plan for "growth in his life's calling," might unsettle romantics. But the remark is characteristic of Reinhold Niebuhr, who never permitted himself heroics, and refused to cultivate the patience to endure those who did. Unless he were being dishonest with himself and others in believing that he had a call to preach, then he must have a church, and he must make a "success" of himself within it. It seemed to follow that he must be acceptable to his congregation; they could not be expected to buy his bread if his ministry brought them no comfort. And that, in turn, meant that *he*—not the denomination —would be failing if, by reason of deviant theology, he failed to rise within the church. Today it is easy—indeed, it is downright *incumbent* upon a young preacher in most mainstream Protestant congregations, to stand to the left of the published (and of course unread) theological position of the denomination he serves, and to behave as though he is shocking everybody by his forthrightness. That is in most instances what he is there for. But when Reinhold Niebuhr went out of Yale seeking a church in 1915, the Protestant congregation was an altogether different thing. People believed that the theological statements of their church contained vital truths; they felt they had a right to expect their pastor to defend and affirm these truths. Such a state of affairs did not lead to the smothering of creative and inspired preaching. (We will soon find that Niebuhr's own thirteen-year career as pastor to one congregation proves that point.) It did, however, discourage heroic posturing.

Since each party understood so clearly what was expected of it, negotiations between a board and candidate-preacher could be businesslike. When Reinhold Niebuhr presented himself in the spring of 1915 as such a candidate, his confidence in his own integrity and loyalty to his denomination had been freshened by the experience of having recently turned down a position at $1,500 in another denomi- nation.[16] The Mission Board of his denomination assigned him a con- gregation in Detroit at a salary of $600—the usual starting salary for a bachelor, they said—and immediately pulled out all the stops on the theme of his indebtedness to the denomination for his free education at Eden. Whereupon, "quite a scrap" ensued[17]—from which the young preacher emerged victorious, but not exultant: "I was very sorry that I had to begin my work this way, I was sent here under false pretenses but forced them to make good the promises they made to me. I was very sorry that thereby I was placed in the position of de- manding something that has never been given to a young unmarried man before. But even for a man just graduating from Eden, $600 is too little for a metropolis where over half has to go for board. Perhaps it is a good thing therefore that I forced them to break this rule. They are now giving me $800 and the district board $100."[18]

Reinhold Niebuhr's career as a preacher is a most unusual one. He did not work his way ahead in the denomination up the steps of brief apprentice-ministries, beginning with the smallest congregation around and promoting himself to larger and more promising ones. He was *assigned* to his first church—that was the rule in his denomination—and he stayed with it for thirteen years, the whole of his congregational ministry. From the beginning, he bent his energies to building Bethel Evangelical church; his own stature as a pastor and as a preacher was a by-product of the growth of his church.

Bethel Evangelical was founded a mere three years before the Mission Board assigned Reinhold Niebuhr to it. In view of the hard bargaining he had put them all through, the Mission Board and the Board at Bethel must have felt they had a right to expect results. The German Evangelical population of Detroit was meager, but was expected to grow along with the city, already the center of the new automobile industry. (The Olds Motor Works was established in 1899, Cadillac in 1901, and both Packard and Ford in 1903.) Barring the horrible (but for a fledgling congregation not improbable) possibility of a string of incompetent or immature pastors, the congregation could *expect* to grow, even if it recruited only from the ranks of German-speaking birthright Evangelicals moving northward out of mid-west farm country in search of city jobs. To some, this seemed justification enough to continue the old ways—and particularly the German character of their denomination. The significant fact about Reinhold Niebuhr's ministry at Bethel is not, therefore, that he left a congregation so much larger than the congregation he came to, but that he led the leaders of the original congregation through changes of expectation, and indeed changes of value and of character.

Certainly the growth in numbers is astounding—though Niebuhr always protested that the sheer growth in numbers of the city of Detroit should be considered the primary cause. Between its founding and Niebuhr's arrival (that is, the first three years as a Mission church) the membership had grown from 16 to 65.[19] A brick chapel costing $5,650 had been built on a lot just outside the then limits of the city and costing $2,880. In 1928, the membership was 656, and the current expense of the church had risen from $957 to $18,397. Through the benevolence of one wealthy member, drawn to the congregation by Niebuhr's soon-celebrated preaching, the congregation received in 1921 a new church site in a much more central location (West Grand Boulevard), where an impressive new building was built at a cost of $128,000. *That kind* of growth was only possible because the pastor's personality and strength of faith were such as to persuade the congregation into taking steps that they could never have been brought to take alone. Early in 1919, Bethel became the first congregation in the Michigan district to discontinue the use of German in services—a hard blow for older members. From the pulpit and at Board meetings the pastor argued the case for letting go of practices and forms which, while they still engaged the nostalgic loyalties of birthright members of the denomination, obscured the church's claim to adherence of newcomers who were not of the "Evangelical" family, not German, and (in gratifyingly large numbers) not previously churchgoers. The result was no milk-and-water, creed-less, form-less "community church," but rather a congregation that would be ready for the mergers that lay ahead for the Evangelical Synod as a whole. Niebuhr's success was such that in 1925 he could give this statement of his congregation's position: "We at Bethel are trying to exploit the good in the denominational tradition without insisting on denominationalism. We believe in the fullest measures of cooperation with all Protestant churches and have in our membership persons who have been raised in almost every Protestant communion. The denomination helps us to keep contact with the various Kingdom enterprises of the Christian church, but in the community itself we strive to be interdenominational. . . . Hence our only form is 'The mind of Christ' which we try diligently to understand and implant in the lives of men."[20]

It must be appreciated that what was at stake was not just the ordinary sort of denominational loyalty that operated among, say, Baptists or Methodists, but a very special kind of tribal loyalty. This was not the most propitious time to be attempting to lead a German-American congregation into the mainstream of the Anglo-Saxon world. German-Americans were still indignant at the abuse they had recently suffered when the Anglo-American majority had closed ranks to fight its War to End All Wars against the Hun without and the Hun within.

Evidence of the continuation of these wartime feelings into the era of normalcy had appeared, for instance, at the meeting of the Federal Council of Churches in Boston in 1921. A suggestion came from certain members that a resolution be forwarded from the Council to German churches "offering the hand of brotherhood." On the surface, it seems to have been meant merely as a fraternal gesture. Speakers for the majority affected to find unfortunate political implications, however—given the fact that a final Peace had not yet been ratified by the Americans; and so the proposal for the "fraternal letter" was voted down. We have evidence of Niebuhr's reaction to this unfortunate incident, in the form of a letter to Dr. Robert E. Speer, dated March 4, 1921, expressing Niebuhr's resentment at the "considerations of expediency that were advanced against the proposed action." It reveals Niebuhr's preoccupation in those early years with the question of the future of his denomination and of his own future within it:

> I myself represent very poorly the sentiment in our churches in regard to the matter. My own interest in it is that of a Christian internationalist who fears that the church is not sufficiently detached from national animosities and is too ready to abandon and too slow to reassert its international consciousness. The interest of my church naturally arises chiefly from its sympathy for the sorry plight of the churches in Germany from which many of our members and ministers came. Many of our older men were educated in the "Missionshaeuser" of Germany and the suggestion that no action can be taken because the German churches might use such an effort toward reconciliation to press their claim for the return of their missions makes them particularly bitter.
>
> It may surprise you to know that many of our older men are hoping to effect a secession from the Federal Council on that ground [sic] that it is doing nothing to right what they regard as a great wrong toward the German mission. I write this in confidence for I have, of course, no sympathy with their viewpoint or at least not with their intentions. Many of us feel so strongly upon this matter that we would resign from a denomination that cut itself loose from organized protestantism. I do not know how strong the sentiment which I have mentioned is and I am not asking that action be taken upon this ground but I thought it would be well for you to know the problems with which we are contending and how our problems are made more difficult by the reluctance of the council to take any action in a matter that is so vital to many of our members.[21]

The challenge presented by the congregation at Bethel Evangelical was, then, of an unusually high order. Fortunately, we have a record of some of his experiences, in the form of a little book of excerpts from the diary which he somehow found the time and the stimulus to keep during the thirteen years of his pulpit ministry. The anecdotal substance and the private quality of the observations in this book make it an altogether unique item in the Niebuhr canon, so that it never fails to surprise students of Niebuhr who come to it late in their reading. Some idea of its quality will be gained from these excerpts from the first two entries:

1915

There is something ludicrous about a callow young fool like
myself standing up to preach a sermon to these good folks. I talk
wisely about life and know little about life's problems. I tell
them of the need of sacrifice, although most of them could tell
me something about what that really means. I preached a sermon
the other day on "The Involuntary Cross," using the text of
Simon the Cyrene bearing the cross of Jesus. A good woman, a
little bolder than the rest, asked me in going out whether I had
borne many crosses. I think I know a little more about that
than I would be willing to confess to her or to the congregation,
but her question was justified.

Many of the people insist that they can't understand how a
man so young as I could possibly be a preacher. Since I am
twenty-three their reaction to my youth simply means that they
find something incompatible even between the ripe age of
twenty-three and the kind of seasoned wisdom which they expect
from the pulpit. "Let no one despise thy youth," said Paul to
Timothy; but I doubt whether that advice stopped any of the old
saints from wagging their heads. I found it hard the first few
months to wear a pulpit gown. Now I am getting accustomed
to it. At first I felt too much like a priest in it, and I abhor
priestliness. I have become reconciled to it partly as a simple
matter of habit, but I imagine that I am also beginning to like the
gown as a kind of symbol of authority. It gives me the feeling
that I am speaking not altogether in my own name and out of my
own experience but by the authority of the experience of many
Christian centuries. . . .

I am glad there are only eighteen families in this church. I have
been visiting the members for six weeks and haven't seen all of
them yet. Usually I walk past a house two or three times before
I summon the courage to go in. I am always very courteously
received, so I don't know exactly why I should not be able
to overcome this curious timidity. I don't know that very much
comes of my visits except that I really get acquainted with the
people.

Usually after I have made a call I find some good excuse to quit
for the afternoon. I used to do that in the days gone by when
I was a book agent. But there was reason for it then. I needed the
afternoon to regain my self-respect. Now it seems to be pure
laziness and fear. The people are a little discouraged. Some of
them seem to doubt whether the church will survive. But there

are a few who are the salt of the earth, and if I make a go of this they will be more responsible than they will ever know.[22]

The reader will be able to see the resources there are in this little book for personal biography. These resources June Bingham has combined with the findings of her interviews with family and members of Niebuhr's congregation to produce the most valuable chapters of her biography of Niebuhr.[23] The relative thinness of the later sections of the Bingham biography is largely owing to the fact that the diary project was abandoned as Niebuhr's reputation as a writer reached the point (about the time of the publication of the *Leaves*) that he could be assured of publication of whatever he cared to write. The impulse to write for his own eyes alone was apparently not very strong—which is to say that he does not seem to have needed the therapy of diary-writing once outlets into public print became available to him.

In his "Preface and Apology" to the original edition, Niebuhr writes: "It must be confessed in all candor that some of the notes, particularly the later ones, were written after it seemed fairly certain that they would reach the eye of the public in some form or other. It was therefore psychologically difficult to maintain the type of honesty which characterizes the self-revelations of a private diary. The reader must consequently be warned (though such a warning may be superfluous) to discount the unconscious insincerities which no amount of self-discipline can eliminate from words which are meant for the public."[24] These are not the words of a true diarist. More than one admirer has sought Niebuhr's cooperation in the preparation of his biography, and all have been discouraged. There are scattered remarks in Niebuhr's writing on the subject of history which suggest that, at the philosophical level, Niebuhr shared the view of the great British philosopher-historian, R. G. Collingwood, regarding the essential irrelevance of biography to the quest for historical meaning.[25] As for the thought of writing his own autobiography or of cooperating in a biography of himself, he would later dismiss such work as inherently "dishonest."[26] But putting aside the question of full-gauged biography, students of Niebuhr are bound to feel rather short-changed by their subject in the matter of documentary evidence sufficient for tracing the connection between Niebuhr's interior life and his public acts—and to feel, therefore, some considerable indebtedness to June Bingham for providing as much of this interior biography as the little evidence allows. Niebuhr was not, after all, one of life's detached intellectuals: he was no Immanuel Kant, deliberately disengaging himself from life's affairs so as to protect the disinterestedness of his philosophy.

Historians are beginning to note the unprecedented difficulties that are shaping-up for the recovering of evidence substantial enough for filling-in the personal or interior dimension of the biographies of twentieth-century public figures. The simple fact is that such lives do not afford the time nor the tranquillity that in earlier days public figures used for keeping diaries.[27] But more basically, Niebuhr seems not to have had the sort of character that is required for the patient recording of one's daily interior life. Everyone in a position to know tells us that he never developed the knack of merely sitting and thinking. His former parishioners remember that routine pastoral visits began with the sudden rush of a motor's engine outside, the screech of brakes, and footsteps literally running up the front steps—sounds more appropriate to the arrival of a doctor on an emergency call. Old friends recall him pacing the vestibules of the concert hall despite a genuine love of good music, and maybe *because* of his very responsiveness to it—incapable of staying for long in his seat.[28] There is as well the recollection of Paul Tillich: "Niebuhr and I often walked through nature. It was mostly Riverside Park, but anyhow there are some very beautiful trees; and while he developed his future big book, I sometimes was deviated by a tree, or the river, or clouds behind it, and suddenly I noticed he didn't care for this at all. When I told him that I cared for this, he called me a German Romanticist. Now this very nice controversy has much deeper philosophical implications."[29] It has indeed. But it has some psychological ones, too, which are surely germane to this matter of Niebuhr's character. As more and more of his energies were channeled into activities of a public and outward sort, the capacity for quiet and interior self-examination seems to have withered away—that is, until the series of attacks from which he began to suffer in his fifties compelled him to redirect the flow of these energies more and more into interior channels. Niebuhr's confession of the difficulties that convalescence caused him is evidence supporting the arguments of this paragraph: "I am ashamed [he wrote at the time to a friend] that my convalescence proves to be spiritually so hard because it reveals a lack in me, a reliance upon jobs and pressures rather than on inner calm."[30]

The argument is not that this restlessness bespeaks a *weakness* of character—certainly not that it is a weakness in a religious character. It surely must be said of the most valuable religious figures (historically speaking) that they relied upon jobs and pressures rather than upon inner calm: I suggest (at random) the names of St. Paul, Charles Wesley, Martin Luther. Whitehead's famous dictum that "religion is what a man does with his solitariness," sheds no light whatever upon an examination of the historical impact of such men. For them, religion was what a man did about what he had learned in his solitariness. More "inner calm" and a lesser drive for external accomplishment would have made Reinhold Niebuhr much less interesting, if *interesting at all*, to an historian.

After the *Leaves*, Niebuhr has left us virtually nothing upon which to base an appraisal of the "inner happenings" of his life. There is much in his correspondence as it survives in the Library of Congress collection that reveals aspects of his character and personality, but nothing that charts their development. That a biography such as June Bingham's is possible at all is owing to the fact that Niebuhr's basic character and personality were established earlier in life than is the case with most of us. For this conclusion we have the evidences of his *Leaves* which throw as much light as an historian is likely to have upon his mental processes.

The evidence of the *Leaves* is unmistakable: the pastoral ministry is the matrix of Niebuhr's philosophy. There is no understanding Reinhold Niebuhr without that appreciation. The spiritual and ethical questions raised again and again in those few pages foretell the characteristic preoccupations of Niebuhr's mature work. When Niebuhr talks of the individual's capacity for heroism and for self-transcendence he is generalizing upon discoveries that he first made in the course of serving his parish. When he develops the contrast between private virtue and group narrowness (the central theme of his first major work, *Moral Man and Immoral Society*, 1932) he is developing themes which make their first appearance in those sections of his *Leaves* where he is to be found brooding about the unresponsiveness of his congregation to the urgings of his preaching on social and economic issues. We shall return to these matters shortly.

# A THEOLOGIAN'S APPRENTICESHIP

Mention of Niebuhr's *Leaves from the Notebooks of a Tamed Cynic* has caused an unavoidable warp in the chronology of our narrative, for they were published in 1929 but deal with the experiences of his pastoral ministry which began in 1915. With *Leaves*, we reach the point of transition between Niebuhr's years in the pastoral ministry and those of what I believe we should call his extra-mural ministry.

The emphasis we have given so far to Niebuhr's ministry at Bethel Evangelical has not been meant to imply that his energies and ambitions were confined to that small orbit. "There was nothing I wanted so little as anonymity," Niebuhr confessed years later.[1] From the day he had established himself in his new study at Bethel, he was bent upon establishing a reputation for himself outside the congregation, primarily by means of writing. In his correspondence with Professor Press, he speaks of his inadequate preparation as a writer in the English language, for German had been the basic language of his college education. The way to conquer that deficiency, he knew, was to find good models and emulate them. His father's model, among others, was Macaulay.[2] It has to be admitted that Niebuhr's style has little of Macaulay's grace, however. His own models seem to have been in the then passing generation of American essayists in religion —William James, Josiah Royce, William Ernest Hocking.[3] The rest was accomplished by faithful application of the seat of the pants to the seat of the chair (as Somerset Maugham has it). Accordingly, we should think of the diary that became the *Leaves* as, in part, a style book.

Niebuhr in his old age claimed that the decisive factor behind his early fling at writing was the money.[4] He was, after all, carrying on his share of the support of his widowed mother, and retiring the considerable debts left over from his two-year stint at Yale. The sixty dollars he made on his first article "looked so big" (as he later put it).[5] A young man of such hard-headed ways would, one supposes, have given considerable thought to the production of that first article. It is worth noting, therefore, that Niebuhr decided to make his first bid for recognition as a writer in the capacity of an expert on the German-American. Though Niebuhr, in later years, was to have much to say on Germany, and was indeed to make a small contribution to the formulation of the United States government's German policies in the post-Second World War years, he never wanted to be thought of as a German-American spokesman. Though there may be occasional references to the German-American and his ways in later writings, there is not another piece, of any size, devoted to the German-American or to German-Americanism.[6] It is curious, in short, that it occurred to him to make his entrée into the world of high-priced and high-quality journalism as a student of the problems of an important ethnic minority in America—only to drop the subject as soon as he was in the door.

The answer to this riddle is to be found in the article itself. It is, in fact, Niebuhr's manifesto of rebellion against German-Americanism. Niebuhr had chosen to write upon the theme of German-Americanism *now*, at the outset of his career, for the very reason that he did not want to write upon it ever again. It was not out of respect or fear for vulgar anti-Germanism that Niebuhr was casting off his hyphen: had that been a consideration, he would have acceded to the suggestion of the federal agent who was to come to him some months later urging that he change his name "to prove my loyalty."[7] Not fear but idealism turned him against his hyphen.

The first article presents a bitter indictment against the German-American community. Their sin, however, is not in their continuing sympathy for Germany, which Niebuhr finds to be only "natural." Quite the contrary: the German-American is guilty of a lack of commitment to Germany—to the best that Germany has accomplished. The German-American has proved "untrue to the virtues of his race." While most Americans are disposed to favor the cause of Germany's enemies in this hour, Niebuhr is bold enough to suggest that Germany has been a great benefactor of mankind. In the movement away from individualism and toward greater community (which Niebuhr is convinced is the movement of greatest moral significance in his generation) Germany has pioneered in establishing "methods of humanizing industry": she has been "a clinic for the world." In the sphere of religious learning, too, Germany is the pioneer, being "the foremost protagonist of liberal Christianity." If the German-American community were faithful to Germany, she would deserve our praise, for she would then have resources for serving America well. She would be helping to sensitize the social conscience of a nation which is much too individualistic; and she would be liberalizing America's too-dogmatic religion. The German-American thus deserves to be censured by Americans—but not because he is guilty of the garden-variety sort of treason. He is guilty of treason to "the ideals of his own people."

Thus, while the German-American may seem to be guilty on two counts, there is, in fact, only the one charge expressed in two ways. He is guilty of "betraying the ideals of his own people." What American life most needs is precisely what a twentieth-century German ought to be best equipped to provide: namely, idealism. America, with all its resources and all its opportunities for new beginnings, suffers from a lack of imagination, attributable to the Anglo-Saxon's congenital incapacity for accomplishing great objectives in community. The Germans, being in the forefront of modern thinking, have seen that the new day lies on the road away from individualism. Serving that truth, German-Americans can best serve America.

Thus, to opt for America and to reject German-Americanism is to accept the promise of American life. Whether one expresses that hope in secular or in religious terms, the essence of it is community ("communism" is the term he uses in this maiden article). To choose America is to affirm the infinite possibilities of human community: to reject America is to accept limits to the possibilities of community. To choose America is to affirm the best hope of mankind.

Obviously, Reinhold Niebuhr's first article commended itself to the editors of the *Atlantic* in large part because of its extraordinary topicality. It is not difficult to imagine the editor's satisfaction at having an issue in the mails with an article having such a title as "The Failure of German-Americans," signed with such an obviously German name as Reinhold Niebuhr, in the weeks following the renomination of Woodrow Wilson for the Presidency, in the very month when German saboteurs blew up the Black Tom, New Jersey docks of the Lehigh Valley Railroad; and still current to the sort who are always trying to "catch up" on the *Atlantic* in those very weeks when Woodrow Wilson was persuading forty-nine percent of those voting that he had kept them out of war, and that only he could keep them out. A few weeks later, the *Atlantic* accepted Niebuhr's second offering, "The Nation's Crime Against the Individual," a rather unoriginal piece which rings the expected changes on the accepted themes of the American liberal's outrage at the unnecessary war now raging in Europe: "It is unnecessary to establish here that the principal cause of modern warfare is commercial rivalry. . . . What a pitiful thing it is that the Pomeranian peasant or the miner of Wales is asked to sacrifice his life in a struggle that is to determine whether future generations of Hamburg or Liverpool merchants shall wax rich from overseas commerce and the exploitation of undeveloped countries."[8] After that, Niebuhr's offerings did not fare so well. Several articles were sent over the next three years to the *Atlantic*, *New Republic*, and *Biblical World*, but without any success until 1920.[9] Until mid-1923, the batting average was discouragingly low— six articles published over seven years: two in the *Atlantic*, one in the *World Tomorrow*, one in *Biblical World*, one in the *Nation*, one in the *Christian Century*. But by the end of that year (1923), Niebuhr had won his way onto the editorial board of the *Christian Century*, and his galling "anonymity" was forever behind him.

While his literary career appeared to have entered the doldrums (temporarily, as it turned out) after the initial heady experience with the *Atlantic*, Niebuhr was building a reputation for himself as a speaker both within and without church circles. That he was able to accomplish this without neglecting his responsibilities to his parish was in large part due to the friendship of Sherwood Eddy, one of the greatest figures in twentieth-century American Protestantism. An older man than Niebuhr (he was born in 1871), Eddy had responded to the call of the Student Volunteer Movement as a young student of engineering, and had spent the years between 1896 and the end of the War as a dramatically successful missionary in India, China, Czarist Russia, and the Middle East, and with the troops overseas. Now back in America as an officer of the Y.M.C.A., he was rapidly becoming one of the boldest of the spokesmen of Social Gospel radicalism. Greatly impressed by the young Niebuhr, Sherwood Eddy persuaded the Bethel congregation to retain an assistant minister to carry the bulk of the parish duties; Eddy paid the assistant's salary out of his own pocket.[10] (This was not the last of the important services Eddy was to perform for Niebuhr.) Now Niebuhr was free to accept invitations to other pulpits, to address gatherings of church-men and especially young people, and to spend some part of prac-tically every weekend lecturing or preaching in the colleges.

Nothing substantial survives as evidence of the message that he brought to those audiences of church young people and college students in his "circuit-riding days" (as he liked to recall them). The published *Leaves* therefore remain the primary evidence for the contents of Niebuhr's mind in the early twenties. The problem of dealing with his German heritage is, as the *Atlantic* article attested, very much to the fore. Several passages in the *Leaves* reveal his concern

that his German-American origins are making it difficult to judge the
rights and wrongs of the great political issues of the day in un-
hyphenated, American terms. Occasionally (though more rarely) he
talks as well of the risk to clear thinking that lies in the opposite
direction of over-compensation for his hyphen in times of national
peril, when the pressures for conformity are going to be increasing.
There is, for example, an illuminating entry on the confusion of heart
and mind that he suffered as a young minister visiting the war-
training camps:

> Out at Funston I watched a bayonet practice. It was enough to
> make me feel like a brazen hypocrite for being in this thing, even
> in a rather indirect way.[11] Yet I cannot bring myself to associate
> with the pacifists. *Perhaps if I were not of German blood I could.*
> That may be cowardly, but I do think that a new nation has
> a right to be pretty sensitive about its unity.
>
> Some of the good old Germans have had a hard time hiding
> a sentiment which borders very closely on hatred for this nation.
> Anyone who dissociates himself from the cause of his nation
> in such a time as this ought to do it only on the basis of an
> unmistakably higher loyalty. If I dissociated myself only slightly
> I would inevitably be forced into the camp of those who
> romanticize about the Kaiser. And the Kaiser is certainly nothing
> to me.[12]

If the opening of the World War drove Niebuhr to weigh the
claims of German-Americanism upon him and to declare himself for
Americanism, America's entry into that war raised a more difficult
dilemma still. What part should Niebuhr, a Christian and a clergyman, play in it? Niebuhr regarded himself as a pacifist. Indeed, he
was convinced that a disciple of Jesus could not be anything else
but an absolute pacifist. Yet 1918 found him making trips to the war-
training camps in the services of his denomination, as Chairman of
the Wartime Commission of the denomination,[13] and justifying his
work there as an opportunity to explain Wilson's program to the
soldiers: the war would "serve a good purpose," he would tell them,
"if Wilson's aims are realized." [14] Niebuhr was painfully aware that,
given his pacifist convictions, there was no possible defense for his
trying to sell Wilson's program to the soldiers; for this was to set a
merely human program against the absolute love-command of Christ.
It would be more honest, he admitted, to serve in the ranks as a
private, and cease trying to make Mr. Wilson's war a Christian
crusade.[15] He would then have only his own conscience to account
for.

At war's end, Niebuhr shared the disillusionment of liberals in the debacle of Wilson's program. Like the others, he had a great deal of explaining to do. Looking back in 1928, Niebuhr was little inclined to give himself the benefit of the doubt: "Being a German-American I was more than ordinarily patriotic during the war. My jealous love for my own nation created such a resentment [in me] against the members of the German group who spoke critically of my country that I forgot my pacifism and was driven into the arms of the war enthusiasts. Perhaps [this decision for patriotism was] merely a rationalization to justify my apostasy from principles [i.e., pacifism] which I had professed before the war. Perhaps I was just too cowardly to remain true to my principles which had taken form after the beginning of the war but before our entrance into it."[16]

Here was a lesson that Niebuhr would not soon forget: no man's reason is disinterested. He had allowed himself to believe that he had been won to patriotism by its claim upon his reason. But his reason had deceived him by persuading him to see the issue as one between Americanism and German-Americanism; this spurious dichotomy had kept him from examining first principles—his religious principles. Now that he had some perspective on the events, he could see that his reason had been in thrall to self-preservation, the basest of instincts. In the long run, this insight was to flower into his mature critique of what he would call the "liberal illusion" regarding the innocency of reason. For the moment, the experience was to spur him to a greater effort to maintain the innocency of his reason.

The decision to atone for his wartime lapse from pacifism began to take shape in the immediate wake of the War. It had hardened to the firmest resolution by the time he returned from a trip to Germany in 1923 (which we shall be considering later).[17] Traveling through the Ruhr, he reported, "you could see hatred with the naked eye. . . ."

This is as good a time as any to make up my mind that I am done with the war business. Of course, I wasn't really in the last war. Would that I had been! Every soldier, fighting for his country in simplicity of heart, without asking many questions, was superior to those of us who served no better purpose than to increase or perpetuate the moral obfuscation of nations. Of course, we really couldn't know everything we know now. But now we know. The times of man's ignorance God may wink at, but now he calls us all to repent. I am done with this business. I hope I can make that resolution stick. . . . For my own part I am not going to let my decision in regard to war stand alone. I am going to try to be a disciple of Christ, rather than a mere

Christian, in all human relations and experiment with the
potency of trust and love much more than I have in the past.[18]

These, then, appear to have been the main preoccupations of the
apprentice theologian during his twenties. It is instructive to notice
that these preoccupations were rooted in the experience of his
pastoral ministry. But nothing that Niebuhr wrote in those days was
*merely* about Bethel or his ministry at Funston. It is the hallmark of
Niebuhr's occasional writing from the beginning to the end of his
career that he refused to deal with the contingent as merely contingent. The mode of expression is always and inescapably theological. There is not one of Niebuhr's nine-hundred occasional pieces
written over the next fifty years, however ostensibly "secular" the
theme, that does not depend for its very intelligibility upon the
whole repertoire of statements that are made within the Protestant
tradition about God's purposes for man. It is as true of his observations on the political and sociological behavior of the German-
American as it is of his articles, fifty years later, on the Vietnam
policies of Lyndon Johnson. That large company who believe that
his "merely political" or "merely sociological" statements are valid
without reference to his theology, are deceiving themselves: that is
the entire argument of this book. The vital point, for present purposes, is that the theological dimension is evident at the very outset
of Niebuhr's writing career. Thus, the argument of Niebuhr's first
article moves swiftly from the particular questions forced upon him
by his situation—the question of his German-American loyalties, the
war, the issue of American Protestant unity—to the roots of these
questions in historic Protestant theology.

The whole point is, however, that these gifts were not then, and
are not now, generally prized among liberal-intellectuals. The fascination of Niebuhr's career lies precisely in the fact that he won his
place in the front ranks of major political thinkers in the face of the
ostensible contempt for theology which marks our time. In the beginning, the theological dimension of Niebuhr's writing was simply
ignored for the sake of the topicality of his first submissions: this,
I believe, explains the acceptance of his first two articles by the
*Atlantic*. After an interval, the *Atlantic* used occasional pieces of his
again.[19] But in view of Niebuhr's developing interest in politics and
social issues, the audience whose attention he desired most to have
was that served by the *Nation* and the *New Republic*. With two
exceptions,[20] his frequent submissions to the liberal journals were refused, and those doors would remain closed to him for a decade.
It takes only a little reading between the lines of the replies of the
editors of the liberal journals to his submissions to cause the suspicion

that it was his theologizing that inspired the qualms that inspired the rejection slips.[21] In retrospect, it seems incredible how long it was before Niebuhr won entrance to these journals—for he was eventually to be among the most prized exhibits between the covers of the liberal journals, ranking with such idols of the liberal left as Charles Beard, John Dewey, and R. H. Tawney. On the other hand, we have the larger question: how a theologian came to be admitted at all to this eminence in a company which, for the most part, regarded theology as so much mummery. The fact is that Niebuhr forced himself upon this company, despite his uncomfortable theologizing. During the years from about 1923 to 1930, Niebuhr gathered to himself a faithful clientele which consisted of the readership of certain journals of opinion that served primarily the radically-oriented clergy: the *Biblical World*, *World Tomorrow*, and the *Christian Century*. By 1930, that clientele was of such irresistible proportions that it became necessary for the liberal journals to co-opt Niebuhr and his clientele. By the mid-thirties, a liberal journal of opinion simply was not plausible without Niebuhr's clientele in tow. The theologizing just had to be lived with; for Niebuhr would not, *could not*, write anything that made sense without his theology. From that time to this, the liberal-intellectual camp has been divided three ways on the question of Niebuhr's significance: that he made sense in spite of his theologizing (which I submit is a delusion); that he made sense because of his theology (which is a tribute to the missionary impact of Niebuhr within the liberal-intellectual community since the 1930s); and that he makes bad sense. Liberal-intellectuals who tried simply to ignore him altogether had their cards taken away from them long before the thirties were out.

But this is getting ahead of our story. We must now say something of how Niebuhr acquired his first hold upon the community of liberal clergymen in the 1920s. And for that we must turn to consider the *Christian Century*.[22] The story of the *Christian Century* cannot be told apart from the career of Reinhold Niebuhr. Its success in the 1920s and 1930s was in large part owing to Reinhold Niebuhr—to his own lively and (in that company) radical contributions to its pages, and to the influence that he had on scores of others who were drawn into its pages by the lively discussions that followed in the wake, it seemed, of everything that he wrote there. The style and the substance of the best that the *Christian Century* offered was an amalgam of the style and substance of Reinhold Niebuhr and the editor, Charles Clayton Morrison. During those two decades, the *Christian Century* had a devoted readership of about 30,000 including many outside the ranks of the clergy and a good number outside of the churches altogether. When Morrison and Niebuhr fell out, owing

to their diametrically opposed views on the European crisis of the late
thirties, Niebuhr left to form a rival journal, essentially a rib out of
the side of the *Christian Century*. (These events are discussed later.)
From that day, the quotient of liveliness sank steadily, until the
*Christian Century* lost most of its appeal to the politically-oriented
clergy, and virtually all of its interest to the world outside the
ministerial ranks. It was, by the 1940s, much the same bland, dull,
proper, benignly moderate voice that it had been before.

Originally the voice of the Disciples of Christ, the *Christian
Century* began its career as the major journal of non-denominational
Protestant opinion in 1919, when its editor and owner since 1908,
C. C. Morrison, recruited the help of certain wealthy laymen in a
massive circulation-building drive. Nineteen-nineteen was the *annus
mirabilis* for bold, fund-raising, trail-blazing Protestantism, as we
shall shortly be pointing out.) When Niebuhr first began knocking
on the editor's door, the circulation drive had reaped its first harvest.
Niebuhr's first submission met with rejection on the grounds that
"it does not seem quite available."[23] This is (to me at least) an un-
familiar use of language, and its exact import escapes me. Perhaps
"availability" refers to style ("presentability," "readability"?)—or
perhaps to content ("topicality"?). But more likely it refers to
nothing at all; I suspect, in other words, that the curiously worded
rejection was meant as a lesson in humility to a young pastor with a
weakness for cosmic themes. Morrison admits (in the same letter) to
having "read your writings in the *New Republic*[24] and elsewhere"
(presumably the *Biblical World* article of November, 1920 or the
*Atlantic* articles—although these last had appeared six years earlier)
—and thus he did have more to go on than the one submission in
hand. In any case, Morrison swiftly changed his tune.

The *Christian Century* had, of course, to depend for copy upon
the contributions of part-time writers—preachers and academics,
mainly—and a man in Morrison's situation must soon develop an
instinct for the recognition of reliable, steady help. The mainstays of
such semi-professional journals have got to be able to turn out plenty
of copy in little time. Reinhold Niebuhr was the type *par excellence*
—a writer whose first draft is usually his last—and he has, as is
often remarked, both the weaknesses and the strengths of that type
in heroic proportions. At the height of his career as a writer (roughly,
1940–1942), he wrote the bulk of the editorial material, the book
reviews, and in every issue at least one article for *two journals*—
one a bi-weekly, the other a quarterly—this on top of a major book
every other year, all done in and around the edges of a full-time
teaching week! This sort of energy is, to say the least, rare. And it
was C. C. Morrison who first recognized it and tapped it.

The invitation to contribute editorials to the *Christian Century* came in September of 1922, together with the information that there could, of course be no remuneration.[25] While we do not possess Niebuhr's reply to that letter, we do have later correspondence from Morrison to Niebuhr which makes it clear that the younger man somehow outfoxed the older on the matter of payment, because by February of 1923 something had been "worked out"[26] and Niebuhr was writing reguarly and being paid. This is early evidence for the toughness in Niebuhr's nature that we shall see more of. He apparently knew, in this instance, that Morrison *did* have the money, and while his appetite for literary success was great, his sense of his own worth was more than a match for it.[27] When Morrison saw that his bluff was called, he backed down. It was a wise retreat—for the impact of the new contributing editor was immediate. If Niebuhr lacked something of the literary grace that Morrison admired and himself possessed, there was nonetheless a power about his writing that commanded the attention. Readers were pleased, and wrote to say so. The editors were soon wondering how they had ever gotten along without him. His name on the masthead was a valuable property.

Bethel's pastor was rapidly becoming a famous man, at least, in the company of preachers. Greater fame was soon to come, however, and that would extend to a more mixed company. Before that came about however, there was to be a dramatic adjustment in his thought. Reinhold Niebuhr Part One would scarcely be recognizable to the disciples of Reinhold Niebuhr Part Two (the mature Theologian/Political-philosopher)—and for that reason, if for no other, it is necessary that we make some effort here to summarize the principal features of Niebuhr's thought in the 1920s, as it stands in the record of his published articles and his first three books.[28]

Like all modern-minded American preachers of his day, Niebuhr started from the proposition that it was "the religion of Jesus" that was normative for Christians, and that contemporary historical science had made that message at last unambiguous.

During the 1920s, Niebuhr's description of the religion of Jesus was along the following lines:

[Jesus] believed that the universe itself must be interpreted in terms of a personality which expresses itself in love and he

believed in the practical and redemptive efficacy of love in all
human relationships.[29]

[Jesus was] a great moral adventurer insisting that love is the
ultimate rule of human conduct.[30]

Modern religion is too sophisticated and circumspect really to
share the religion of Jesus, for that demands a love and a faith
which will seem foolish rather than wise to the obvious-minded
man.[31]

Jesus was a "great moral adventurer." He taught the ethic of absolute
love—and He believed in its practicability. How, then, shall we explain
the failure of His followers to live up to this ethic? It is fascinating
to leaf through Niebuhr's writings at this time, to see him tacking
back and forth between two quite contrary answers. The one obvious
answer, and the one to which he seemed to be attracted when he
was counselling his parishioners, or preaching, is described in this
excerpt from his diary:

In the young men's class this morning we continued our
discussion of the Sermon on the Mount. The boys have been
making some interesting contributions. On the whole they are
skeptical of the practicability of the demands which Jesus makes
in the matter of trust and love and forgiveness. It is rather
interesting to have this revelation of the basic cynicism of even
the adolescent mind. They think that to follow Jesus "would put
a business man out of business in no time," as one expressed it
today. Of course, it is better to see the difficulties than to engage
in some kind of sentimental avowal of Christian faith without
realizing how stubbornly life resists the ideal.

"Maybe it would work if we tried it hard enough," thought
one of the boys today when we discussed the practicability of
trusting people. That may be the answer to the whole question.[32]

Thus, as someone has said, Christianity has not been tried and found
wanting; it has been found hard and not tried. Christianity is perfectly practicable. Thus (to take the question of war and peace), there
is no doubting that Jesus stood for the ideal of non-resistance; there
can be no doubt that He meant it to be followed by His disciples;
therefore, it must be practicable.[33] Similarly, there are no grounds for
believing that we have to fix any limit to the possibilities for community inherent in Jesus' love command: all human relationships
could be redeemed—"if we tried hard enough." "Modern sociology's
demand that the social motives of primary social groups shall become
the motives of secondary groups is identical with the demands of the

sermon on the mount. The progress of civilization depends upon the expansion of attitudes which now characterize family life.... Reason and experience will contribute to the attainment of the ideal of human brotherhood; but spiritual religion must make the major contribution. Every essential of that contribution is in the gospel of Jesus."[34]

The dominant theme in Niebuhr's theological expression during his apprentice years is one of sturdy commitment to the practicability of Jesus' love-command. Yet it is significant that Niebuhr felt it necessary to go beyond the simple evidence of the gospel ethics to *supporting* evidence alleged to come from social science.

The perfectionist response to the challenge of Jesus' love-command is thus the dominant theme in Niebuhr's thought in the 1920s. There is an alternative response, however, to which Niebuhr was, in some moods, much tempted:

There is a discouraging pettiness about human nature which makes me hate myself each time I make an analysis of my inner motives and springs of action. Here I am prodding and criticizing people continually because they have made too many compromises with the necessities of life and adjusted the Christian ideal until it has completely lost its original meaning. Yet I make my own compromises all the time.

It is Christian to trust people, and my trust is carefully qualified by mistrust and caution.

It is Christian to love, and to trust in the potency of love rather than in physical coercion. Logically that means non-resistance. Yet I believe that a minimum of coercion is necessary in all social tasks, or in most of them.

It is Christian to forgive rather than to punish; yet I do little by way of experimenting in the redemptive power of forgiveness.

I am not really a Christian. In me, as in many others, "the native hue of resolution is sicklied o'er by a pale cast of thought." I am too cautious to be a Christian. I can justify my caution, but so can the other fellow who is more cautious than I am....

A reasonable person adjusts his moral goal somewhere between Christ and Aristotle, between an ethic of love and an ethic of moderation. I hope there is more of Christ than of Aristotle in my position. But I would not be too sure of it.[35]

This more hard-headed, less idealistic response (we might tentatively identify it as the theme of "realism") comes more and more to the fore towards the end of the decade. During the twenties it remains a nagging, willful companion, one that will not heel, though it remains on a short leash. By 1930, however, it will have gained its head, and will send the perfectionist theme from the field. It will be the business of a later chapter to describe how this happened.

"I am not really a Christian!" What then of the Church: is it "Christian"?

Significantly, Niebuhr tended to be more optimistic about the resources for perfection which the Church possessed than about his own. While conceding that popular religion "frequently reveals disappointing characteristics," he could write in the early 1920s of the "social gospel" as the leaven within the Protestant Churches, and of the evident "social vision" of the churches.[36]

Niebuhr's first book, *Does Civilization Need Religion?* (1927), provides us an opportunity to consider the drift of Niebuhr's thinking as he approached the end of his service as a pastor. It is (except for *The Contribution of Religion to Social Work* [1932], a slimmer book, hurriedly written and superficial in its arguments) the only one of his books which reads like the product of a working clergyman. That is, it shows us a man trying to make sense of his experience with church people, setting out with candor both the virtues and the defects of the religion which he has found in his people, against the background of what he believes to be the needs of America and of Western civilization.

Relentlessly, Niebuhr presses one question: is religion relevant to the world's needs? This is, as Niebuhr acknowledges, really two questions—the one addressed to religion as it is ideally, and the other to religion as it is practiced. As for the first: "The religious interpretation of the world is essentially an insistence that the ideal is real and that the real can be understood only in the light of the ideal."[37] As we have seen, Niebuhr is committed at this stage to the proposition that what America needs is more idealism. This faith he affirms, by-and-large gladly, in these pages. The negative component of his message is small, but worth pausing over since it bears hints of his future disenchantment with idealism. The basic fault of church people is that they are wont to confuse idealism with optimism. We are called by Jesus to be idealists; but we are explicitly told not to expect the triumph of this program in this world. Christians must be prepared to experience the appearance of failure, as well as ridicule —and possibly crucifixion. All men (but Americans especially) value the appearance of success too highly. Their strategy is to stake out certain limited areas of obvious sin for conquest; then, mastering these, to claim an unmixed triumph for their religion. This is done at the cost of neglecting the larger areas of sin, the areas less immediately impinging on their consciousness—social issues, in short.

The theme is not an original one—as Niebuhr himself would have been quick to acknowledge. It had been impressed upon him again and again by the men to whom he looked for guidance as a preacher and as a Christian: by Bishop Scarlett and Bishop McConnell; by Kirby Page and Sherwood Eddy; and, in his reading, by Walter Rauschenbusch. It was the whole burden of the Social Gospel. It was, indeed, one of the oldest themes of self-criticism within the church. Moreover, there is a considerable ambiguity in Niebuhr's presentation of the theme in this book. Basically, he is arguing that the religion of Jesus is an *unfailing* source of truth for personal purity and for right social action. For example: "It is difficult to escape the conclusion that the reverence for personality which is implicit in religion is necessary to establish an adequate motive and an adequate method of social reconstruction. . . . In the religion of Jesus both a social and an individualistic emphasis issue from a spiritual appreciation of human spiritual personality." (page 61) Despite the revealingly slow wind-up, the point, once it is delivered, is that the Gospel of Jesus is "adequate," both as "motive" and as "method" for social reconstruction. Again: "the art of forgiveness can be learned only in the school of religion. . . . The creative and redemptive force is a force which defies the real in the name of the ideal, *and subdues it.* [Emphasis added.] Since the family relation is the most ethical relation men know, religious faith interprets all life in terms of that relation. . . . The races and groups of mankind are obviously not living as a family; but they ought to. And as the necessity becomes more urgent the truth of the ideal becomes more real."

Boiled down, this ought to mean that if Henry Ford's workers, for instance, wish to bring their boss to a more benign policy in the matter of wages and fringe benefits, they ought to be applying the strategy of religious non-resistance advocated by Jesus. This would, of course, rule out any policy of applied force, such as the strike; for whoever heard of a strike in a family, "the most ethical relation men know"? If the strategy of religious idealism is "adequate," it must be adequate all round: in family relations, in social conflicts within the nation, and in international conflicts. Let us therefore trust our enemies, he argues, and achieve thereby domestic and international peace; for the "attitude of trust . . . once it is assumed, is inevitably verified." (page 153)

That, at least, is the major theme of this book, as it is the major theme of Niebuhr's writing, taken as a whole, to this point in his career. But there is a minor theme to this book as well: "When Jesus rebuked the young man for his anxiety about an equitable division of his inheritance, he took a high spiritual ground which easily lends itself to abuse in the disillusioning realities of economic and social life. Obviously an attitude which represents a high spiritual achievement in the individual instance has its limitations when raised to a general social policy." (pages 180–81) This minor theme seems to have a robust will of its own, indicating that Niebuhr can find no way of bringing it under the discipline of the major theme. (It would take a subtle philosopher indeed to make these two themes lie down together!) Niebuhr simply will not part with his religious idealism, and he cannot quiet the voice of realism within him.

Readers who know Niebuhr only on the basis of his reputation as a mature thinker, and who have failed to recognize him in the expressions of religious idealism we have so far dealt with, will begin to recognize him now. Before another five years have gone by, he will have resolved this dilemma—in favor of what has hitherto been the minor theme. There will then be no more heard of "faith which defies the real in the name of the ideal, and subdues it!"

In these years of Niebuhr's apprenticeship as a social critic, Protestantism had not yet yielded its place as the predominant religious force in America. There was much to suggest (as we shall be indicating later in these pages), that the Protestant clergy were about to enter upon a great age of hegemony over the political and moral life of America. Despite the manifest shortcomings of pulpit and pew, Niebuhr believed in the possibility of a Christian solution to the problems of America.

The best evidence for Niebuhr's views on the political role of the Protestant clergy at the beginnings of his ministry is an article which he wrote for the social gospel organ, *Biblical World*, in November, 1920.[38] It is addressed "to those who believe in the kingdom mission" —that is, the progressive or social gospel clergy who read the *Biblical World*. The article has its pessimistic side; it contains harsh warnings that the task of the Protestant clergy is considerably sterner than clergymen are wont to admit: "The wrongs of modern civilization cannot be righted without fundamental and constitutional changes in our whole economic order which will involve a radical reapportionment of social privileges and economic rights." The issue is the preservation of democracy against the selfish designs of the holding classes (the classic "social gospel" description). Even the most progressive churchmen have been acting as though the whole of their concern were "to hold the workingman for the church"—thus laying the church as a whole open to the charge that "it is more interested to allay social unrest than to eliminate social inequalities." But outweighing this is the great and unquestionable fact that the Protestant leaders command the attention of the possessing classes in 1920; the great task that lies ahead is to "sensitize" the middle-class conscience. In accomplishing this, the clergy must go beyond their characteristic preachments of stewardship and philanthropy and win the bourgeoisie "to the uncompromising application of the principle that 'whosoever would be first among you shall be your servant.'" It is an awesome responsibility, for if Protestant clergymen fail in this, class warfare, he insists, lies ahead for America.

It was in this mood that Niebuhr did his political apprenticeship in 1924. As he later recalled it, Niebuhr was persuaded by Jane Addams to serve as Detroit chairman of the La Follette campaign.[39] How optimistic he may have been about the prospects of victory for his candidate we have no way of knowing. But he was presumably persuaded that he was implementing the call he had made in his *Biblical World* article for political action for the sake of "the kingdom mission." Service in the cause of La Follette and Wheeler he saw as a long stride toward accomplishing the triumph of altruism in the realm of politics.

Our best evidence for his motivation at the time of his political debut is a lengthy article[40] which he wrote for the *Christian Century* about the time that Jane Addams was recruiting him for the Progressive cause. The boldest product of his idealistic period, it is a call for "a Christian political party" informed by the purest "spiritual idealism" in program and in methods. The great hope for political reform lies in the fact that the middle class "is not prompted by its needs, for they are not sufficiently acute, but ... may be enlisted through its ideals, once they are awakened, to support a program of thoroughgoing political and economic reconstruction."

As we have already noted, there is now no way of knowing how seriously Niebuhr had considered the prospects for La Follette in 1924. We cannot, therefore, determine whether the unhappy outcome of the Progressive race had anything to do with the striking change which becomes obvious in Niebuhr's critique of church and society in the months that followed that election. "One gets the impression from this gathering of wholesome virtue rather than rebellious heroism": this, according to the *New York Times*, was Niebuhr's testy greeting to a gathering of Christian students at

Evanston, Illinois, in 1925. "The Church," Niebuhr warned the
students, was "predatory"—as were "the family, the nation, and
other organized groups." Although it existed to maintain the Gospel,
the church had "corrupted the Gospel to maintain itself."[41] The
church had knuckled under to nationalism in wartime and was now
hopelessly enslaved.[42] The church was enslaved to the values of the
middle-class, from whose ranks it almost exclusively draws its membership: its so-called message is not the gospel at all but a variation on
middle-class moralism.[43] The church is contributing virtually nothing
to the moral reform which is necessary if America is to be redeemed.[44]

If we did not have the confirmation we have from other evidence,[45]
it would be easy enough to guess that these newer judgments owed
something to Niebuhr's reading of Max Weber, whose essay *Die
Protestantische Ethik und der Geist des Kapitalismus* first appeared
in book form in 1920 (in Volume One of his *Gesammelte Aufsätze
zur Religionssoziologie*). It was not to be available in English translation until the latter part of the decade.[46] Niebuhr must have had
many a conversation with his younger brother Helmut Richard
Niebuhr who was then preparing his first book, which drew heavily
on Weber; it could, indeed, be called an essay on the applicability of
the Weber thesis to the American scene.[47] The Niebuhr brothers seem
thus to have been among the first Americans to have read Weber,
and, more important, to have made serious use of his thesis. Another
evident inspiration for Niebuhr's critique of American Protestantism
is, of course, Walter Rauschenbusch.[48] At this point Niebuhr was not
nearly so "hard" as that prophet of social gospel in his analysis of
the social antagonisms which lay behind America's present discontents; soon he would be a good deal "harder."

Niebuhr's confidence in the church as an agent of social redemption became more and more qualified as the decade went on. It would
not be unfair to suggest the word "cynicism" for this new sub-theme.
(Niebuhr himself, speaking of the collapse at mid-decade of the
prestige of the erstwhile wartime heroes, recommended "the wholesome cynicism that feeds on such history as Philip Gibbs' 'Now it
can be told' and hails Lytton Strachey's biographical art.")[49]

At the time of his service in the La Follette cause, Niebuhr was in
his ninth year as pastor of Bethel Evangelical. This was the only
pastorate Niebuhr was ever to have, and he held it for thirteen years.
Niebuhr's first biographer, D. R. Davies, has described Niebuhr as
serving a "slum parish."[50] In point of fact, the parish contained

something like a cross-section of Detroiters—"everything from auto workers to two millionaires."[51] His parish was not Walter Rauschenbusch's in Hell's Kitchen, nor Norman Thomas's Spring Street Settlement House. While those two prophets of the Social Gospel, like so many others manning similar cockpits, frankly used the language of the class struggle in their preaching and writing, Niebuhr (while he was in Detroit) did not. It is crucial to understand that when Niebuhr recalled that "Ford made [him] a Socialist," a phrase often cited by students of his life and thought[52]—he was talking about a decidedly pre-Marxist brand of socialism. Niebuhr's discovery of the class struggle apparently had to await his translation from his Detroit parish to his New York professorship.

The name of Reinhold Niebuhr first came to the attention of the press as a result of a squabble among Detroiters which, boiled down, came to a question of the right of organized labor to bring its case to the people in an open-shop town. Niebuhr came down firmly on the side of the labor leaders in this question—and since this was the occasion for his first real notice in the press it is tempting to see this event simply as an expression of his identification with the cause of the working man.[53] It was that, in part, of course; but it was much more an expression of his concern for freedom of discussion. The upshot of the whole affair, in fact, was to impress upon him the woeful narrowness of mentality of the would-be leaders of the working-class. If anything, the whole affair lessened any inclination he might have had to identify the worker with virtue and the employer with evil.

In October of 1926, the American Federation of Labor came to Detroit for its annual convention.[54] It had been the custom for many years for A.F.L. leaders to have themselves invited, through the local ministerial association, to speak in city churches at Sunday services during the convention. The business community of Detroit, however, found this prospect an alarming one, and determined that Detroit should break the tradition—once and for all, if possible. The Board of Commerce, through its official publication, the *Detroiter*, bluntly called upon its members to corner their pastors and talk them out of allowing their pulpits to be used by the A.F.L. spokesmen, "men who are admittedly attacking our government and American Plan of employment."[55] All but six of the city's pulpits were closed to the A.F.L. speakers[56] and these were opened by the efforts of the officers of the Federal Council of Churches—the Detroit Ministerial Association, which had originally issued the invitations, having retreated ingloriously.

Niebuhr's diary makes it clear that the affair caused him to lower his estimation of all concerned: the capitalists who threw their weight around; the clergy who allowed them to do it; and, not least, the would-be leaders of labor, who could make no good use of the few pulpits that were opened because they held to the same primitive ideals as the ownership classes: "I attended several sessions of the convention and the men impressed me as having about the same amount of daring and imagination as a group of village bankers."[57] The affair thus did nothing to improve Niebuhr's opinion of the American worker: all about them, American capitalism is tottering, but the self-styled leaders of American working-men cannot find words too glowing for the system.

Detroit was, of course, the unchallenged bailiwick of Henry Ford —and Niebuhr's residence in Detroit coincided with the nation-wide cult of Henry Ford so well described by William Leuchtenburg in his *Perils of Prosperity*.[58]

Popular adulation of Ford impressed Niebuhr as a revelation of the incorrigible materialism of the people. Why is it, Niebuhr wondered, that Americans have been so indulgent of Henry Ford, while nowhere so indulgent of Carnegie and of John D. Rockefeller, Sr.?

> In spite of libraries and colleges, the two wealthiest men of the last generation were reviled almost as much as they were praised. Henry Ford is wealthier than either and is nevertheless the hero of the average American. The reason is that he is supposed to have accumulated his fabulous fortune without ruthlessness, and to have preserved a generous heart in the money-getting process. To pay high wages, sell a cheap product, and yet accumulate vast riches—that is a miracle which fires the imagination of every mother's son who, if the truth were known, indulges both spiritual and worldly ambitions in the secret of his heart.[59]

Ford had cultivated this goodwill through deliberate self-advertisement. But Ford's claims regarding his own philanthropy were almost complete eye-wash—as Niebuhr undertook to demonstrate (by means of some case studies from his own parish, and some plain arithmetic) in two articles and several unsigned editorials written for the *Christian Century*.[60] Ford, Niebuhr found, had indeed increased the daily wage. But he had at the same time brought ruthless speed-up techniques into his plants, which allowed him to turn his cars out faster and to send his workers home sooner, with smaller take-home pay, physically worn out, and spiritually deadened. The speed-up had also made possible extensive lay-offs—for which Ford had never felt any need to apologize to anyone. Old men could not stand up under the strain of the speed-up and in any case were soon dismissed in favor of young men from the always long lines of job-seekers at the door. Ford, of course, assumed no responsibility for the welfare of burnt-out employees; neither would he contribute when the community which he thus dominated sent around the hat for the relief of the unemployed and unemployable—this on the specious grounds that his "adequate" wage scale made any kind of philanthropy redundant and insulting to American males of good character. Ford was only able to get away with it because he had so successfully sold himself to the American public, and had so effectively rung the changes on the American myth of the self-made man as to persuade his dupes that they too might some day enjoy his wealth and know his powers.[61] If the cult of Ford contains valuable lessons on the theme of the plight of the American worker, it contains as well, Niebuhr thought, more important lessons on the broader theme of human frailty.

Plainly, the worker needs guidance—and firm guidance. The masters of this world are far too subtle for him. Significantly, Niebuhr observed that only the Communists seemed to have the spirit that was called for by the Detroit situation.[62] They were, of course, not in the least tempted by the alleged charms of the middle-class paradise. No Ager-myth for them. A worker is a worker; an owner is an owner. It was this cornerstone of the Marxist faith—the identity of interest which unites all who labor—which made the Communist leadership proof against petty-bourgeois thoughts and gave realism to their reporting of the situation in the Ford plants. Such is the force of ideology.

It is important to recall here Niebuhr's conviction, recorded as early as 1920 and repeated with regularity throughout the decade, that the alternative to a conversion in the hearts of the middle-classes, accomplished by the Protestant clergy, must be class warfare.[63] As things now stood, Niebuhr admitted, the church was weakened for her task of reconciliation by the fact "that she is not a proletarian institution."[64] There seemed to be nothing presently standing in the way of a complete conquest of the working-men by "cynical," "class-conscious" labor movements.[65]

The more he pondered the cynicism of the proletariat, the more Niebuhr felt impelled to speak for the power of the gospel to transform the oppressor: "There can be no social salvation without sacrifice, without a love that is willing to sacrifice not merely surpluses of wealth but the very economic power by which inequitable surpluses are created. Salvation through sacrifice is a truth that has been regarded as revealed finality by the church for centuries and it ought to be the more eager to be guided by it in the present crisis. What the world needs is not only the gospel specifically applied but the gospel undefiled."[66] In the meantime, "the intensive development of the kingdom waits upon the establishment of more equitable relations in business and industry."[67]

Yet there were times when Niebuhr had to confess the temptation to cynicism. The will to believe in the perfectibility of the middle-classes carries with it, he admitted, the risk of "sentimentality" —the distinctive "middle class vice."[68] While he continued to be impressed with the enthusiasm of the preachers and their "social vision," it became increasingly difficult for him to retain patience with "the rank and file of the church."[69] If "credulity" and "sentimentality" are the diseases, then some degree of "wholesome cynicism" might seem to be called for.

Marxists, however, are highly selective about their cynicism. But deep in his heart, as Niebuhr has been insisting, the worker is as materialistic, as selfish, as the worst banker. And (if we are to judge by the performance of the A.F.L. leaders) he can be counted on to turn a deaf ear to the cause of his proper comrades once he gets one foot on the ladder. How can the worker's friends serve him whole-heartedly without falling into the deceit of pretending that the worker's cause is more virtuous than it is?

Marxists, of course, have an answer for this. It is plain that Niebuhr, in his Detroit period, knew nothing of that answer. In the Marxist dialectic, it is the very poverty of the worker that declares his objective virtue. Possessing nothing, and without prospect of any material improvement, he does not need to appeal to "morality" to justify himself. Objectively, the proletarian is the only pure force in the "works" of history—precisely because he is materially interested. He provides the dynamic of history and commands its destiny because none of his energy is dissipated in ideological mummery. To the Niebuhr of the nineteen twenties, this logic seemed mere "cynicism."[70] Middle-class America, as it appeared from West Grand Boulevard in Detroit in the 1920s, was not without its redeeming qualities. For a few years longer he was to remain resistant to social cynicism and the blandishments of Marxism.

All things considered, Niebuhr's experience as a pastor had been a perplexing and, at times, a frustrating one. The church is entrusted with the supreme truths about life; yet the social imagination of its members, Niebuhr found, is no greater than that of secular citizens. Conventional Christianity, the Christianity of the average man, never gets beyond the most limited risk-taking; the average Churchman honestly believes that he has applied his religion to the limit when he has brought the more obvious personal vices under discipline. It is plainly too much to hope of the average man's intelligence and will that he should be able to see the social applications of his faith. This insight and this will are confined to the few who are specially endowed: to an elite, in short.

There has always been an elitist strain to Niebuhr's thought. A classmate of Niebuhr's at Eden Theological Seminary recalls the reaction of the young seminarians to the news of the sinking of the Titanic in 1912:

> We were deeply shaken by this tragedy in which more than a thousand people perished. I was moved by the sheer numbers of this awful tragedy. Reinie kept commenting on the loss of some of the leaders in the realms of art and science that went down with the ship. I protested that all men are equally precious in the sight of God. But he insisted with his passion for realism that the loss of men and women who are making a great contribution to the welfare of their fellowmen is infinitely greater than the loss of the rank and file of the human family. For me democracy and religious concern for human personality were equated with a kind of hazy egalitarianism, but Reinie's keener insight recognized an aristocracy within the framework of democracy, namely an aristocracy of character and service to humanity.[71]

It is this elite, Niebuhr believed, which must within the ranks of the church give expression to the larger implications of Christianity—its social and political implications. But, given the weakness of the leadership principle within Protestantism, there seems little hope for success. Egalitarianism is too powerful within Protestantism, precisely as it is in the democratic community as a whole. In America, the capitalist philosophy conspires with Protestant individualism to deprive the community of its social conscience. Any clergyman who seeks to apply the Christian message to the problem of social injustice is either driven from his pulpit or (more regularly) simply ignored.

> In these questions it is the laymen who fancy themselves the experts and who are the traditionalists, resenting interference from amateurs who may know religion but who "don't know business." If the pulpit is to speak bravely on economic and moral problems it ought to have the support of the entire Christian community against the semi-pagans who fill its pews and represent not so much an army to be enlisted as an enemy that must be converted. Both the Catholic and Anglican churches have better records for courage in social and economic issues than

> congregationally organized communities in which the individual
> prophet is frequently at the mercy of a congregation which
> may contain many men who do not want religion to "interfere
> with business."[72]

Something must therefore be done to strengthen the leadership principle within the church.

We should note here the parallel between Niebuhr's diagnosis of
the spiritual failure of the church and his diagnosis of the political
failure of the working-class. Both the working-class and the rank and
file of the church suffer from a lack of deference. As we have seen,
Niebuhr found the working-class unqualified for enlightened direction
of its own struggle for justice. The would-be leaders who emerge
from its ranks are quickly claimed by the enemies of the working-
class as salesmen for their capitalist values.

Thus, all that Niebuhr had observed to this point (the late 1920s)
of the economic, social, and political facts of life reinforced the lesson
he had learned from his practical experience in the ministry. The
church, which incarnated the great spiritual truths, was at best
irrelevant to the needs of the American community—unless the
ministry accepted larger responsibilities of leadership and unless the
rank and file learned the wisdom of deference to it. Similarly, the
working-class, whose cause is objectively the cause of justice, is
entirely without hope of rescue from material and spiritual poverty—
unless it can be brought under the direction of responsible leadership
*outside its own ranks.*

Niebuhr's plea for a recovery of the leadership principle in democracy was very much in tune with liberal-intellectual thinking of his
day.[73] In fact, Niebuhr is here sounding the distinctive note of the
whole Progressive tradition. It is necessary to say something about
that tradition here, before the onset of two movements of the 1930s
—the socialist enthusiasm of the early thirties and the great inter-
ventionist debate of the late thirties—which would change forever
the character of American liberalism.

# THE PROTESTANT-PROGRESSIVE MATRIX

*"The ideal of the kingdom of God*
*built the holy commonwealths of New England,*
*provided the core of the 'social gospel',*
*and is the cardinal ingredient even in American*
*secular idealism today."*

ROLAND BAINTON[1]

From time to time in this book we shall find it useful to turn to European observers for help in identifying features of the American religious scene which were not obvious to American writers lacking their comparative perspective. The first of these is Willem A. Visser 't Hooft (later General Secretary of the World Council of Churches) in whose book, *The Background of the Social Gospel in America* (1928), we find an early and valuable discussion of the situation of the Protestant clergy in the first quarter of this century.

Religion in the United States is popular in the best sense of the word. It is not confined to a small section of the population but has a generally accepted and generally recognized value. It is therefore not compelled to adopt a defensive attitude as it is in many countries in Europe where it has to fight for its life, but can claim the sympathy of the nation as a whole and aggressively enter the field of nation-wide moral and social issues.

Though there is a distinct opposition to a participation of the church in political affairs as such, there is a deep and widely held

conviction that the underlying principles of social and political
life depend for their permanency on religious influences and that
therefore the underlying moral issues of national life rightly
belong to the sphere of interest of the church.

The church therefore has always felt free to influence public
opinion on matters where it has felt convinced that important
principles of moral and religious life were at stake.[2]

All things are, however, relative. Even as Visser 't Hooft was recording these observations, the company of preachers was losing its hold
on the public attention. Reinhold Niebuhr stands virtually alone in the
middle decades of this century as a Protestant clergyman exercising
substantial influence upon reform thought and action. The fact is that
by the 1930s leadership no longer came automatically or even easily
to a Protestant clergyman, and Niebuhr was required to win his
audience in the American reform community *in spite of* his cloth.
Nonetheless, Niebuhr's message depended for its impact upon the
continuing vitality of the Protestant ethical tradition. In other words,
while there was little force left in the old notion that "the underlying moral issues of national life rightly belong to the sphere of
interest of the church," there was, and perhaps there is still in
America, "a deep and widely held conviction that the underlying
principles of social and political life depend for their permanency on
religious influences." It is only the conjunctive "therefore" of Visser
't Hooft's statement that stands discredited by the politics of the
middle decades of this century.

In our study of Reinhold Niebuhr, we are dealing with a man who
came of age a little too late to be active within the original Progressive
movement but did arrive in time to do his political apprenticeship in
the camp of La Follette and Wheeler (in 1924), and who came to
stand in the front ranks of the intellectual leaders of the post-New
Deal years.

Niebuhr was the son of a clergyman, and became a clergyman
himself. He later recalled that when he announced to his father his
intention to follow his father's career in the ministry he was best
able to express his motivation by declaring that it was "because
you're the most interesting man in town."[3] Anyone familiar with
Richard Hofstadter's *Age of Reform*[4]—the work which instigated the
contemporary re-interpretation of the Progressive movement—will be
reminded by this comment of Hofstadter's description of the social
role of clergymen in the years of the senior Niebuhr's ministry.[5]
Niebuhr's father is the prototype of the man that Hofstadter had in
mind—and this is all the more worth recording because Pastor
Niebuhr was an immigrant (he had come from Germany at the age

of seventeen). Gustav Niebuhr's parishioners were mainly retired farmers who (as Reinhold Niebuhr bluntly expressed it) "had made their pile"[6] and, regarding their wealth as the due reward for hard work and simple virtue, were determined to resist any claims upon it of community and government. Gustav Niebuhr believed that his ministry required him "to spend a good deal of time trying to beguile them from their unconstructive conservatism."[7]

It is Richard Hofstadter's conviction that this conception of the preacher's task was generally held by Protestant clergymen of the Progressive age. For the most part, they themselves lived what Reinhold Niebuhr remembers as a life of "genteel poverty."[8] During the last quarter of the nineteenth century, as the cost of living rose, and as the wealth and comforts of the sort of men who were chairmen of church boards rose steadily, the salaries of clergymen improved hardly at all.[9] More important, like other representatives of the older professional classes, they were being brusquely shoved from their positions of leadership in the community at large. They were, says Hofstadter, "probably the most conspicuous losers from the status revolution ... that took place in American society and intellectual life in the last three decades of the nineteenth century."[10] Thus, for example, in the field of education, trustees of colleges were being chosen less and less often from the ranks of lawyers and clergymen, and more and more often from the ranks of the businessmen who were footing the bills and who would, it was feared, capture the schools, along with the political parties, the press, and everything else, for their money-grubbing way of life.

In the years between the Civil War and the late 1880s, the Protestant ministry had presented (in the words of Henry F. May) "a massive, almost unbroken front in its defense of the *status quo*";[11] then, "Beginning slowly in the 1890s and increasingly in the next two decades, members of these professions deserted the standpat conservatism of the post-Civil War era to join the main stream of liberal dissent and to give it both moral and intellectual leadership."[12] Just as the Anglican Church in the eighteenth century could be seen as "the Tory party at prayer," so a case could be made out that Progressivism was the Protestant establishment in political action. "In the Progressive protest," Richard Hofstadter writes, "the voice of the Christian conscience was heard more clearly than at any time since the days of the abolitionist movement."[13]

Most of the American clergymen who were swept into the political wars during the Progressive era were moved by enthusiasm for the "Social Gospel."[14] Genetically, Social Gospel was Reform Darwinism, coupled with Christian Socialism.[15] To Social Gospelers, it seemed clear that God had placed America in the forefront of the struggle for the accomplishment of His Kingdom on earth. The Kingdom lay ahead—but quite within reach, some felt.[16] Perhaps no better summation of the Social Gospel can be found than an editorial manifesto appearing in Shailer Mathew's journal, *Biblical World*, in 1920: "The bottom of society has broken loose and is coming up.... Social reconstruction means that the man who works the machine shall be at least part owner of the product of his toil.... Social reconstruction needs the dynamic of the cross of Christ.... God works through social evolution.... The saved world will not be an exhumed, resuscitated past. It will be a Christian social order in which men shall be given justice.... For men shall have the attitudes and the behavior of Jesus Christ."[17]

Before the consummation of the Kingdom, however, America must experience the judgment of God upon America's social shortcomings. Social Gospelers agreed that that system lay under judgment. Capitalism was doomed and must disappear. But would the transition from capitalism to socialism be peaceful or must it be accompanied by violence? It was on this question that Social Gospelers differed most strongly. Indeed, an individual Social Gospeler could regularly be found tacking between the two alternative possibilities which this question suggested.

On the one hand, it was argued that chastisement was the inescapable fate of capitalism and of the capitalists. It would be naive and unrealistic to anticipate some change of heart which might cause the capitalists to join hands with the proletariat and to avoid retribution for their past. Many Social Gospelers were drawn to Marxism as a tool of social and political analysis. A *consistent* use of Marxism was never essayed by even the most radical, however. The basic obstacle in the way of marrying Social Gospel to Marxism was Marx's conviction that the bourgeoisie would resist to the death. The basic idealism of the Social Gospel encouraged its followers to believe that the hard hearts of the owners could be softened by appeals to their better nature.

This difficulty about the matter of violence is perhaps not as obvious to us today—and this quite apart from the fact that the predictive uses of Marxist science have been so much discredited by intervening events. For there exists today a formidable corpus of literature defending the tragic necessity of the Christian's undertaking force to achieve relative goals in an imperfect world. The most impressive of the items in that literature are from the pens of former Social Gospelers, of whom Reinhold Niebuhr is the foremost. It is, indeed, a large part of our task in this essay to describe the circumstances which brought about this turn of affairs. In the days of which we are speaking now, however, it went without saying that a liberal-minded American clergyman was, at least in theory, a pacifist. The mainline Social Gospel scenario for social reconstruction ran along these lines.

> [The] economic millennium must be reached, first of all, through the consecrated initiative of component individuals. . . . The pillars of modern industrial life are securely set in the moral stability of the vast majority of business lives. Millions of such persons, as they scrupulously discharge their business obligations, are meeting the demand of Jesus, "Whosoever would be first among you shall be your servant" [Matt. xx. 27]. . . . The Christian problem of the industrial world is to multiply lives like these. If any revolution in the industrial order is to overthrow the existing economic system, the new order must depend for its permanence on the principles of the teaching of Jesus; but if the principles of the teaching of Jesus should come to control the existing economic system, a revolution in the industrial order would seem to be unnecessary.[18]

Thus, the judgment against capitalism *could* work itself out; a more Christian social order *could* come to replace it—if only sufficient well-placed capitalists would apply the ethics of Jesus to their daily lives. This was, of course, a far cry from the adulation of the business leader indulged in by the conservative clergy. No Social Gospeler could escape the conclusion that for American civilization—capitalistic, individualistic, materialistic, as it was—judgment lay ahead. The only point worth arguing, they felt, was whether judgment necessarily would involve chastisement of the capitalists themselves.

When Reinhold Niebuhr was beginning to make his mark as a spokesman for Social Gospel, the Protestant clergy appeared to be on the threshold of their greatest period of power. The War was doing worlds of good for the morale of the clergy. The War years were years of happy cooperation between the American community as a whole and organized Protestantism; for no segment of the community had better served the cause of rallying the community behind the war effort.[19] With a few exceptions (the Fellowship of Reconciliation, the Friends, and the Mennonites), the legion of peace groups which flourished before the War (and whose leadership was drawn largely from the clergy, when they were not altogether Church-oriented)

abandoned their witness—or, as they preferred to describe things, adapted their message to the times. Government officials appealed to the church—and never in vain—for its help in bond drives and in spurring citizens to a variety of vital activities, from distributing literature to collecting vital statistics.[20] In return, government sources repeatedly expressed their gratitude to the church for its cooperation. The whole experience had been a heady one—and had left Protestant leadership convinced that it now enjoyed the deference of the American community as a whole. Now it could undertake to stamp its ideals on the American civilization.

Thus, when the War ended, Protestantism appeared to be entering a day of great vitality and maturity. This was the period when the most ambitious experiments in interdenominational cooperation were launched. It was a period of spectacularly successful fund-raising drives launched by the major denominations for the expansion of their work.[21] Above all, it was the age that saw the Protestant establishment's greatest legislative victory—national Prohibition.

James H. Timberlake has demonstrated[22] the remarkably broad appeal of the Prohibition "crusade" to the American people in the first two decades of the century, and has thus challenged the notion (most readily associated with H. L. Mencken) that Prohibition was merely the vengeance of the countryside being wreaked upon the city. Timberlake has found widespread Prohibition sentiment within the ranks of business and labor, and within the Catholic Church, and within the middle-class elements from which the Progressive movement as a whole drew its strength. Most interesting, for our purposes, is Timberlake's demonstration of the enthusiasm for Prohibition within Social Gospel ranks.[23] Social Gospelers, like the Protestant leadership generally, spoke out against drink as a hazard to the soul; but the Social Gospelers added to this an extra bitterness, deriving from the conviction they shared with Progressive leadership as a whole, that the liquor traffic was marked by the worst vices of big business: monopoly, and corrupt liaison with politicians. "Alcohol is a spirit born of hell," Rauschenbusch charged, "but he [who sells it] is merely a satellite and tool of a far greater devil, and that is Mammon. . . . The private interest that has invested its money in the wholesale and retail liquor business is seeking to fasten on an angry people a relic of moral barbarism which the awakened conscience and the scientific intellect of the world are combining to condemn."[24]

The triumph of the Prohibition movement in 1919 is correctly seen as a triumph of organized Protestantism over those elements in the American community that did not share its scale of values. But it must be realized that in its crusade for Prohibition Protestantism had the good will of the Progressive movement as a whole. It marked, therefore, an apparent double-triumph for Protestant leadership: it seemed to vindicate Protestantism's claim to speak for the community as a whole in matters of morals and at the same time it seemed to place Protestant leadership in the company of the most enlightened forces of the time. A statement from a young Social Gospel clergyman of the time illustrates the point in all its naïvete: "The prohibition movement has come to express the most enlightened conscience of the American people."[25] The author of the statement is Reinhold Niebuhr—then aged twenty-four.

A curious chapter in this account of Protestantism's heyday belongs to the brief career of the "Interchurch World Movement"—a story that is now all but forgotten but which was one of the big domestic news stories of 1919–1920. Anyone pursuing this story through the pages of the newspapers of those months finds himself skipping over headlines and lingering over photographs (still restricted, in those days, to the weekly rotogravure sections, and still brown and white) that document the big story of the year—the Versailles Treaty and how Wilson and the other Irreconcilables did it in together. Interestingly, the climax in both these stories comes at about the same time —in the spring of 1920. In both cases, the climax was marked by the collapse of high hopes. In both cases there is a long anti-climax, an unseemly funeral with everyone pushing forward to make the funeral oration, and nobody left in the ranks of the mourners. The public lost interest in both stories at about the same time, in the fall of 1920, when the national election swept all the issues of the Wilsonian age into limbo.[26]

"The Interchurch World Movement" was organized late in 1919 to pool the money-gathering talents of all the major denominations for a dramatic final push against the challenge of foreign and home missions.[27] Encouraged by large donations from John D. Rockefeller, Jr., and by the willingness of that same noted Baptist layman to serve as chief fund-raiser, Interchurch set itself a budget of $400,000,000 for the next five years only, and pledged to collect several times that amount over the next few years. A ten-year lease was taken out on a five-story headquarters, at an annual rent of $350,000.[28] Soon the movement was claiming to speak for thirty million persons (the total population of the United States was then 106 million).[29] The directors radiated confidence in the American people, in the loyalty of churchmen, and in social science; working in harness, these forces could not fail. Interchurch would survey "all the facts about the religious, social, moral, physical and economic environments of humanity through the world [so that] from these facts a unified program shall be worked out in which all can concur." The result would be "nothing less than the complete evangelization of all of life."[30]

In the course of their fact-finding, Interchurch investigators took it upon themselves to enquire into the circumstances behind a burning public question of the hour: working conditions at United States Steel, at that time being struck by its workers. The investigation had been prompted by no less a power than Secretary of Labor Wilson.[31] In the opinion of Donald Meyer, the Interchurch Report on the strike "remains to this day one of the best inquiries into a specific strike situation."[32] By the time the Report was published, however, Interchurch had collapsed.[33] It seemed natural enough to assume that the preparation of the Report and the sudden drying up of funds in support of Interchurch were connected. It was said then—and is still widely believed—that Interchurch was destroyed by Judge Gary, Chairman of the Board of U.S. Steel, who bruited it about the halls of big industry and big finance that the Interchurch investigators were Kremlin dupes.[34] Certainly, the big contributions stopped coming in, and Interchurch was soon facing appalling financial troubles—not the least of which was that five-story headquarters building with its six-figure rental. Other factors were involved, of course: notably the withdrawal of the Presbyterians and Baptists, in protest over the unrealistic financial goals set by the directors. Yet it would be difficult to underestimate the significance of Gary's lobbying against the Interchurch probers. Certainly, the liberal magazines were convinced that Gary's vendetta was the full and sufficient explanation.[35] The great experiment had lasted just twenty months.

The collapse of Interchurch struck a great blow to the morale of all Protestant churchmen. To Social Gospelers, the blow was no less hard than it was for the conservatives. It revealed a shocking resistance in the hearts of capitalists to even the most distant effects of the social message of Jesus.

The Report had not, after all, included anything very subversive: it had recommended little more than that U.S. Steel catch up with the times in its labor policies.[36] Yet how quickly the appreciation of the captains of industry for the high ideals of Interchurch had evaporated! How quickly their enthusiasm for the evangelization of everything on the landscape had cooled when it appeared that the church was in a mood to enquire about matters private to the captains of industry—such matters as labor policies! It seemed almost as if the leaders of the American economy hardly trusted the leaders of the church. But were these latter not, by general consensus, the moral leaders of America?

The real significance of the Interchurch affair was that a good decade before the collapse of Prohibition (which signalled the collapse of the dream of imposing Protestant ethics on a post-Protestant civilization) Judge Gary and his friends had blasted the myth that Protestant pastors could speak "to and for the whole population in the same tone of voice which they direct[ed] to their own memberships."[37]

Actually, Protestant leaders were rapidly losing their hold over the thoughts and actions of their congregations. Protestant denominations were becoming increasingly "confessionless." Protestant preachers and writers drew more and more upon a vague moralism for sermon content, which moralism was a barely sanctified version of nineteenth-century prudential morality. Although Protestant affiliation grew absolutely during the twenties (and would continue to grow at least through the early 1960s), Protestant Americans were already a minority. The great gains in membership made by the Catholic Church and the striking revival of religious affiliation among Jews, in the same period, were to put the Protestants in a minority position, despite the continued growth of Protestant membership. Protestantism, wrote André Siegfried in 1927,[38] is America's "only national religion, and to ignore that fact is to view the country from a false angle." It is impossible to be precise about the timing, of course; but it is probable that this statement had already become out of date by 1927, when Siegfried expressed it. As Alfred North Whitehead observed in 1933: "[Protestantism's] dogmas no longer dominate; its divisions no longer interest; its institutions no longer direct the patterns of life."[39] The "national religion" was by that date well on its way to becoming "the fourth religion," which Will Herberg describes as a consensus of the supposedly non-controversial tenets of Protestantism, Catholicism, and Judaism—creedless sentimentalism whose principal feature is its ready identification of God's purpose with America's.[40] This "national religion" is identical with "The American Way of Life": "From the very beginning the American Way of Life was shaped by the contours of American Protestantism; it may, indeed, best be understood as a kind of secularized Puritanism, a Puritanism without transcendence, without sense of sin or judgement."[41]

Somewhere in the first quarter of the twentieth century—the World War is probably the turning point—Protestant America's concept of the Kingdom of God in America came to occupy the same ground in the American consciousness with secular America's patriotic concept of the nation's "exceptionalism." The Protestant leadership, having behind it centuries of experience in preaching, exhorting, and haranguing multitudes, quickly found itself commanding the platform. The experience was a heady one. It left the Protestant clergy believing that all Americans—or at least its better elements—had gone under the yoke of its discipline. The surest proof of this seemed to be the success of Prohibition, a cause that seemed to combine the best of American prudential morality with the "most enlightened conscience of the times," and one for which the Protestant churches had long provided the leadership.

Richard Hofstadter, in his *Anti-Intellectualism in American Life* (1963) describes the growing alienation (beginning in the twenties, increasing in tempo in the thirties) between the rank and file of the Protestant churches and the intellectual element within the clergy. Laymen generally were suspicious of the "social gospel" which had been the love of clerical intellectuals. They feared, too, that these same intellectuals were spreading a disturbing liberal theology which endangered the "fundamentals" of the faith. Social gospel was creating a "priestly class" that no longer spoke the language of the lay churchgoers.[42] While Hofstadter singles out the great Fundamentalist controversy as the critical occasion for this parting-of-the-ways between the intellectual leadership and the ranks, it seems clear that there was involved as well a conflict regarding the role of the church in capitalist society. Within the ranks of the Social Gospelers themselves there was emerging a radical wing which recognized the peril of the old habit of identifying the Kingdom with the Promise of American Life. These radicals argued that the church was deceiving itself to think it was setting the moral tone or the intellectual tone of the American community, when in fact the community was using the church to sanctify materialistic values.

Radicals wondered how much longer they could hope to defend a church which seemed so given over to the celebration of the American system and its leaders, the businessmen. Indeed, many of them (Norman Thomas is the best-known example) did soon leave the church in despair over the possibility of getting the Babbitts to come to terms with what they regarded as the social teachings of Jesus. Those who remained in their pulpits thought of themselves as committed to uncompromising struggle against the values which commanded the allegiance of their parishioners—values celebrated in the astonishing works of Bruce Barton, advertising man and church-layman, whose best-selling contribution to the quest for the historical Jesus (*The Man Nobody Knows*, 1925) "assimilated Jesus Christ into the new cult [of the businessman], observing admiringly of the Son of God that He had 'picked up twelve men from the bottom ranks of business and forged them into an organization that conquered the world.' "[43] With the world-view of the Founder of Christianity so entirely in harmony with that of the age of prosperity, there was, of course, no place for any thought of judgment.

Thus, radicals warned, the church's values were increasingly being set by the business community which were, they said (and Bruce Barton notwithstanding) essentially at odds with the ethics of the Kingdom. The Interchurch debacle, they argued, had proved that point. "Radicals" were that self-conscious minority who *welcomed* the recognition by their congregations that they, the clergy, did not "speak the language" of their semi-pagan congregations. During the twenties, they separated themselves from out of the ranks of the conservative clergy—and from out of the ranks of the old-line Social Gospelers as well, for these shared the illusion of harmony between Christian views and the best values of American civilization—to essay the role of the prophet, setting their faces against the values celebrated by the capitalist system.[44]

"If the pulpit is to speak bravely on economic and moral problems," Niebuhr had written in 1924, "it ought to have the support of the entire Christian community against the semi-pagans who fill its pews." Niebuhr, in this appeal to the clergy, was using the language of the new radical wing. This conviction of alienation from the values of the American community marks the end of the Progressive era of American reform.[45] A man who saw so deep a gulf as that between the values of the pulpit and the values of the pew was as remote from the world of Walter Rauschenbusch as he was from that of Bruce Barton. The clue to the differences between this new "radical" minority—of whom Niebuhr was to become the leader in the thirties but whose leaders during the twenties were such men as Harry Ward and Kirby Page—is to be found in the reaffirmation of judgement against contemporary civilization. Rauschenbusch's conviction of a continuum between the best values of American society and the Kingdom-message was no longer very convincing to the radicals of Niebuhr's generation.

Yet Niebuhr's declaration of judgment against the man in the pew is not without a certain (apparently unconscious) nostalgia. Niebuhr was very much a child of the twilight years of the Protestant hegemony. What can he mean by "the entire Christian community" whose values are somehow not those of "the semi-pagans in the pews"? The Progressives loved to talk in this fashion of the entire Christian community—of the Christian conscience of the community —and so on; and what they meant by it was the respectable element of Americans. And that, we must conclude, is what Niebuhr meant by it. This nostalgia for "the Christian community" is part-and-parcel with Niebuhr's lingering indulgence for the bourgeoisie and his expressions of faith in their continuing idealism. By the end of the decade, Niebuhr's total disenchantment with both the Christian laity and the bourgeoisie (who were, after all, the same persons) was accomplished. It was then—and only then—that Niebuhr found himself ready for socialism.

The new dawn of Protestant hegemony had been a mirage. Social drift had undone its majority position, while intellectual drift had deprived it of a hearing on social issues. A clergyman could no longer claim leadership in political opinion by reason of his cloth. If he desired to play a political role at all, he had to overcome a powerful, double-edged prejudice against him in the political community. On the one side it was felt that he should keep out of politics for the sake of the purity of his message; on the other, it was held that his cloth automatically marked him as a servant of the most formidable of all the engines of social inertia.

Reinhold Niebuhr was remarkably quick to read the signs of the times. He was a deeply political animal—not for any of the reasons known to Aristotle, but because, with Péguy, he believed that everything that begins in mysticism must end in politics. Deep religious seriousness made him a politician. But that same religious seriousness convinced him, by the end of the decade of the twenties, that the Protestant community had long since ceased to be a helpful instrument for political righteousness. He was further convinced that his cloth gave him no claim to the ear of the American community as a whole. Thus, he took his burden of concern for human society into the political arena as a citizen, where, he believed, a loving God would teach him how to use his reason to wring answers to political questions from the same materials that proved so recalcitrant to secular progressives in the dreary age of Harding, Coolidge, and Hoover.

# THE WORLD OF POLITICS

From the perspective of old age, Niebuhr remembered himself in the twenties as "a simple-minded socialist,"[1] or (on another occasion) "a socialist, though not yet expressing myself in socialist terms."[2] Looking over the record of his words and deeds, one has to conclude that no good purpose is served by calling him a socialist before the end of the decade. The label he regularly used during the twenties to define his position on political issues was "radical." And that label, in view of the philosophical inconsistencies in his social analysis in the twenties, is precise enough for our purposes.

Niebuhr's first published comment throwing light on this matter of political labels is a letter to the editors of the *New Republic*.[3] The letter begins: "Of course all of us who were pleased to call ourselves 'liberals' are greatly disappointed with the peace treaty," and goes on to make clear that the young writer identifies liberalism with Wilsonianism, and expects both to be soon repudiated by the conscience of mankind. Wilson's failure, he writes, is the failure of a political tradition (liberalism) which thrived on compromise and is thus disarmed by the new ruthlessness of the twentieth-century situation (incarnated in Lloyd George and Clemenceau). As the use of the past tense implies ("those of us who *were* pleased to call themselves 'liberals' "), Niebuhr is done with such compromise:

There is a gray spirit of compromise in most liberalism, ancient as well as modern. It is afraid to tear down old houses and build new ones. It just tinkers around on the old ones and has no better luck with them than the architects have. It lacks the spirit of enthusiasm, not to say fanaticism, which is so necessary to move

the world out of its beaten tracks. Liberalism is too intellectual
and too little emotional to be an efficient force in history. It is the
philosphy of the middle aged, lacking the fervency of youth
and its willingness to take a change and accept a challenge. It
approaches the old order with a friendly mien, tries to blindfold
it and lead it upon a new track without hurting the old order's
feelings or losing its friendship. But the old order is never the
doting fool that it seems to be. Either it humors and fools
liberalism by changing its course so imperceptibly that it has no
value or, if liberalism proves itself too persistent, it gets angry
and gives the reformers a slap in the face. In the peace treaty the
old order seems to have defended itself quite successfully by both
methods. We need something less circumspect than liberalism
to save the world.

Statements of this sort—condemning the old order for its injustices, and commending something variously described as "industrial
democracy" or "socialization"—can be garnered with ease and in
great numbers from Niebuhr's writings in the early twenties.[4] Significantly, however, Niebuhr does not undertake anything like a full-
length diagnosis of society's sickness until October of 1928, in an
article, "Why We Need a New Economic Order," in the *World
Tomorrow*.

Though somewhat lacking in internal consistency, this essay on
the sins of capitalism could stand up well in comparison with the
essays of better known American radicals whose thoughts were
appearing in the *New Republic* and the *Nation* of the day. (Let us
note, in passing, that this article appears just one month before the
Presidential election of 1928, and just one year before the stock
market crash.) Niebuhr has obviously read and understood the history
of capitalism's origins. We have already noted his acquaintance with
the works of Max Weber—and certainly there are overtones of
Weber here. There is as well a large debt obvious to R. H. Tawney's
*Religion and the Rise of Capitalism*.[5] One could hardly hope for a
clearer description of the fundamental flaw of the American economy
which would lead in a very few months to the great depression:
"As industry continues to perfect its machines it arrives at a production capacity which the wants of the community cannot absorb
except the buying power of the workers is greatly increased. . . .
With his present buying power the worker cannot absorb the products of his own toil. . . . When competitive industry deals with this
problem it easily aggravates it, for it meets the problem of restricted
markets by lowering wages and cutting wages, thus further restricting the buying power of the public."[6]

Niebuhr proposes not to tear down and build anew, but "to modify the present system step by step." He acknowledges the possibility that the despair of the unprivileged may swell to such proportions that the opportunity for step-by-step reform may be lost, and revolution will ensue. But he clearly does not want revolution and he does not regard revolution as inevitable. He shares the conviction of Social Gospelers that a bold employment of "imagination and intelligence" will avert the need for revolution.

There is not a hint of Marxism in this gas-and-water socialism. There was enough Marxism in even the mildest American socialist of the 1920s to balk at this:

> Whether the present system will succumb to violence or be gradually changed and modified by social and political action will not be decided by those who suffer most from its limitations. The decision may seem to rest with them. But it really rests with the community in general and with the holders of privilege and power in particular. A society which is able to modify its processes and relationships to fit new situations may gradually evolve new systems out of old ones. Only if it is too stubborn or too inert to attempt such modifications will the old be destroyed for the sake of the new. It might be added that the widespread belief among radicals that a violent change is preferable because more thoroughgoing is not borne out by history. The more complex economic and social relationships become the less forceful is the logic of the revolutionists.

To speak of the power of "decision" resting with "the community in general" is to part company with everything recognizable as Marxism. The key to understanding Niebuhr's politics is still, in October of 1928, what it was a decade earlier: namely, religious idealism. It is curious, therefore, that in later years Niebuhr would regularly remember his position as a moral critic in these days as being characterized by reaction against the "soft utopianism," and "idealism" of liberalism.[7] While he frequently lapsed into moods of "wholesome cynicism," the predominant mood was clearly one of idealism; and it is a very liberal sort of idealism, deriving from a faith in the goodwill of the community as a whole and from Niebuhr's conscious repudiation of the temptation to see a particular virtue in the dispossessed. Putting the problem of social inequality in its proper perspective, he said (about this time), we "are confronted with a civilization . . . so wealthy that it obscures social inequalities."[8] Affluence, thus, is the real enemy. Compared to the baneful effects of American affluence, social friction (arising out of differences of

opinion as to how to distribute the wealth) is a secondary blight. Or
so it seemed to Niebuhr on the eve of the Great Depression.

In addition to the evidence we have of Niebuhr's expressed views in
the 1920s, we have to consider the evidence of the political company
he kept. We have already alluded to his service to the Progressive
cause in 1924. There is no evidence of his membership in the Socialist
Party in these years.[9] He is included, however, in a list of members
of the faculty of Union Theological Seminary supporting Norman
Thomas for the Presidency in 1928.[10] Niebuhr was a member of the
League for Industrial Democracy[11] which began life in 1905 as the
Intercollegiate Socialist Society, under the aegis of Jack London,
Upton Sinclair, Morris Hillquit, and others. The I.S.S./L.I.D. had
never been under the discipline of the Socialist Party, however, and
included many who were not Socialist Party members.[12]

Socialist Party membership and electoral strength were both at
their lowest ebb in those years.[13] To accommodate social democrats
and radicals who were unwilling to declare themselves socialists,
Norman Thomas, in the weeks immediately following the election of
1928, was lending his formidable energies to the development of a
new third party movement. He found a happy meeting of minds in
discussions with Paul Douglas, John Dewey, W. E. B. DuBois, and
others associated with the L.I.D. Out of these discussions came the
League for Independent Political Action, in December, 1928.[14] Reinhold Niebuhr was, from the beginning, a member of the L.I.P.A.[15]

Socialist and quasi-Socialist enthusiasm ran very powerfully in
ministerial ranks in the 1920s. Yet clergymen, like the run of the
middle-class intellectual spokesmen, were usually reluctant to accept
the Socialist Party tag. Here again we find Niebuhr to be typical
of his profession. He was a member of the most lively of the
socialist-oriented forums which the clergy provided for themselves in
the 1920s: the Fellowship for a Christian Social Order, organized in
1922 by Sherwood Eddy, Kirby Page, and others, and including such
formidable spokesmen of the Social Gospel as Francis J. McConnell,
Charles Clayton Morrison (of the *Christian Century*), A. J. Muste, and
Harry Ward.[16] He was, as well, an editor of the *World Tomorrow*.
This fascinating mirror of the left-wing clerical mind of the 1920s
had begun in 1918, under Norman Thomas's direction, as the voice
of the pacifist Fellowship of Reconciliation. Its emphasis was as much
socialist as pacifist, however; its editors regarded the two as inseparable. Its masthead described it as "A Journal Looking Forward to a

Social Order Based on the Principles of Jesus." Its socialism was quite flexible and attenuated, however—like Niebuhr's own.

The L.I.D., F.C.S.O., and the editorial community of the *World Tomorrow* provided Niebuhr with abundant opportunities to share thoughts about politics, economics, and social problems with educated and sensitive students of life. None of these associations committed him to anything that can accurately be called socialism. The furthest he had gone in that direction was to recommend the election of Norman Thomas over Al Smith or Herbert Hoover—which is, after all, not very far. But the effect of all these associations—and possibly most significantly the association with Norman Thomas—was to prepare him for a decision he was soon to make in favor of socialism and Socialist party membership.

Sherwood Eddy, who was so instrumental in launching Niebuhr's career as a writer and lecturer, was also responsible for Niebuhr's first travels outside America, an experience which was to be of decisive significance in his development as a moral philosopher. In 1921, Eddy had devised the plan of his European Seminars, to acquaint a select group of American intellectuals with the European situation and with the European politicians, intellectuals, and other leaders upon whom Europe's future would depend. Niebuhr was included in the select company for the Seminar of 1923.[17] Niebuhr —always one to improve an opportunity—brought back materials and memories for several excellent articles on the European scene.[18]

These articles, together with the references to his trip which we find in his published diary, illustrate at least three effects that his trip had upon his thinking. The first of these (as we have already had occasion to mention) was to strengthen his pacifism. His encounter with French ruthlessness in the Ruhr[19] seems to have dealt the final blow to the illusion that had hitherto kept him from complete cynicism about the outcome of the War to End War—the illusion (as he had expressed it on an earlier occasion)[20] "that, bad as the peace is, it is better than the Prussian variety offered us."

The second effect of Niebuhr's exposure to Europe was to improve his sensitivity to certain unpleasant facts of political and social life which he had been inclined to discount. The European trip, in short, began that education in social realism which was not completed until the end of the decade. "The moral limitations of modern life" (as he put it) were undoubtedly kept from impressing themselves on Americans as starkly as they should, by the fact of America's "tremendous wealth, the production of which is almost the sole achievement of modern industrialism."[21] Europe's experience, and more especially that of Germany, contained some terrible warnings for Americans. In Germany he had learned the most unexpected and the most unwanted lesson of his trip; namely, the fact of class hatred as a dynamic political factor. "In Germany," he discovered, "the various economic and political groups contend for their rights and support their prejudices with a vigor and venom which make ordered government well-nigh impossible.... The industrial worker of the Continent is probably permanently alienated from the nation."[22]

Niebuhr, as we have seen, had regularly discounted the factor of class antagonism in his analysis of America's discontents. Yet, even in America he had been able to detect a hint of social bitterness (which, he had noted, only the Communists had seemed capable of using). In Germany, it seemed that one's class loyalty was the only fact that counted. The workers, brutally pushed to the wall by the middle-class in the scramble for the little that Germany's pinched economy afforded, now so despised the system that they were "probably permanently alienated." American workers, schooled in the Alger-myth and infinitely better-off economically than their German brothers, showed little of this "alienation." Only the pitiable remnant of Communists actually used the slogans of the class struggle in broad daylight; and they lived from day to day in fear of molestation at the hands of Red-baiting union members. However, while there seemed little class antagonism in the American scene, Niebuhr argued, there was every reason to doubt that America's present "opulence" (as he called it) could last much longer. Against that time, the need now was to improve the moral tone of the nation, so that class antagonism will find no place in American hearts. This will take both "social imagination" and "spiritual passion," the "morally redemptive forces."

We are thus driven back upon Niebuhr's primary concern: the matter of religion's role as a "morally redemptive" force. Niebuhr's European trip was to do much to clarify this issue in his mind. Precisely as Europe's greater poverty heightened social conflict, high-lighting the stark fact of class selfishness in the political equation, it equally threw into relief the question of the social relevance of religion. At first blush, the European evidence appeared contradic-tory. Niebuhr's German experience demonstrated to him that the sort of social obtuseness which one finds in church people in America can take on diabolical proportions in a setting where life is more pre-carious and the relations of man to man are harsher. In Britain, on the other hand, there seemed to be a greater sense of social responsibility than among Americans—which was a blessing that

Niebuhr was inclined to attribute to the religious tradition of the British.

It seems to boil down to a matter of grace. The resources for social revolution are there in Christianity: indeed, Niebuhr insists that these resources can only be found in religion, and supremely in the religion of Jesus. But when a nation turns its back on these resources, religion seems only to give an edge of self-righteousness to the clamor of selfish individuals and classes, making social reconciliation more difficult than it would be in a frankly secular context. Religion (as someone has said) is a good thing for good people but a bad thing for bad people. And (the grace of God being the mysterious thing it is) it would appear that Germans are capable only of exploiting the negative side of religion while the British seem wonderfully responsive to all that is positive.[23]

"England," Niebuhr finds, "gives the promise of developing a political policy which approximates the Christian ideal."[24] On the other hand, "the democratic forces of continental Europe lack confidence in Christian method." In Britain's Labour Party Niebuhr was certain he had discovered the secret of "Christian politics." "It believes in a thoroughgoing and fundamental change in our social and political order, in order that competitive strife may be discouraged, unequal economic and social privilege divided and unjust economic authority destroyed. But it will not grow impatient [as continental radicals are doing] and try to reach its paradise by the short cut of revolution. This patience in the face of a great task is a spiritual achievement."[25] This "patience," it is clear, is a gift of God's grace: Niebuhr is unable to explain why the English have it and the continentals do not have it, other than to say that it has always been there in the English make-up.[26]

In Germany, Niebuhr found, Protestantism had proven itself utterly incapable of "mak[ing] the inspiration of a spiritual interpretation of life available for the problems of social life."[27] Yet, he was convinced, Protestantism in America was failing even more miserably than in Germany, though the severe economic disorder of Germany made Germany's case appear worse. In an extremely revealing article,[28] Niebuhr compares what he regards as the most vicious political force in Germany (Hitler's *Deutsch-Voelkische Bewegung*) with the most vicious political force in the United States, the Ku Klux Klan. The Hitlerites get the better of the comparison. The Klan's greater viciousness he attributes to the religious commitment of the Klansmen. It would thus follow that, should some economic calamity befall America, unleashing the social passions from which her widespread prosperity presently shields her, we should expect to find in American politics a viciousness greater than what Germany has experienced, and we should also expect to find that the religiosity of Americans will serve to aggravate rather than alleviate the bitterness.[29]

Thus, we must not assume that the vitality of religion in American life will guarantee peace and justice in our present or in our future. The continuing loyalty of Americans to the religion of their fathers (in which loyalty upholders of the faith of American exceptionalism have been wont to find the secret of America's happy destiny) in fact guarantees nothing at all. American Protestantism, *because it lacks idealism*, may yet prove an engine of oppression. The problem of religion is thus no different from the problem of politics, and the program we must follow in both spheres is the same. Religious statesmen, like political statesmen, must learn to appeal to the idealism of the nation. Since Christian idealism conflicts at no point with that idealism which is vouchsafed to secularists in their best moments, nothing should stand in the way of launching a Christian political party.[30]

Unhappily (Niebuhr noted) there was no evidence that anyone other than Niebuhr himself was thinking along these lines: "We [Americans] are blind to the visions of a new and better world which intrigue the soul of the European. There is no real radicalism in America, the fears of our councils of defense and boards of commerce notwithstanding. Of late a new agrarian radicalism has developed[31] but it is based upon immediate economic needs. It lacks every note of authentic idealism and will probably be as transient as it is immediate.[32] It is important to stress here that while Niebuhr admires the "vision" of the European radical and wishes he could impart some of his fire into the soul of American radicals, he refuses to believe that the European's radical faith is exportable to America. *America needs a radical idealism, and Europe has only radical Marxism to offer.* Niebuhr's European impressions had confirmed him in his conviction that Marxist "cynicism" must be resisted like the plague. The first question that must be answered by a would-be reformer is whether he will seek the willing acquiescence of the middle-class, or whether he intends to have his revolution over the dead body of the latter. The first course is the way of idealism, the second of "cynicism."

> [The] dogma of the class struggle has built up walls of
> mutual distrust between the classes which is making orderly
> parliamentary government almost impossible in Germany. The
> Marxian prophecy that modern industry would expropriate
> all classes but a small holding class which could finally be
> expropriated has not materialized. The modern industrial state, in
> fact, maintains and creates a large middle class which is not

prompted by its needs, for they are not sufficiently acute, but
which may be enlisted through its ideals, once they are awakened,
to support a program of thorough-going political and economic
reconstruction. In Germany this class has been alienated by the
theory of the class struggle and has been driven into the arms of
conservatism. In England, on the other hand, it is the very middle
class which is gradually throwing its support to labor. . . . [T]he
frenzies of Winston Churchill could not dissuade the average
Britisher from giving labor its chance.[33]

The very intransigence of the continental radical has served
to withhold the power from him which his British brother is
gradually assuming.[34]

A revolutionary solution of society's wrongs is clearly out of the
question for Niebuhr. It is important to note that there is an evident
connection between this rejection of revolution and Niebuhr's pacifism. ("I am done with the war business," Niebuhr was promising
himself, in these very months.)[35] Conveniently, Niebuhr discovered
that the same Labour Party which showed such "promise" as an
agent of social regeneration within England had a clean record as
well on the matter of war.[36]

But British political methods could no more be translated to
America than continental European ones. The happy conjunction of
religious idealism and political realism which marked British politics
was, Niebuhr found, a unique "spiritual achievement," springing
from an historical experience that took place long before America
was ever dreamed of: it is simply not exportable. An American
equivalent of this accomplishment is needed; but it must be built
from the ground up.

American experience, it seemed, was not a mere extension of
European—neither on its bad side nor its good. While an examination of the German experience provided useful warnings of the cost
to be paid for religious conservatism and class selfishness, it could
offer Americans nothing of value in preparing them to meet their
own political crises. Similarly, an examination of the British experience could provide cheering illustrations of constructive possibilities
of idealism in politics, but it could offer nothing in the way of
political method for Americans whose historical experiences had been
so different. In the mid-twenties, it was the contrasts between
European and American civilization that most impressed Niebuhr

—and in this he was a true son of the American liberal-progressive tradition.

The European trip had thus done nothing to qualify Niebuhr's commitment to the conviction of America's "exceptionalism." It had, indeed, strengthened that conviction. Yet the time was not far off when Niebuhr would abruptly abandon that faith for a new faith which would affirm the continuities and deny the discontinuities between European and American experience. The occasion for this conversion (the word is not too strong) was not to be some outward experience at all, but an inward one—an intellectual and a spiritual crisis. It is this inward crisis which marks the inauguration of Niebuhr's mature philosophy; and to this we now turn.

# PART

# II

# APOSTLE
# TO THE LEFT

*Chapter*

# 5

# THE MAKING OF A SOCIALIST

Reinhold Niebuhr entered upon his academic career at a remarkably late stage in his life[1]—remarkable, that is, when we consider how thoroughly he is identified in most men's minds with the academic life. It was not unusual in those days for preachers to be invited into the academic wing of the American Protestant church establishment on the basis, essentially, of their reputations as preachers. In the fundamentalist branches of the Protestant church that is still basically the pattern. It is not surprising, given the greater strictnesses that applies to academic matters these days, that Niebuhr would always feel a bit embarrassed by the circumstances:

> I became a member of the faculty of Union Theological Seminary in 1928, largely at the instigation of my friend Sherwood Eddy, who persuaded the seminary faculty to call me to a Chair of Christian Ethics. This was a hazardous venture, since my reading in the parish had been rather undisciplined and I had no scholarly competence in my field, not to speak of the total field of Christian theology. . . . It was therefore a full decade before I could stand before a class and answer the searching questions of the students at the end of a lecture without the sense of being a fraud who pretended to a larger and more comprehensive knowledge than I possessed.[2]

It was characteristic of Niebuhr (and it does him credit) that he should protest his lack of qualifications for a position as a teacher of theology. It does no credit to the sponsors of his candidacy for the position at Union that they insisted that much formal competence was not needed—that a man whose qualifications as a preacher were proved could learn the necessary theology on the job. Such a thing could not happen today in a respectable theological seminary—and Reinhold Niebuhr's intervening career is one of the principal reasons. Niebuhr, despite his admitted deficiencies in formal theological training at the beginning, was to provide leadership to a new generation of American teachers of theology who brought home to American Protestant seminaries the intellectual shallowness of their product and subsequently brought about its improvement.

But even at the end of his career, Niebuhr was still insisting on his own lack of qualifications as a theologian:

> I cannot and do not claim to be a theologian. I have taught
> Christian Social Ethics for a quarter of a century and have also
> dealt in the ancillary field of "apologetics." My avocational
> interest as a kind of circuit rider in the colleges and universities
> has prompted an interest in the defense and justification of the
> Christian faith in a secular age, particularly among what
> Schleiermacher called Christianity's "intellectual despisers." I
> have never been very competent in the nice points of pure
> theology; and I must confess that I have not been sufficiently
> interested heretofore to acquire the competence.[3]

It is essential that we understand the point of Niebuhr's refusal of the title of theologian—since it is honestly made, and since so much of our story hinges on this matter. The unifying theme of Niebuhr's life-work is preaching—not theology. That he is described in reference books as a theologian is owing to the public's unfamiliarity with the fact that theology is a systematic discipline—that to speak about theology, or to draw upon theology in one's preaching, is not the same thing as to be doing the work of theology. There are large areas which are traditionally and correctly held to be of central concern to theology about which Niebuhr has written nothing—or (more to the point) about which he has written that he is uninterested. Niebuhr nonetheless contributed mightily to the making of an American community of theologians—by blowing the whistle on all the preachers (including himself) who have been passed off as theologians merely because they have written at length about theological problems. He forced American Protestantism to acknowledge that it had virtually been doing without honest academic theology since the eighteenth century. In his characteristically conscientious way, he made some major contributions towards a definition of the theological function. He has left the task of systematic theology to others, for the good and sufficient reason that it was (as he has said) secondary to his "avocational interest" as a preacher. It reveals much about the academic confusion of our age that the historians, political scientists and philosophers—let alone the publicists—would not take him at his word.

It might puzzle the young, academically-trained theologian of today that the faculty of Union Theological Seminary could casually hand over a license to teach theology to a man whose formal preparation in theology was as slight as Niebuhr's was in 1928. In those days, however, very few of the men who taught theology in American seminaries took theology seriously as an "avocation." The prevailing attitude was that theology was the handmaiden of the church's "true work," which was pastoral and apologetic. The attitude of the German theologians (who, of course, dominated academic theology in Europe), that the work of theology was justifiable on its own terms as an intellectual discipline, was regarded by Americans as gravely misplaced. Eventually the Germans won out in the American seminaries—as they had *already* won in such other humane disciplines as history, economics, and philosophy. The American theologians were the last of the academic communities to capitulate to German scholarship, however, because they possessed in much larger measure than the others the bias that all American scholarship shared to some degree against "intellectualism" and in favor of what was, in the nineteenth century, thought to be the redeeming practicality of American learning. Teachers in American theological schools were inclined, indeed, to assume a certain tone of moral superiority as they compared their wholesomely amateur and practical approach to questions of theology to the disengaged abstruseness of European scholarship. In return, European scholars dismissed the American theologians as a pack of amateurs.

Having already claimed for Niebuhr a major role in persuading American Protestantism of the urgency of developing sound theological scholarship on the German example, I must make clear that he was always equally adamant against adopting the German view of the place of theology in the total work of the ministry. If in my recital of the theological career of Reinhold Niebuhr over the next two decades I have to emphasize his affinity with the continental side of the confrontation between the continental theologians and the Americans, it is because it was on that side, as a proponent of certain aspects of the European "dialectical" theology, that he made his impact on American theology—and ultimately upon American intellectual and political history. To the Europeans, Niebuhr's affinity with the traditional American pragmatic approach was much more obvious.[4] In arguing for greater integrity in theological study, Niebuhr never repudiated the traditional American view of the purpose of theology.[5]

Time has brought about great changes in the reciprocal assessments of American and continental theologians. German standards of scholarship were, by the end of the 1930s, securely established in the American seminaries. By the 1950s, European theologians had, to some degree at least, abandoned their formerly patronizing attitude toward American Protestantism. Reinhold Niebuhr played perhaps the principal role in both processes.

The German theologian who undoubtedly did more than any other to discomfit traditional American theological habits and to commend the European tradition to American theologians was, in his latter years, full of praise for "the glory of American theology."[6] Paul Tillich held a very low opinion of the American religious scene when he came to it in 1933:

> When, soon after the victory of the Nazis in Germany and after my removal from the chair of philosophy at the University of Frankfort, I decided to accept an invitation from Union Theological Seminary in New York, I wrote to a friend who had already left Germany: "There is everywhere in the world sky, air and ocean." This was my consolation in one of the most tragic moments of my life. I did not write: "I can continue everywhere my theological and philosophical work," because unconsciously I doubted whether one could do this anywhere except in Germany.[7]

Tillich's name was becoming important in German theological circles by the late 1920s, primarily because of his indictment of the church's social and political conservatism. He claimed to be condemning the Protestant churches in the name of the "Protestant principle" itself, which he identified throughout his lifetime with the prophetic principle within the Judaeo-Christian tradition. As the Protestant church of Europe had come to terms with bourgeois civilization and was thus aligned against those political and social forces which were undertaking the overthrow of that society, the "Protestant-prophetic principle" thus became the enemy of bourgeois society and of the Protestant churches. It was only among the intellectuals, therefore— among those who could grasp the paradox that the Protestant principle itself condemned Protestantism—that the hope of the purification of religion could be seriously held. Faithfulness to the intellectual formulations of the church made the theologian (in his own imagination, at least) the enemy of the bourgeois culture that thought he was its servant. Hence, the habit of these contemporary European

theologians—the theologians of "crisis," as they called themselves—
of identifying themselves with the unchurched "proletariat," as
fellow "outsiders"; hence, their enthusiasm for "socialism"—of
which more shortly. At the same time, these preoccupations made the
"crisis" theologians urgent in a way that American theologians could
not grasp, about the intellectual and academic soundness of their
work. Their work was presented as something carrying conviction
only because it came out of earnest debate within the intellectual
community, conducted on the ground rules worked out by the labors
of the past century of academic scholarship. As the young Dutch
theologian Willem Visser 't Hooft discovered and published in 1928
(in the work from which we have already quoted), leaders of the
American Protestant community did not share this conviction of
"alienation" that gripped their European brothers. Indeed, they could
not even understand it. Far from recognizing any radical gulf separating them as intellectuals, or as defenders of the prophetic religion,
from bourgeois society, the American clergy thought of themselves
as the spokesmen of the best values of the society around them.

It is no coincidence that during the very months when Niebuhr was
mulling over the implications of a commitment to socialism (in the
half-way house of Norman Thomas's L.I.P.A.) he was groping with
his new responsibilities as a teacher of theology. By the time he came
to New York to take up his teaching at Union, Niebuhr was thoroughly disillusioned with what he called the "nineteenth century
religion" of the Protestant churches.[8] His observation of church-
going Americans had convinced him that the message which their
pastors brought to them was irrelevant to social and political responsibility. For this failure, he had come to blame the liberal, idealistic
theology in which he had himself been instructed at Eden Theological
Seminary and at Yale. Niebuhr's younger brother Richard was in
those years at the beginning of his career as a theologian and was
already beginning to goad Reinhold to a greater intellectual tidiness
in his theology.[9] Their precocious intellectual curiosity, together with
their command of German had brought both brothers into touch with
the newest currents of continental theology sooner than any but a
handful of American scholars.[10] Thus Reinhold Niebuhr came to
learn very early in the 1920s of the assault which continental
theologians were then mounting against the American Social
Gospel.

In January, 1925, a First World Conference on Life and Work was held at Stockholm for the purpose of helping theologians and church-men to define the social responsibilities of the churches.[11] Here (in the words of the historian of the American Social Gospel) "for the first time American church leaders had to reckon with the new 'crisis theology' in full dress debate."[12] Two years later, at Lausanne, the debate was resumed during the World Conference on Faith and Order, Methodist Bishop Francis McConnell leading the defense of the Social Gospel against the continental critics. The event proved to be the beginning of the end for the Social Gospel theology: "It was after Lausanne that Richard and Reinhold Niebuhr began to be heard from as, in effect, mediators between the European theologians and their own countrymen."[13]

There is no understanding the life-work of Reinhold Niebuhr without taking account of the fact that he entered the ranks of the professors of Protestant theology at the *precise moment* when that tradition was undergoing its most vigorous shaking-up in four hundred years.[14] A single book of a unique religious genius is said to have started it all. This was Karl Barth's *The Epistle to the Romans*[15]—of which it has been said that it "fell like a bomb upon the playground of the theologians."[16] While we cannot, in these pages, begin to account for the significance of this book in twentieth-century religious thought, we can hardly manage without a few observations.

First, as regards nomenclature. In the effort to come to terms with Barth's radical challenge to the settled habits of nineteenth-century Protestant thought, his critics (rather too quickly) settled upon him-self and his circle certain labels which, in retrospect at least, can be seen to have missed the mark: among them, "dialectical theology" and "neo-orthodoxy." The most appropriate label—the one which, if pressed, Karl Barth allowed, was "crisis theology."[17] Following Kierkegaard's example,[18] Barth describes the wisdom of Christian faith as coming into view only as one is convinced of the failure of reason to provide answers to the question of personal existence. Secular humanism is seen as entailing a conspiracy to conceal the whole range of negativities affecting our lives, and whose keystone is the riddle of suffering and death.[19]

The "crisis" for the individual has its counterpart in the "crisis" of civilization—the crisis of morality, of community, of intellectual tranquillity which had marked the years since the outbreak of the Great War. For Barth himself, the discovery of this larger "crisis" could be precisely dated:

One day in August 1914 stands out in my personal memory as a
black day. Ninety-three German intellectuals impressed public
opinion by their proclamation in support of the war policy of
Wilhelm II and his counsellers.[20] Among these intellectuals I
discovered to my horror almost all of my theological teachers
whom I had greatly venerated. In despair over what this indicated
about the signs of the time, I suddenly realized that I could not
any longer follow either their ethics and dogmatics or their
understanding of the Bible and of history. For me at least,
nineteenth-century theology no longer had any future.[21]

"Nineteenth-century theology" means, for Barth, theology conformed to one version or another of that heresy which inspired the
Enlightenment: that man was meant to be conformed to this world.[22]
"Nineteenth-century theology" means all talk of "objective knowledge of God";[23] it means "that well-known 'awe in the presence of
History' ";[24] it means the "meaningless . . . attempt to construct a
religion out of the Gospel . . . [setting] it as one human possibility in
the midst of others."[25]

It is above all in the evaluation that it placed upon religion that
nineteenth-century theology betrayed its captivity to mere humanism:

Religion is [indeed] the supreme possibility of all human
possibilities . . . [but] Grace is man's divine possibility, and as
such, lies beyond all human possibility. . . . Forgetting the awful
gulf by which they are separated from Him, [men] enter upon a
relation with Him which would be possible only if He were not
God. They make Him a thing in this world, and set Him in the
midst of other things. All this occurs quite manifestly and
observably within the possibility of religion. Now the prophetic
KRISIS means the bringing of the final observable human
possibility of religion within the scope of that KRISIS under
which all human endeavour is set.[26]

Thus, nineteenth-century man had lost his perspective on himself
when he lost the sense of sin. Yet theologians, deceived by the same
evidences of progressive improvement of the material circumstances
and of the civility of men, had acquiesced in the mood of optimism,
and read out of their Bibles the God of Wrath. Having thus brought
their Bibles into tune with the prevailing optimism of secular philosophy, the theologians had abandoned the role of prophecy. Theologians had come to believe that it was their responsibility to justify
their faith to their secular contemporaries in terms that appealed to
secular man's own view of his situation.

In a work written a few years later than the *Romans*,[27] Barth likens the Word of God to a stone which is "thrown into" the cultural situation. Nothing in the cultural achievement of man prepares him to find God as the Word of God declares Him to be. God was revealed by Scripture to be "Wholly Other" than what human culture—any culture, even the most accomplished and humane—guesses that He must be. This being the case, the preacher's task is to confront civilization in all its arenas with the word of judgment, drawn from dogmatic Truth, having no points of tangent with the ideals, ambitions, and accomplishments of civilization.

Barth's theology provided Niebuhr with his first challenge as a professional theologian. When Barth's *Das Wort Gottes und die Theologie* became available in English translation in 1928 (that is, five years before the publication in English of *Romans*) it was given to Niebuhr for review in the pages of the *Christian Century*.[28] It is clear that Niebuhr had already heard a good deal about Barth's impact among German theologians and churchmen. Some comments of Emil Brunner's, made many years later, help us in reconstructing the chronology for this story of Niebuhr's exposure to the crisis theology:

> It was in the autumn of 1928 [that is Niebuhr's first term at Union] that I first met Reinhold, at an evening discussion group after a lecture I had given at Union Seminary in New York. There were three of us (the third being Professor Van Dusen, now [in 1956] president of the Seminary) who sat together and discussed the theme of original sin. At that time both Karl Barth and I were known to these men in little more than name only. What I had said in my lecture about sin led to an animated and passionate discussion. The concept of sin in those days had almost disappeared from the vocabulary of enlightened theologians. But I sensed how this basic term seemed to stimulate Niebuhr and set fire to his imagination.[29]

It must be admitted at the outset that Niebuhr seems to have missed something of what Barth was getting at. He seems to have gone at Barth's early books (*Romans* and the *Word of God*) impetuously—perhaps in the very wake of that "animated and passionate discussion" which Brunner later recalled—and predisposed to find certain things. Niebuhr's own passion was for politics. He had already heard about Barth's background in socialism. And there was much grist for the mills of political radicals of Niebuhr's generation in Barth—as we shall shortly be pointing out. But the political message (if we can call it that) is peripheral at best in these books. The part of Barth's message which was most important to the continental theologians and which would prove to be the enduring portion of his work was not in his political observations but in his critique of religion— some characteristic passages of which we have just been considering. Niebuhr seems to have missed these passages. Indeed, we find Niebuhr commending to readers of the *Christian Century* the "re- ligious advantages of Barth's theology"![30] Among other principles of "Barthian theology" which Niebuhr discovers are: that "religious experience will at least help us to see that moral limitation involves perversity, that it is in a sense treason against the highest we have conceived";[31] that "it is the business of religion to create a sensitive conscience,"[32] that "True religion does save man from moral conceit in the attainment of his relative goals"[33]—principles diametrically opposed to Barth's critique of religion. He speaks of Barth's offering, in place of "the subjectivism and relativism in which religious know- ledge, together with all other knowledge is involved,—one absolute— the Christ-idea"—a "doctrine" which commends itself to us "because it is a doctrine which meets a human need."[34] The best that can be said of these observations is that they are not recognizably Barthian.

Niebuhr had already concluded, evidently, that Barth's greatest influence was going to be in the area of ethics—and particularly in politics. He was excited to discover that all of the members of the Barthian circle were Socialists—and Niebuhr would invariably revert to this matter of the socialist grounding of Barthian ethics in all his later commentary. Barth's socialism was real enough, deriving in part from Marx,[35] but primarily from a substantial tradition of German and Swiss "Religious Socialism."[36] Religious Socialism fastened upon the spiritual insensitivity of bourgeois society, and blamed the rule of money. The capitalists had bound the political authority and the schools and the church to their purse-strings. Their sway over all arenas of modern life was irresistible and spiritually irresponsible. This alliance was so vicious, Barth said, that Christians must resist absolutely any claim that the powers of this world make in defense of their authority: "Must not the existing order, the order that has already been found, seem the very incarnation of triumphant un- righteousness to the man who is seeking after God and His Order? . . . Is there anywhere legality which is not fundamentally illegal? Is there anywhere authority which is not ultimately based upon tyranny?"[37]

But, while a first reading of those lines might cheer Marxist hearts, it can be seen that the drift of this thinking is ultimately fatal for the socialism which set it in motion. All civilization, in Barth's scheme of things, stands under the judgment of God, who stands utterly beyond the distinctions which men make in this world between relatively good and relatively bad accomplishments. Thus (in Charles West's words), socialism awoke in Barth "a metaphysical sense of the crisis of all humanity before God,"[38] which ultimately swallowed up everything else, including his confidence in socialism. Barth came to believe that socialism, like any other system of arrangement of rights and responsibilities that men might come to among themselves, would inevitably prove to be as far removed from God's perfection as the present or any previous social system. The end-product of Barth's political theorizing seems thus to be Christian quietism.

The truth seems to be that, for all of his traffic with socialism and socialists, Barth lacked—indeed, always would lack any sense for politics and (in the opinion of the present writer) anything very worthy of consideration in the way of political theory. For him, history was, as Will Herberg put it, essentially a realm of life "characterized by a pervasive 'monotony'; ... politics and political questions [were] 'fundamentally uninteresting' ... [and] theologically tolerable only when carried on as 'essentially a game.' "[39]

Later on, his eminence as a Christian thinker forced him into taking a position of leadership on the question of Nazism (as early as 1933) and on the issues of the Cold War in the forties and fifties; and while these positions will seem to many to be correct and courageous, it must also be said that they are not in fact, supported by any clear social or political theory. Niebuhr was quite correct in accusing Barth of being "more concerned with the problem of his inner life than with the effort to protect and advance moral values in society."[40] (Barth himself later conceded the criticism in effect, as it touched his early writing at least, when he came to repudiate his early infatuation with "Kierkegaard's pronounced holy individualism.")[41]

While Niebuhr recognized this failure in Barth at the outset, he does not seem to have wanted to accept the obvious conclusion: namely, that Barth's politics should be ignored. Instead, he kept coming back to the matter of Barth's socialism—sometimes to congratulate him for it, and at other times to deplore his lack of seriousness about it. Karl Barth's socialism would always be like King Charles's head with Reinhold Niebuhr. The point seems to be that Barth had gravely disappointed Niebuhr. He desperately wanted to believe that the socialism followed from the theology. But, the arguments of *Romans* and the *Word of God* are of no use whatever for the construction of a social or political philosophy.

A series of essays on the subject of Barth's challenge to American Protestantism constituted Niebuhr's first contribution to theological discussion in America, establishing him in the role of "mediator" described by Paul Carter.[42] Niebuhr welcomed Barth's restoration of the Biblical themes neglected or denied by the ascendent liberal-Protestant theology: the themes of tragedy and human guilt. ("It is the highest function of religion to create a sense of guilt," Niebuhr discovered.)[43] Niebuhr's net assessment of Barth's ideas is curiously ambivalent, however. He cannot deny what he calls the "religious advantages" of Barth's proposition: that we must put away the relativism of theology which tries to come to terms with secular knowledge, in favor of dogmatic theology based upon Absolute Truth, tossed into the human situation "like a stone." "There is, as a matter of fact, no way of escaping relativity except through dogmatism or magic. There is always a danger that a religion which makes or has made its adjustments to society, to culture, to science, and to thought in general will degenerate into nothing more than a sentimental glow upon thought and life. In contrast to that kind of insipid religion, Barthian religion has the note of reality in it."[44] Yet, he was not sure that the Barthian proposition would prove the right one for Americans: "[U]ltimately there is no more peace in dogmatism than in magic. We can escape relativity and uncertainty only by piling experience upon experience, checking hypothesis against hypothesis, correcting errors, by considering new perspectives, and finally by letting the experience of the race qualify the individual's experience of God."[45]

It is curious that he offers no explanation for this paradox: that Barth's dogmatism is religiously sound yet irrelevant, even dangerous, to Americans. He suggests that Barthianism arose out of the present need of disillusioned continentals[46]—the clear implication being that, had things not gone badly for Europe, "the sense of tragedy" would not be as relevant for them! This theme is developed at length in the later articles on Barth, with special reference to Barth's socialism. Niebuhr was puzzled by Barth's continued identification of himself as a socialist throughout the thirties. Barth's interest in socialism, as Niebuhr saw it, was largely a case of *auld lang syne*. Barth offered a rather feeble explanation about the Christian's responsibility "to seek a social order which will throw the most effective restraints about the sinfulness of man and establish the most tolerable communal life"—a highly negative motive for political concern, deriving from what Barth saw as the Christian's primary need to be let alone in the contemplation of his own unworthiness and God's vast and inexplicable love for him.[47]

Niebuhr saw two great and related dangers in the Barthian defini-

tion of the Christian's role in politics. The first was that Barthianism set so small an evaluation on political concern (in fact, it set
*no* positive evaluation on political action, *per se*) that it could not
fail to deprive its adherents of enthusiasm for politics. The leaders
of the movement—Barth himself and Emil Brunner—were not
being followed in their rather vague and incidental support for
social reform; instead, their more basic preachment of "submission
to the powers of this world" was being cheerfully accepted by their
German disciples, particularly among the clergy.[48] In fact, Niebuhr
reported from Germany in 1934, "all the epigones of Barthianism
are using that doctrine to justify the efforts to establish a state
absolutism in Germany under Hitler.[49]

Yet Niebuhr could not shake off the conviction of the religious
soundness of Barth's central challenge against the accommodations
which liberal theology inevitably made to the values of society.
How could a Christian preserve the prophet's conviction of the
unbridgeable gulf between man's works and God's commands, while
not succumbing to despair about the political life? If Christians are
to serve just causes in this world, they must act with other men in
the arena of the possible—in politics, where their own convictions
regarding God's purposes are not generally shared. But that would
involve making compromises—an impossibility for religious perfec-
tionists of the stripe of Barth.

Thus, while Barth's message, taken alone and as a whole, would
make life more and not less difficult for Niebuhr, Barth's anathema
against the accommodations which liberal theology inevitably made
to the values of society was welcome to Niebuhr. Barth's view of
the Gospel played havoc with all efforts at accommodation between
the doctrine of progress and the concept of the Kingdom of God.
The Social Gospel of Walter Rauschenbusch was thus a heresy. The
Kingdom lay beyond human history, and would emerge in judgment of mankind's failures, which would be just as evident at the
end as at the beginning of the human story.

It was Karl Barth who provided for Niebuhr the theological
weapon for puncturing the complacency of American liberal churchmen. The vocabulary employed by Niebuhr in his critique of
American civilization is henceforth noticeably enlivened by the sort
of language that Barth himself employed. The rather tentative tone
of Niebuhr's early critical writing is now quite gone, and he is
suddenly the "American Amos" (to use the phrase of one historian),[50] the "Prophet from America" of D. R. Davies' pioneer
biography. The very dogmatic character of Barth's own language
and his thought-patterns, coming in such contrast to the amiable,
undogmatic, accommodating tone employed by theologians and

writers on the American side, stimulated Niebuhr to a new critical sharpness. The effect is remarkable and impresses itself on anyone who cares to compare the language and the argument of Niebuhr's *Moral Man and Immoral Society* (1932) with the language and the argument of either of his now-forgotten books of the 1920s.

The challenge of Barth precipitated the rejection of liberal theology that had been preparing itself within Niebuhr for some time. More important, for our purposes: it brought to his attention, as nothing before had done, the intellectual and moral dilemma in which he stood as an avowed enemy of the capitalist system and as a free-loader (so to speak) upon socialist rhetoric.

In the last paragraph of his first review of Barth's writing, we find Niebuhr trying to reconstruct his native, Social-gospel faith in social action on the intellectual ground cleared by the encounter with Barth. Barth's pessimism, he concludes, is the authentic "fruit of moral sensitiveness.... And there is certainly more religious vitality in such pessimism than in the easy optimism of evolutionary moralism." But how can we afford this kind of moral sensitivity "without tempting the soul to despair of history and take flight into the absolute?"[51] His own answer to that question took shape over the next few months, and is clearly established in his article of 1935, "Marx, Barth, and Israel's Prophets." With this article, he shakes off *forever* the temptation to affirm, with Barth, "the absolute transcendence of God," and announces his affiliation with a political philosophy that effectively mixes the moral positivism of social gospel with the messianism of Marxism.

What, then, did Niebuhr owe to Barth? Karl Barth made Niebuhr aware of a question that had never occurred to him before, and which is never raised in the literature of social gospel, because it could not occur within the thought-world of liberal optimism. Why, when "our life is so debatable"—when it is "defined and constituted by ambiguity"—when "our whole concrete and observable existence is sinful"—when, that is, life is so manifestly under a curse, do we strive nonetheless to set this world aright? The question derives from Barth. Niebuhr's answer, however, does not. For this, Niebuhr fell back upon two quite independent arguments, and combined them into a unique political philosophy, that itself owes nothing to Barth.

The one line of argument comes straight out of William James—Niebuhr's long-standing favorite source for natural theology; it is the line of argument that James himself called "radical empiricism."[52] It is impossible to imagine Barth approving of James' answers to "the question of existence." But that is not the point; Niebuhr never accepted the absolute distinction that Barth *always* made between natural and revealed theology. Niebuhr had always been interested in William James,[53] and the influence of James now would become increasingly evident in his work.

The other argument derives from Karl Marx. For Marx, as for James, human history "*feels* like a real fight"! But whereas James listened for the still, small voice of his conscience for direction in sorting out the *possible* meaning of historical events, Marx had his infallible dialectic. In Marx's system, there are social forces which *objectively* bear the purposes of history; and to act positively as an historical agent is to attach oneself to those objectively discoverable forces. Mixing James and Marx, Niebuhr had developed a theory of the meaning of history which, in its use of social realism, departs from liberal Protestantism, while retaining a thorough-going transcendental aspect which puts it beyond the reach of the secularist. "It is only because life is moral and men feel that an unjust civilization ought not to survive that the scientific evidence can be finally adduced that it will not survive."[54] There speaks William James. "The destructive and constructive forces must come from below."[55] There speaks Marx. "Modern radical Christians are not wrong in affirming the fateful mission of the victims of injustice in our present civilization. The prophets and Jesus blessed the poor, not because they were morally superior as individuals to the privileged, but because they are by virtue of their position in society [i.e., objectively] the forces of progress and creativity in it."[56] There is Niebuhr's mix.

"Radical empiricism" alone cannot generate such a dynamic theory of history, for it requires the added perspective of Barthian "neo-supernaturalism" (to use Henry Nelson Wieman's term). Nor will "neo-supernaturalism" alone yield this philosophy without the addition of Marxist historical theory. Admittedly, these three disparate elements do not blend altogether homogeneously. Over a long career as a writer on theological and political themes, Niebuhr would be constantly adjusting the proportions in the mix. But the three elements are there at the end, as at the beginning: Jamesian pragmatism; Marxism; Barthian supernaturalism. In my opinion, Barthianism *requires* "mixing" with something or other out of natural theology or secular philosophy if it is to yield anything of value for politics or ethics. Turning away, finally, from the seductive, mathematical vocabulary which he had originally preferred for describing "God's equidistance from all human programmes," Barth himself would eventually acknowledge that there must, after all, be some *social content* to the Gospel of Christ. How else can one describe the turnabout represented by his final position on politics? "The Church is witness of the fact that the Son of Man came to seek and save the lost. And this implies that—casting all false impartiality aside—the Church must concentrate on the lower and lowest levels of human society. . . . The Church must stand for social justice in the political sphere."[57]

The difference between Niebuhr and Barth is that Barth, a systematic theologian, was dogged, all along the way, by the terrible responsibility of bringing each part of his theology into line with every other part. And, while he showed extraordinary inventiveness *and courage* in his revision of his theological positions, he never went so far as to allow that the admission of a *social* content to the Gospel requires different views of history than his theology permits; and thus, his social theology would always have about it a certain quality of adventitiousness—indeed, of opportunism. The saving grace of Niebuhr's situation was that, not being a systematic theologian, he was not obliged to make all the pieces fit together. He could, for example, use as much of the logically antagonistic arguments of natural theology and of Marxism as seemed comfortable to the immediate text of his preaching—without being obliged to rebuild his theology to accommodate the questions implied in their contradictions. This would give him a great and perhaps unfair advantage in his later, much-publicized controversies with Barth on current political themes—of which, more later.

It is impossible to say whether Niebuhr's intellectual development owed more to Karl Barth or to Paul Tillich.[58] Tillich (1886–1965) shared with Barth the earnestness about philosophical consistency that stamped the products of German universities. It is fair to say that Tillich was always a more political animal than Barth. He was deeply committed to the doctrines of the same German religious socialists who affected Barth's early thought. Tillich, like Barth, regarded capitalist civilization as marked by an almost hopeless "emptiness." The high-water mark of that civilization had been the last years of the nineteenth century, "a time . . . in which the forms of life were self-sufficient and closed against invasions of the eternal."[59] The capitalist civilization represented the apparent eclipse of the transcendent God. Capitalist-bourgeois man is convinced of his self-sufficiency, and without contrition. Confident in his ability to satisfy all the needs of his life by the accumulation of goods, of "things," he "does not see the abyss which opened before every time and every present."[60] But precisely for this reason Tillich sensed that history had come to a decisive turning-point. God would surely

take pity on mankind in its bankruptcy of spirit and there would
be a sudden invasion of a new creative energy into the situation.
There is no way of demonstrating this truth, Tillich admitted. It is
a conviction that seized religiously sensitive persons when they
contemplated the barrenness of the present human situation and
remembered that God is love. This is Tillich's doctrine of *Kairos*
(the fullness of time).

Tillich, like Niebuhr, welcomed Barth's rediscovery of the theme
of judgment in the Christian tradition: Barth's theology, he wrote,
"lets the judgment of the unconditionedly transcendent God fall
upon every attempt of culture or religion to claim value before
him;"[61] a statement that could not be improved upon as a thumbnail
introduction to "crisis theology." Tillich soon emerged as a rival to
Barth for the distinction of being the scourge of liberal theology in
general and of American Social Gospel in particular.[62] To Tillich,
the dream of the establishment of the Kingdom of God in America
revealed the "happy backwardness" of the American intellectual
climate.[63] Both Tillich and Barth assumed an impassable gulf between the purposes which God has for history and even the most
worthy of political programs. But with that declaration, Tillich
veers sharply from the path of other-worldliness which Barth follows.
For Barth, faithfulness to the transcendent God made it impossible
for the Christian to take the political sphere of life with real seriousness, since consistent political action would compromise his submission to the absolute will of God. To Tillich, however, it seemed
that the very spiritual sensitivity that made so clear the failures of
capitalistic society ought to point the Christian to the force which
most effectively bore the spirit of protest against that society; the
appropriate political program would consist in support of the bearers
of that protest. In the present context, that force would be the disinherited, the proletariat—the same proletariat identified by Karl
Marx.

Unlike Marx, however, Tillich did not hold the proletariat to be
a "pure" force. Though they are without power in contemporary
civilization and cannot, therefore, be saddled with responsibility for
its political or social forms or for its cultural barrenness, the workers
are made of the same clay as the owners, and they are implicated in
the sinfulness of the present situation, by dint of having succumbed, out of envy, to imitation of the ways of the capitalists;
they have become "bourgeois in ... temper."[64] In fact, the whole
socialist movement had, by and large, "fallen prey to the spirit of
the nineteenth century."[65] The best hope for redemption of proletarian and capitalist alike at this hour is in the movement called
"religious socialism."[66] Religious socialists see in "the proletarian

situation" the outcome of the degradation of humanity caused by the acquisitive spirit; but their strong sense of the imperfect virtue of all human instruments prevents them from idealizing the workers. Thus, Tillich sees the creative task as one for non-proletarian forces, particularly the Protestant intellectual, to serve as the vanguard for the proletariat.[67]

To act in imitation of the disinterestedness of Christ, the Protestant intellectual must act in the vanguard of the proletariat. Since the existing order was the absolute antithesis of the prophetic spirit, any expression of religious "seriousness"—even in such peripheral areas as artistic expression[68]—was ultimately subversive of the existing structure of power and privilege. This was what Tillich meant by the "proletarian situation."[69] In the true sense of that ancient word, the "proletarian" is one who stands outside civilization and, merely in being himself, threatens the continuance of that civilization. Similarly, true religious action, since it calls for the substitution of the spirit of love and mutuality for the spirit of economic competition upon which capitalism is reared, is subversive of the present order.[70]

Tillich's formula thus gives benefit of clergy to the central Marxist description of the appointed role of the proletariat, while repudiating the materialistic categories which Marx employed. Marx's argument that the proletariat does not need to defend the virtue of his cause before history (the "objective" fact of dispossession does that for him) has its parallel in Tillich's argument that the proletarian is presently under divine commission as the appropriate agent of deliverance, whose cause every religious man serves whether he knows it or not. This is true even though the proletariat is explicitly antireligious in its view of itself—even though the proletariat, because of his irreligion, regularly justifies himself in terms of the selfish-materialistic values he has learned from the world of the bourgeoisie.[71] At this hour, "the movement most strongly conscious of the *kairos* seems to us . . . to be socialism."[72]

Reading Tillich, Niebuhr made the great political discovery of his life: religious Marxism. His review of Tillich's *Religious Situation* in the December, 1932, issue of *World Tomorrow* marks Niebuhr's declaration of discipleship to religious socialism of the European stamp: "Paul Tillich is the intellectual leader of the little group of religious Socialists in Germany who are trying to understand our modern civilization and the proletarian protest against it in religious terms. . . . It is an analysis which could not possibly have been written in America and which many liberal, semi-radical and unreligious radical Americans will find meaningless. America is still too thoroughly immersed in the illusions and superstitions of liberal-middle-class culture to appreciate just what Tillich is trying to do. But his book points the way in the direction of which [sic] our thought must ultimately go."[73] In one assault, the German theologians had levelled all of Niebuhr's defenses against radicalism: his religious idealism, his bourgeois gradualism, and his American exceptionalism.

It cannot be stressed too strongly that Niebuhr's new political creed was won in the resolution of theological difficulties. Students of American political philosophy who are willing enough to admit Niebuhr's great influence in the shaping of political discussion in America have failed to make enough of the conjuncture of these two intellectual discoveries—the one a theological discovery ("crisis theology") and the other a political one (Marxism). One gets the impression from many such discussions that their authors feel there is something indecent about attempting to treat these developments in tandem. Thus, critics of Niebuhr's Marxist phase usually satisfy themselves with the explanation that it was the depression which made Niebuhr a Marxist.[74] The reorientation in Niebuhr's theology (away from theological liberalism, towards "neo-orthodoxy") is separated from his Marxist phase and treated as a purely internal crisis that would not bear political fruit until Niebuhr's later repudiation of Marxism (at the end of the decade). Thus students who are loath to think of religion as anything but a socially stabilizing force manage to see Niebuhr's religious orthodoxy emerging in step with his later political neo-orthodoxy. But it has become perfectly clear in recent years as a result of the work of such historians as Robert Miller, Paul Carter, Donald Meyer, and others, that the religious faith of American Protestant leaders during the 1930s often made for radical opinion and radical social action. Not a little of this radicalism is traceable to Tillich's religious socialism, made relevant to the American situation in the words and activities of Niebuhr.

The discovery of Tillich's religious socialism came in time to rescue Niebuhr from the effects of doubts which had been afflicting him for some years—not only political doubts but essentially religious ones. Tillich satisfied Niebuhr that the only force powerful enough to rescue civilization from the political lethargy induced in it by its liberal-optimism was a recovery of the sense of urgency which New Testament Christianity has in its expectation of the imminent end of the world. The contemporary counterpart of that expectation, Tillich insisted, was the Marxian apocalypse. Tillich's religious socialism provided Niebuhr with the insight that rekindled his religious fervor and galvanized him into political action.

Expressed in secular terms: Niebuhr's interest in Marxism "suggests his shocked fascination with the possibility of some basic turn, some drastic judgment in history."[75] But, it would be a serious mistake to believe that Niebuhr could simply have thought himself into Marxism and into the flurry of political action that now followed. A deeply religious man, Niebuhr was taken into the political wars by a deep religious conversion. Whoever misses this link between religious conviction and political action in Niebuhr's life utterly misses the most striking feature of his intellect—which is (in the proper sense of the word) its integrity. The effort of applying religious concern to secular descriptions of American society made him a Marxist. The impact which Marxism could make upon a sensitive religious intelligence of the inter-War period is something not properly appreciated by historians of American intellectual life in the inter-War period. To grasp this side of the appeal of Marxism, one has to turn to European models—to Hromadka in Czechoslovakia, to Tillich in Germany, to John Macmurray in England, or to Berdyaev, the Russian exile.[76] These religious thinkers, combining Marxist descriptions of the alienation of the proletariat with pronouncements of judgment upon the rich culled from the Scriptures, were the intellectual masters of Niebuhr in the 1930s. And it was Niebuhr who bore their message to America. With arguments deriving from European Marxists and European theologians, Niebuhr shaped a political creed which soon attracted the enthusiasm of a loyal coterie, made up at first principally of clergymen, but coming at the end of the thirties to include great numbers of lay intellectuals.

*Chapter*

# REFLECTIONS ON THE END OF AN ERA

*If a season of violence can establish
a just social system and can create
the possibilities of its preservation,
there is no purely ethical ground upon which
violence and revolution can be ruled out.*

MORAL MAN AND IMMORAL SOCIETY (1932), PAGE 179.

Historians who have dealt with the stampede of American intellectuals toward socialism in the months following the stock market crash of 1929 usually imply that there was something superficial about the conversion, *in the typical case*.[1] It is very much in the American character to make the pragmatic test the conclusive test, in politics as in other matters. The "system," however defined, had failed the pragmatic test—and economic depression and human suffering had been the outcome. No wonder that the intellectual community was now prepared to give a hearing to a program which had systematically excoriated the system and had confidently predicted that its defects would be betrayed in just such a turn of affairs as had now taken place. The wonder is only that so few of these same intellectuals paused to tidy up behind them, as they dashed from one camp into the other. The typical American socialist of the 1930s had been a typical liberal-progressive of the 1920s. As he leapt from one camp to the other, he abandoned the grab-bag of liberal-progressive phrases and outfitted himself with a grab-bag of ill-assorted tag-ends of all the schools of socialist thought, from the gas-and-water socialists through the spectrum to Lenin.[2]

It is precisely because ante-depression socialists talked so much of ideology that American intellectuals had found them unattractive. The vigorous idealism of American liberal-progressivism had seemingly dissolved all need for ideology. What makes Reinhold Niebuhr a special case, a quite remarkable and refreshing contrast to the typical socialist convert of the thirties, is his courage and his frankness in dealing with the issue of ideology. He confronted the challenge of socialism with the seriousness bred in him by deep religious intelligence. It was the philosophical challenge of his life. His mature philosophical method was shaped in this encounter—and, while he lived to repudiate his socialism, his political and social thought would always display the effects of the encounter. The problems which Marxism raised for his philosophical method were the problems which occupied him throughout the remainder of his life. We have thus reached the beginning of our discussion of Niebuhr's intellectual maturity.

In the months that followed Niebuhr's arrival in New York, the new experiences we have described were compelling him to a systematic review of his commitments. Within the L.I.P.A., he was constantly tilting with mature and experienced politicians and political thinkers in debates about the practicability of socialism and the limits and possibilities of parliamentary socialism. (Barely had he launched into his second year at the Seminary before the Stock Market Crash took place, adding urgency to this debate.) Within the lecture halls of Union Theological Seminary, he was struggling to give expression to his theological views, measuring the stern "Biblical theology" of Barth against the benign and liberal theology of the seminary textbooks; seeking as well, to find a place for Tillich's religious socialism,[3] without succumbing to Marxist "dogma." One result of all of this—and probably the most enduring result—was his first important book: *Moral Man and Immoral Society* (1932).

Niebuhr was to admit in later years that his title was a misleading one; that its thesis might better be summarized as "immoral man and even more immoral society." In this book, Niebuhr puts an end to that nagging inner debate about the perfectibility of man, and commits himself to an acceptance of the concept of "original sin." This commitment reflects the impact upon him of the crisis theologians, and it reflects as well the interest he was developing about the same time in the works of St. Augustine.[4]

*Moral Man* is meant to be Niebuhr's parting blast at liberalism, and a defense of Marxism, both undertaken in the name of a more "realistic" view of human nature made possible by a reaffirmation of central Christian themes. The basic illusion which hobbles our political thinking is the one about the essential reasonableness of men. Lurking behind that illusion is a subsidiary one—namely, that reason is disinterested. But, the beginning of political wisdom is to recognize that, while individuals may strive to act disinterestedly and may within limits and on occasions succeed, there is a certain "inevitable hypocrisy" (page 8) which besets every similar effort of *collective* man. Individuals can act disinterestedly, up to a point; but groups, never. This is an observable fact of life and of history. More than that, it is the principal lesson of Christian scripture and is known to theologians under the name of "original sin."

Recognizing this, Christians should cease calling for the application of the perfectionist ethics of Jesus to social problems and to politics. Jesus' ethics of perfect and disinterested love are appropriate only to the Kingdom of God (which he expected imminently). The outcome of Jesus' witness to these ethics (his crucifixion) attests that they were ineffectual in this world against the powers of this world. It is the Christian's business to bear witness to the ethics of non-resistance, and in his witness to allow other men a window (as it were) onto the Kingdom. But all of this will not bring the Kingdom closer to historical realization. The Kingdom is "final and absolute," "equally distant from all political programs." (The influence of Barth is obvious here.) "All men cannot be expected to become spiritual any more than they can be expected to become rational. Those who achieve either excellence will always be a leavening influence in social life: but the political structure of society cannot be built upon their achievement." (page 73)

Niebuhr insists that the record of history and the *total* impression of Scripture both bear out his argument that men are basically incapable of sustained altruism. Niebuhr's critics are struck by the categorical nature of these observations on human potentiality. Secular critics talk of "a retreat to obscurantism,"[5] while religious critics aver (with Victor Gollancz) that when they read these words from *Moral Man* they "can almost hear the nails on Calvary."[6] All consideration vanishes with this work of the possibility of making the ethics of Jesus into a political program. One can comb the works of Niebuhr with the finest of combs and one will not find, after this work, any further references to "Christian politics," "Christian solutions," or "applying the rule of love"—or any of the religious-perfectionist phrases that sounded so regularly in his earlier work.

Now, it is the great merit of Marx, says Niebuhr, that he recovered for moderns this fact of the impossibility of disinterested action in the group. (Marx himself was evidence of the occasional possibility of disinterested action *in the individual*.) While Marx claims to have come to this discovery by the application of rigid scientific method, his discovery is best seen as "an apocalyptic vision" (page 155), as the response of a morally sensitive soul to an unjust situation.

"[Marxism] is more than a doctrine. It is a dramatic, and to some degree, a religious interpretation of proletarian destiny. In such insights as this, rather than in his economics, one must discover the real significance of Marx (153–54). . . . The Marxian imagines that he has a philosophy or even a science of history. What he has is really an apocalyptic vision." (155) The celebration of Marxism and of the "proletarian situation" proceeds from this point along Tillich's lines.

The proper course of action for Christians in this hour Niebuhr finds in the creative synthesis of Christian realism and Marxist realism (233ff.). Recognizing that social conflict is inevitable and that a showdown between the proletariat and capitalist civilization is imminent, Christians should ally themselves frankly with the proletarian cause. They should seek to advance the rights of the workingman not by preaching the ethics of non-resistance but by accepting the power realities. This means that Christians must come to terms with "a frank dualism in morals" (271). They must not think that the owners can be talked into an attitude of charity and sacrifice, nor that the proletariat can be talked out of the use of force to overthrow the system in the ultimate encounter which is just around the corner.

Thus, getting down to the concrete situation in which America finds herself, Christian realists must not be deceived by apparent and piecemeal concessions made by the possessing classes in nations where parliamentary forms have survived up to date.

> There is as yet no evidence that a privileged class, which yields advantage after advantage peacefully, will finally yield the very basis of its special position in a society without conflict. (210)
>
> [The middle-class] living in comfort and security, is unable to recognize the urgency of the social problem. . . . (213) It is a question whether any middle-class will ever be more intelligent than that class in England and Germany. In both of these nations the entire middle-class community turned to conservatism rather than radicalism in the moment of crisis; in England in the election of 1931, when it participated in the overwhelming Tory defeat of labor, and in Germany, where it expresses itself through the policies of fascism. (215–16)

Similarly, the farmer is a hopeless conservative in his instincts (as

Marx had said), and will prove himself, in the showdown, an enemy
of the proletarian cause. Thus, the attempt of Paul Douglas (of the
L.I.P.A.) to bring about a New Party based on farmer-labor cooperation is unrealistic (218–18n). The basic fact determining political
allegiance is economics—which means, in the end, class. The failure
of liberals to see this is their cardinal error. "It would be pleasant to
believe that the intelligence of the general community could be
raised to such a height that the irrational injustices of society would
be eliminated. But unfortunately there is no such general community." (213)

To sense the distance that Niebuhr had travelled in a few short
years, we need only compare these words with a passage (already
cited) from his article, "Why We Need a New Economic Order," of
October, 1928: "Whether the present system will succumb to violence or be gradually changed by social and political action will not
be decided by those who suffer most from its limitations. The
decision rests with the community in general."

Only the proletariat, then, is a force for enduring reform in present circumstances—the proletariat, and those very few who ally
themselves to it, detaching themselves in an effort of deepest religious seriousness, from the values of capitalist civilization.

Something very radical had happened to Niebuhr's politics. But
we must be careful about the labels we use. It is not difficult to
compose from Niebuhr's writings of the 1930s a list of his judgments against America's present and predictions regarding her
future that would have drawn the applause of the fondest of Marxist
sectaries. Robert Fitch, for instance, provides us such a list, drawn
from only one work:

> In this mood [Fitch writes] he was able to declare that democracy
> alone could not effect the transition from capitalism to socialism
> (*Reflections on the End of an Era*, 1935, pages 80–81, 156–67), and
> that our world "moves with inexorable logic toward collectivism."
> (Ibid., 238). He proclaimed "a new society such as the workers
> are destined to build," (162), and affirmed "the inevitability of
> the reign of the workers," (147), while he described these workers
> as "those who are destined to become the rulers of society," (148),
> and "fated to contend for a society which the logic of history
> affirms." (143) He assures us that "their victory is as certain as
> their revolt is inevitable when the time is ripe." (142)[7]

Niebuhr himself, in reviewing these expressions, correctly remembered (in 1953) that he "used Marxist collectivism to counter liberal
individualism, Marxist catastrophism to counter liberal optimism, and

Marxist determinism to challenge liberal moralism and idealism."[8]
The operative word here is "used."

But the older he became the more Niebuhr was tempted to recall
his erstwhile commitment to socialism as a dogmatic one. In 1959
he wrote: "We [Christian Socialists] became involved in a politics
which made an absolute distinction between the innocent poor and
the guilty rich. We were thus led astray by a genuine religious and
ethical impulse into utopian politics."[9] The record does not bear out
this picture of ideological captivity. We shall be looking at this more
closely: but for the moment, it can be said that the clearest description of his commitment to Marxism is found on page 277 of his
*Moral Man*; it is "a very valuable illusion for the moment."

Reinhold Niebuhr was never a doctrinaire Marxist. There was a
period in his life (the years with which we are dealing in this chapter) when he thought he saw in Marxism the appropriate instrument
for castigating capitalist civilization and ideology, both of which he
had consciously and explicitly rejected. The most relevant evidence
is a work which follows closely upon *Moral Man*—his *Reflections on
the End of an Era* (1934),[10] in which Niebuhr develops his views on
the uses of this valuable illusion. Niebuhr's reputation in radical
circles owed a good deal to this book. It is unfortunate and somewhat
disturbing that this book remains (at this writing) the one work of
Niebuhr's mature years which has been allowed to go out of print
without reissue. It could not, of course, be reissued without a careful
preface explaining to unwary readers that its author later abandoned
the Marxist-catastrophic view that it so vigorously presents. Yet it
richly deserves revival, for it is the one book in the Niebuhr canon
(not considering the two collections of his sermons)[11] in which
Niebuhr succeeds in wedding the vigorous style of his preaching to
a book-length presentation of his larger views. Of all his books, it has
the liveliest style. Such a product, one supposes, is only possible to
a man in the moment of excitement that follows upon a great doubt-
dispelling discovery. Perhaps its sometimes strident tone embarrassed
Niebuhr in his old age (when he was agreeing to the reissue of the
remaining titles of the 1930s).

"Marxism," Niebuhr had written in *Moral Man*, "is more than a
doctrine. It is a dramatic, and to some degree a religious, interpretation of proletarian destiny" (page 154). By 1934, this hint has been
expanded into this remarkable passage from his *Reflections*:

> However much [Marxism] may claim scientific validity, it is
> clearly a mythological construction. Events in history are read
> from a perspective achieved by an ethical and even a religious
> passion. A force in history is assumed which makes for the

triumph of man's highest social ideals, interpreted by the Marxian as that of equal justice. The Marxian does not share the liberal hope that an ethical ideal is easily achieved in history, nor yet the classical religious belief that only God himself can redeem the chaos of history and reduce it to harmony. The Marxian hope is rather that processes in history support those who are willing to affirm these processes.

The Marxian faith that the "objective" conditions of history support the moral purpose of the proletariat extends even to the hope that his enemies will defeat themselves, an analogue to the Christian idea that God will "use the wrath of man to praise him." The belief of Marx that "when the proletariat proclaims the dissolution of the existing order of things it is merely announcing the secret of its own existence for it is itself the virtual dissolution of this order of things" is an effort of the religious imagination to snatch victory from defeat, and runs parallel to the Christian hope that "the last shall be first and the first last. . . ." The Marxian has a secularized version of the religious assurance, "Fear not, little flock, it is your Father's good pleasure to give you the kingdom."

The analogy between Marxian religion and the more classical religious faith is further revealed in the fact that it has the same difficulty, revealed in the history of Christian thought, in striking a proper balance between voluntarism and determinism. The idea that the downfall of capitalism is inevitable is as powerful an incentive to moral energy as was Calvinistic determinism in the heyday of Calvinistic faith. The belief that determinism inevitably leads to an inclination to take "moral holidays" (William James) is a typical illusion of a rationalistic and individualistic age. On the contrary, men develop the highest energy in the pursuit of a moral or social goal when they are most certain that they are affirming the preordained "counsels of God."[12]

The source of both Niebuhr's enthusiasm for Marxism and of his realism regarding its vices is this awareness—which seems to be unique among American intellectuals of his generation—of the religious depth of Marxism's appeal. "Its virtues and its vices," he had written earlier, "are the virtues and vices of religion."[13]

"Some kind of religion," Niebuhr saw, "is the basis of every potent social programme."[14] Liberal politics, which depends upon the appeal to reason and to self-interest, is incapable of bringing about the needed change in the character of civilization because the reason of the proletarian tells him that his cause is hopeless against the entrenched power of the possessing classes, and the self-interest of the possessing classes tells them to resist every demand of the proletariat. Marxism points to an assurance of success for the proletarian revolution which is deeper than reason can discover. It endows its disciples with a fervor to struggle against all apparent evidence that they are overwhelmed. It gives them fanaticism; and so formidable is the accumulation of power and privilege which supports the capitalist civilization, that nothing short of fanaticism will avail against it. Liberals are hamstrung in the struggle for social justice because they lack fanaticism. Since the capitalist system is doomed, therefore; and since it cannot be overturned except by the fanaticism which is bred by Marxist "mythology"; and since liberal politics, the politics of compromise and strict parliamentarianism, is irrelevant to that accomplishment—it would seem to follow that Marxism provides a full and sufficient program for Christian politics. Here, however, Niebuhr's argument takes a subtle turn.

Fanaticism, while a necessary force at this critical turning-point in history (this "kairos," Tillich would say), is, like everything else human, an ambiguous force: good on one side, evil on the other. The positive side of fanaticism is that it creates energy, an energy that is unqualified because it is uncalculating; on the obverse side, it generates hatred—for fanaticism operates only while the fanatic's attention is trained on the enemy. There is no point talking about tempering the fanaticism of the proletariat with Christian charity: "The moral logic of history is never pure and dispassionate precisely because judgment upon evil cannot be executed without stiffening the spirit of justice with an alloy of the spirit of vengeance. . . . The stubbornness with which social evil is maintained requires that the force which is to dislodge it be propelled by the impulses of nature as well as the ideals of the spirit, by vengeance as well as by justice. . . . In brief, the judges of history are always barbarians."[15] If the spirit of vengeance inspires the proletariat to his *necessary* task of destruction, there must nevertheless be kept in reserve the faculty for compromise and accommodation which has inspired liberals in happier days. The point is, however, that it is in reserve because it is irrelevant in the moment. The duty of those who call themselves liberals is to wait until the destructive task is done—when mankind will once again be able to put them to use.[16]

Liberals are deluding themselves to think that they can offer anything to a situation when capitalism is dying and the new era of socialism is struggling to be born. The proletariat—the "barbarians" —are correct in believing that liberals have some stake in civilization which prevents them from giving themselves unqualifiedly to its overthrow. But when we stand on the other side of the proletarian revolutions, we shall then have need of constructive idealism. For, contrary to Marxist theology, the demise of capitalism will not usher in an age of perfection.

In 1930, Niebuhr was one of a group of United States churchmen who travelled to Russia to study the new society. Out of this there came immediately five excellent articles for the *Christian Century*.[17] Niebuhr was much impressed by the enthusiasm he found among the people for the accomplishments of the revolution. There was, he found, "a boundless enthusiasm among the people which transmutes the necessities of the situation into voluntarily accepted sacrifices."[18] The sense of national pride he found in Russia was a heady experience for one accustomed to the rampant individualism and selfishness of the capitalist world.

How did the Russian common man come by this remarkable and enviable capacity for sacrifice? The answer, Niebuhr argued, was to be found in the perennial need of man for religious faith. Russians were now finding a purpose in life, and what can only be called a religious experience in their present constructive experiment. This constituted a positive religious gain, for the Russian people had long ago ceased to derive religious nourishment from their churches. This failure of the ancient religion of Russia impressed itself upon Niebuhr during an Orthodox service he attended in the Soviet Union:

> Twenty minutes were consumed in robing the bishop in preparation for his entrance into the sanctuary. . . . [E]ach article of ceremonial apparel is blessed and given to him. . . . [S]o remote and unreal [is] all this elaborate eccelesiastical millinery business. The mind wanders to the eager young men and women who speak and work so earnestly for the building of a new Russia in which social justice shall prevail and who, if they lack the tenderness of the gospel which this church ought to be preaching are certainly not without the gospel's passion for social justice.

Then, these words of warning to the readers of the *Christian Century*:

> The logic of revolution while brutal, is not without a kind of rough justice and we should be sentimentalists to forget the intimate and organic relation between the church of these priests and the oppression of the tsarist Russia. If innocent priests now suffer under the wrath of a revolutionary age, that may be one way of purging the guilt of the past. Our groups of liberal clergymen feel a little too superior, I think, to these chanting priests. After all, the liberal church of America is almost as

intimately related to economic reaction as was the Russian church to tsarist oppression.[19]

The article just cited is, incidentally, a revealing source for Niebuhr's now rapidly crystallizing theology. The will to believe (as William James called it) is seen by Niebuhr as a perennial and irreducible element in every man's make-up. Religion is that deep earnestness that possesses a man when he is about the business that he takes with ultimate seriousness. Western man, because he has long since solved the basic problems of survival and creature comfort, reserves his moments of ultimate seriousness for contemplation of the after-life, because this seems to him to be the only aspect of his affairs that he cannot handle for himself. But, where the problems of this world are not all under control—where poverty, ignorance and squalor are the general lot of men—ultimate seriousness is the appropriate attitude toward this world and its business. Because the priests of established religion (whether of tsarist Russia or of liberal America) ignore this truth, workingmen are indifferent to organized religion. The new man of Russia has recovered his religious conviction—though he calls it by an irreligious name.[20]

Recognizing the religious component in Marxism, Niebuhr argued, equips us to accept realistically the behavior of Communists. Thus, we should be on the alert for the symptoms of religious sectarianism among Communists everywhere—such symptoms as extreme self-righteousness, extreme submissiveness in the lower ranks towards the hierarchy, resistance to honest cooperative effort with gentiles, and dogmatism. Niebuhr was inclined to believe that the very fanaticism of Communist faith assured that it would not capture the still pragmatic American proletariat.[21] A more serious threat existed in the prospect that liberals in general, failing to see that the ultimate loyalty of Marxists puts them beyond the rules of decent give-and-take in politics—and, indeed, justifies them in the practice of deceit (as Lenin argued)—will unwittingly allow themselves to be used for Moscow's purposes. Thus, their "dogmatisms and over-simplifications are so false to the political realities of western society, that their political emphasis, for all its vitality, may help to create Fascism."[22] If Niebuhr was (occasionally) betrayed into lapses of his characteristic hard-headedness in dealing with the new order in Russia, he was never the least bit naive about the Communist Party, U.S.A., which he always regarded as an arm of the Soviet policy-makers.[23]

Some element within our doomed civilization must, therefore, hold itself in reserve for the moment when the revolution is achieved as it must inevitably be—and disillusionment sets in among the triumphant proletariat, as it inevitably will. There must be some remnant prepared to teach the lessons of charity and compromise to a proletarian majority which is schooled in vengeance and drunk with expectations of utopia. That remnant is to be found among the "relatively disinterested"[24] within our present system. With this discovery, we find ourselves back on familiar ground.

Throughout his adventure with Marxism, Niebuhr remains what he was at the beginning  the "relatively disinterested" intellectual. The disinterested intellectual, of course, has no place in Marxism. Niebuhr is not talking (on Marxist lines) of the enlightened and sympathetic refugee from the bourgeoisie (like Marx or Engels) who attaches himself to the proletariat. Niebuhr's liberal must hold a part of himself in reserve; he must keep his critical faculty intact, while acknowledging that the proletariat is the wave of the future. Such an insight is possible only to a remnant of society—"its ethically most sensitive members."[25] These are the few who are intelligent enough to perceive "the total social situation,"[26]—which is that capitalism is doomed, and that the proletariat is the "necessary" instrument of its destruction. But to say that this elite comprises the "ethically sensitive" is surely Niebuhr's weekday way of saying that they are educated in true religion. If observation of the corruption of capitalist society has convinced Niebuhr that Marxism is "necessary," it is the Christian doctrine of "original sin"—that *final fact of human nature*—that convinces him that it is illusion.

*Chapter*

# A SOCIALIST POLITICIAN

*It is probably not generally realized,*
*even by his admirers,*
*that in his socialist days [Reinhold Niebuhr]*
*was probably a little to the left of me.*

NORMAN THOMAS[1]

Once the decision for socialism was made, Niebuhr threw himself with astonishing vigor into the job of advancing socialist ideas in the circles where his name was already known and respected. Almost at once, he became one of the best-known spokesmen for socialism among American intellectuals.

The first clear-cut literary product of Niebuhr's Marxism is an article in the *Christian Century* of August, 1931.[2] Regular readers of that paper (mostly clergymen, and mostly of the Social Gospel persuasion) must have been struck by the new note of historical determininism in a writer whose work was already so familiar to them:

As an industrial nation we seem to be placed chronologically about a half century behind England and Germany and we may expect therefore to pass through a stage of development which characterized the life of these nations in the last two decades of the nineteenth-century.

The most outstanding political development in these nations in the period mentioned was the growth of a class-conscious labor movement and the expression of its political aims in terms of a collective social creed. . . . [Thus, we can expect that] the growth of socialistic political philosophy will be the most significant development in our political life in the next decades.

Nothing in Niebuhr's previous work could have prepared them, either, for the Marxist realism Niebuhr was now employing:

The American people, and more particularly the American workers . . . will learn that a dominant political group holds its power because it is the dominant economic group and that, despite its communal and brotherly pretensions, it uses its political power to safeguard its economic interests. . . . Ideally, laws are the conscience of a community, arbitrating the conflicting interests of various social and economic groups. Actually, they are always to some larger or smaller degree a kind of legerdemain by which a dominant group hides its particular interests behind the sanctities of "the general will" or "community interests" or some other pretension of universality.

In political strategy and in political program, too, Niebuhr speaks with unmistakable Marxist accents:

The political power which an economic group has arrogated to itself can be destroyed or abridged only by setting organized power against it. . . . The only way in which political power in the hands of the workers can assert itself is by the continued abridgement, qualification and destruction of absolute property rights. . . . Every industrial state is bound to move in the direction of the socialistic ideal of the progressive communal control of all the significant sources of economic power. The same historical processes which stripped the political autocrats of their power will operate restlessly to qualify and finally destroy the economic and industrial autocrats.

But the most striking aspect of the conversion that Niebuhr has undergone is seen in his resolution of that nagging dilemma—the *leitmotif* of all his early writing—regarding the proper political program for the Christian Church: "The more idealistic element in the Christian Church does not . . . find any difficulty with the ultimate aim of socialism. . . . [That element] recognizes the identity between . . . [the Christian ideal of love] and that of socialism."
This was to be but the first of a long list of articles[3] that Niebuhr

was to do in this, the busiest decade of his career as a writer, in defense of a Marxism that was to be both Christian and American. The audience for these shorter pieces was principally among the Protestant clergy and socially concerned Protestant laymen; but soon large numbers of intellectuals with no church affiliation and no admitted religious concern acquired the habit, in the thirties, of searching out Niebuhr's articles on politics, as the word got around to the intellectual community as a whole.

Niebuhr's synthesis of Marxism with "Christian realism" produced colorful results when he applied it to the theme of domestic politics. He was now an unsparing assailant of the established two-party system and of the entire roster of available politicians. In the final hour of the electoral campaign of 1932,[4] Niebuhr could see nothing to choose between the two major candidates. Both represented "the financial and commercial classes," and both held the support they did among workers and farmers only because of "the political ignorance of these classes." Nothing of importance could be decided by the election, since "the system" itself was not challenged by either candidate: that must await "a social struggle in which power is pitted against power." Niebuhr, thus, resented the decision of the editorial majority of the *Christian Century* to support Hoover (their ground being his soundness on the prohibition issue, which, they claimed, declared his "spiritual nature").

Niebuhr was, of course, for Norman Thomas, and expanded his energies in the political wars of 1932 pouring scorn upon liberals who thought that there could be grounds for choosing between Tweedledum and Tweedledee. Among the most pathetic of these bemused liberals was George Norris, whom Niebuhr had long admired for his independence and humanity, but whose "National Progessive League for Roosevelt" Niebuhr characterized as "the last dying gasp of liberalism in America."[5]

Roosevelt's election altered nothing, so far as Niebuhr was concerned. "Capitalism is dying and it ought to die.... Next to the futility of liberalism we may set down the inevitability of fascism as a practical certainty in every Western nation"[6]—these were Niebuhr's thoughts as Roosevelt was making his way to the White House in March of 1933. Roosevelt had not made much of an impression upon Niebuhr at all before 1932; he was simply another name on an interminable and undefying list of shallow crowd-pleasers standing ready to attempt the reconstruction of capitalism. If anything, Niebuhr had the impression that Roosevelt was a bit shadier than most.[7] But his personal qualifications were, in any case, irrelevant. As the tool of the established interests, Roosevelt would be permitted merely to tinker away the hours until the time was ripe for his masters to establish their overt fascist order. Then Americans would see the end of capitalism, in bloodshed.[8]

"Someone once asked me how I, as an intelligent person, could belong to a political party that is dogmatic. You can imagine what party that is. There is only one party which has real dogmas—I mean, real principles! Why, I am glad to divest myself of some of my intellectual liberty in order that I may express organically with a political group that, I believe, is facing in the right direction in our world."[9]

It should not surprise any reader that Niebuhr's lively commitment to socialism did not translate itself primarily into an active role within the Socialist Party—that is, in the organizational sense. Even during the 1930s, Niebuhr seemed to prefer the company of that larger community of politically concerned intellectuals that clustered about the L.I.D. and the L.I.P.A. (of whose executive committee he was a member.)[10] "He was an active socialist," Norman Thomas recalls, "who was never very active in the Socialist Party as such. He avoided organizational responsibilities but was very helpful."[11] Niebuhr made no secret of his Socialist membership; he does seem, however, to have resisted making himself too much available to the Party. (Thus, in 1930, he tried to scotch a bid to run him as a Socialist candidate for Congress.)[12] Niebuhr was, however, always willing to put himself behind the Socialist ticket—and issued abundant testimonials of this support to all who would hear. In both 1932 and 1936, he led weighty committees of intellectuals in praise of the Socialist Presidential ticket.[13]

Once, for a brief few months, the name of Reinhold Niebuhr does figure prominently in the organizational life of the Socialist Party. This was during the great intra-party fracas that came to a head in the "Militant" revolt of 1934.[14] The "Militants" were the younger generation, clustering about Norman Thomas, most of whom had entered the party since 1930 by way of the L.I.P.A., and who now were determined to see Thomas' labors as the candidate of 1932 and as the architect of the larger policy of courting non-Socialist liberals recognized by his elevation to the chairmanship of the Party. Though the friendliness of the Thomas group toward non-Socialist liberals of the L.I.P.A. camp attracted the scorn of the older Socialists, the younger group nonetheless liked to think of themselves as the "Militants" because of their greater friendliness toward the Communist experiment in Russia. The Militants were, on the average, much younger than the Old Guard (clustered about Morris Hillquit and the needle-trade Socialists), were American-born rather than immigrants, and college-educated.

The surprisingly poor showing of Socialist tickets in the elections of 1932, after the dramatic gains at all electoral levels during 1930 and 1931, gave weight to the arguments of the Militants that the time had come for newer hands to take the controls. The electoral successes of Adolf Hitler in 1932 and 1933, followed by the disastrous rout of the German left, convinced the Militants that American Socialists must cultivate the cooperation of the Communists in stabilizing the left against the growing threat of American Fascism. Though not entirely convinced of the goodwill of the Communists, the Thomas group was convinced that "for the sake of our own members, especially the younger people," a formal overture must be made to the Communists for amalgamation of Socialist-Communist efforts: "It must be made obvious that it is they who sabotage our united front, not we who disdainfully reject it."[15]

What followed needs to be seen against the backdrop of shifting tactics of the Third International in the thirties.[16] The Sixth World Congress of the Comintern (1928) had imposed the obligation of hostility to the non-Communist left upon Communist members. Democratic-Socialist and non-Communist labor forces were to be shunned as "social fascists." By the end of 1933, even Stalin was being forced to realize that this tactic had smoothed the way to power for rightist forces, most tragically in Germany; so that when the Seventh World Congress met in 1935, there was no reason for the surprise that so many Communists in fact suffered on learning that their new marching orders called for cooperation with all progressive forces in the "Popular Front." Well before the Congress of 1935 met, there were substantial straws in the wind, and younger Socialists were anticipating a conflict over this issue with their elders —all of whom, of course, had suffered in one way or another the abuse of the Communists, and many of whom bore real scars from the savage crushing of the left in Austria and in the Reich, for which they blamed the opportunism of Austrian and German Communists, and the machiavellism of Stalin.

At the Party's convention in Detroit in 1934, the Militants made their bid. Devere Allen led the troops into battle with a Militant "Declaration of Principles": under Militant leadership the Socialist Party

will meet war and detailed plans for war . . . by massed war
resistance organized so far as practicable in a general strike of labor
unions and professional groups in a united effort to make the

waging of war a practical impossibility and to convert the capitalist war crisis into a victory for Socialism. Capitalism is doomed. If it can be superseded by majority vote, the Socialist Party will rejoice. If the crisis comes through the denial of majority rights after the electorate has given us a mandate, we shall not hesitate to crush by our labor solidarity the reckless forces of reaction and to consolidate the Socialist state. If the capitalist system should collapse in a general chaos and confusion, which cannot permit of orderly procedure, the Socialist Party, whether or not in such case it is a majority, will not shrink from the responsibility of organizing and maintaining a government under the workers' rules.[17]

The Old Guard, their ranks in disarray on account of the recent death of their leader, Morris Hillquit, saw the Declaration become party policy by a comfortable margin, and a greater number of Militant figures now enter the ranks of the Party's executive.[18] The conflict within the Party continued over the next year, each side preparing positions of strength for the convention of June, 1936. To compound the confusion and the ill-feeling, a third splinter, calling itself the Revolutionary Policy Committee, emerged by early 1934.[19] The R.P.C. scorned the parliamentary road to power, and talked heroically about taking to the streets. This thinking put the R.P.C. in step with the still-effective orthodoxy of the Sixth World Congress. The irony was, however, that the Comintern was already laying the foundation for its shift toward respectability—towards "extending the hand of cooperation toward all genuine Progressive forces," in parliamentary action under a Popular Front. The better-informed American Communists were already beginning to smile on the Militants.

Until the Militants launched their own paper (the *Socialist Call*) early in 1935, Reinhold Niebuhr stood briefly in the editorial cockpit of the Militant cause. This was the office of the *World Tomorrow*, the political journal sponsored by the pacifist Fellowship of Reconciliation. The principal editors were Devere Allen, Kirby Page, Norman Thomas, and Reinhold Niebuhr—all Militants, or friendly to the Militant wing. Niebuhr had been a contributing editor since 1926, and an editor since 1928. Norman Thomas, the original chief editor, had left the editorial board a few months prior to the events we are about to describe, but he remained as a "Special Contributor" and was still the presiding spirit of the enterprise.[20] Niebuhr's most important contribution to the debate was his "Comment" (on the Appeal of the Revolutionary Policy Committee of the Socialist Party).[21] This is the most striking exhibit we have of the intellectual difficulties which Niebuhr's Marxism made for him. To the claim of the R.P.C. that Communists were tactically correct and should be supported whole-heartedly in their refusal to cooperate with the middle-class or to indulge at all in parliamentary action, Niebuhr gives what he considers the reply of realism. The middle-class and the farmers are too much attached to their "cultural inheritance" to be wooed into the ranks of the alienated, the proletariat, by even the most energetic "missionary labors." To have any measure of electoral success, the Socialist Party must avoid revolutionary jargon and excessive dogmatism:

> What we need is a socialism which neither deviates from the central emphases of revolutionary Marxism, nor complicates its revolutionary problems by insisting upon dogmas which accentuate psychological and cultural differences between various classes of the disinherited and prevent them from feeling the common bond of poverty, oppression and the fateful mission of building a new society. . . . [T]o speak of a dictatorship of the proletariat in a country in which there is not yet an authentic proletariat and in which any emerging proletariat will require the help of non-proletarian forces for its victory, is to speak without realism.

Despite these swipes at the left-wing's Marxist dogmatism, the article as a whole took the side of the left-wing against the Old Guard. Niebuhr and his fellow editors pursued these issues energetically for a few weeks longer.[22] There seems, indeed, to have been a determined bid to turn the *World Tomorrow* into the effective spokesman of the Socialist left and, in the same stroke, to wed the whole lively but confused movement of Christian social radicalism, despite its hard-core pacifist concern, to the Socialist Party. But the strain of trying to contain the debate between Marxists and pacifists proved too much for that child of the Fellowship of Reconciliation. Before the year was out, the *World Tomorrow* collapsed under the strain.[23] Henceforth, the pacifist message was carried by *Fellowship*, as the organ of the F.O.R., while the Christian Marxist message was carried over to a new paper founded by Reinhold Niebuhr in 1936, called *Radical Religion* (of which, much more later). The collapse of the *World Tomorrow* was the first indication that pacifism and social radicalism were heading for the parting of the ways that came at the end of the decade.

The routing of the Old Guard, not surprisingly, encouraged the R.P.C. to declare for ever stiffer doses of revolutionary Marxism. The Party, they demanded, must drop all pretense of being interested in the parliamentary avenue to power, and opt once and for all for the

Leninist program. It soon became necessary for Niebuhr, as a
respected member of the party and a powerful channel to the outside
"liberal" community, to make his position clearer. Deprived of his old
forum in the collapse of the *World Tomorrow*, Niebuhr prepared a
statement for the *American Socialist Quarterly*,[24] in which he spelled
out clearly the limits that there were in his own mind to the allegiance which Socialists should admit to parliamentary forms.

> Whatever the values of democracy may be in the struggle of the
> workers for power—and the values are still considerable—it
> ought to be fairly clear that a workers' movement can never
> make democracy an end in itself, nor even go upon the assumption
> that it is a certain means to an ultimate end.
>     No revolutionary group of whatever kind in history has ever
> made obedience to law an absolute obligation. . . . The touching
> devotion of right-wing socialism to legality and the constitution is
> proof either of inability or unwillingness to profit from the clear
> lessons of recent history or is merely a convenient ideological tool
> for suppressing new life in the party.

But, having reached this height of Marxist scorn for legalism,
Niebuhr finds the pragmatist and the American-exceptionalist
within himself taking over. "Our romantic left," he writes, makes
the mistake of praising Russian methods as the only alternative to
Germany's fate.

> Now, the Russian revolution remains a beacon of light to workers
> in the whole world. But it was effected in a country which knew
> nothing of the spiritual, political and economic movements which
> determined the history of the western world. Every effort to fit
> the Russian pattern exactly upon western life is bound to result in
> confusion and imperil the workers' cause. . . . An adequate policy
> means a strategic compromise. It probably means that at the
> present moment socialists ought to help in creating a farmer-labor
> party even if such a party, particularly the agrarian end of it, can
> not be expected to come out for pure socialism. A good socialist is
> not afraid of such compromise.

These two declarations from the moment of Niebuhr's fullest involvement in Socialism show him to be a most curious sort of
Marxist. Two quite irreconcilable tendencies are struggling for
possession of his mind: the one, his determination to be a good
Marxist (with a very special allegiance to the catastrophic message of
that ideology); the other, his incorrigible pragmatism. Perhaps the

fairest comment one can make on these two documents—as on the whole Marxist moment in Niebuhr's intellectual career—is that they are striking testimonials to the impossibility of using an ideology without being used by it.

In the upshot, the Old Guard were squeezed out of the party, the bulk of their leadership heading into the newly-formed American Labor Party.[25] But well before the 1936 convention had accomplished that fact, the fratricidal squabbles had alienated much support from the party. Membership fell by about one-third[26] as did support for party candidates throughout the land. Niebuhr, however, plainly exhilarated by his debut in the ring of party forensics, was sure that it was all for the best: "Many critics of the party think that this split will destroy whatever prospects of future usefulness the party may have had. They are in error. . . . The vital forces of the party are not with the [Old Guard]. . . . In New York there is already a remarkable burst of new energy in the party since the hand of the Old Guard has been removed from the wheel of power.[27] There now began the dual experiment that Norman Thomas had long wished for: the Socialist Party was to become "all-inclusive," welcoming Trotskyites, Lovestoneites, and others without hindrance;[28] and at the same time efforts were begun to bring unity on the left by cooperation with the Communists in anti-Fascist action. All the principals (on the Socialist side) later recognized that this dual experiment was disastrous for the Socialist Party.

These years were the busiest in Niebuhr's entire life. He was in constant demand as a sponsor for causes, as a speaker, as a writer. No one will ever be able to tote up an exhaustive list of causes and committees—so many of them of the shadowy, "letter-head" sort so characteristic of the period of "Popular Front"—to which Niebuhr lent his name, his voice, or his presence.[29] There was the New York Conference Against War,[30] the United States Congress Against War,[31] the Scottsboro Defense Committee,[32] the Interreligious Committee for Justice for Thomas J. Mooney,[33] and others. A supporter of the National Student League, and then of the American Student Union during the years when (according to the later testimony of its then chief spokesman, James Wechsler) it was largely within Communist control, Niebuhr could be found addressing the annual student Peace Strikes in New York City.[34] For these sins, he is much catalogued in the works of Elizabeth Dilling, Henry B. Joy, J. B. Matthews, and John T. Flynn.

Niebuhr's fellow-travelling must be studied within the context of this period of great enthusiasm in Protestant ministerial ranks for radical and, in particular, anti-war causes. "Among all the trades, occupations, and professions in this country, few can produce as high a percentage of socialists as can the ministry," remarked Kirby Page in 1934—and the statistics would appear to bear him out.[35] Even the *Christian Century* spoke with occasional socialistic accents in those days.[36] Part-and-parcel of the enthusiasm for socialism was a tendency to rather uncritical enthusiasm for the Soviet experiment. Niebuhr was quick to confess in later years that he too had some-times been "too uncritical"[37] about Soviet Russia. He might have had in mind (for example) an occasion in 1935 when, on learning that a prominent spokesman of the Old Guard of the Socialist Party had gone on record for the Hearst Press with some negative thoughts regarding the Soviet Union, he had quickly repudiated the man and the thoughts for the benefit of the readers of the *Daily Worker*— without bothering even to examine the context of the critic's charges: it was enough that the critic had "len[t] himself to any kind of Hearst propaganda!"[38] This defensiveness about the Soviet Union, however, could be put down to a normally moderate concern for fairness. Niebuhr had been to the Soviet Union on extended visits and had found much to praise—and much to condemn as well. And if he sometimes gave the U.S.S.R. the benefit of the doubt when the evidence was unclear, he did not cut himself off from the effects of clear evidence when that was available: in the crucial business of the Stalinist purge trials, Niebuhr took a harsh view of Stalin's American apologists, the "liberal sympathizers of the Communist Party."[39]

Even in the months of his greatest availability, some liberals felt that Niebuhr was overly suspicious about the hazards involved in cooperation with Communists. In 1939, he withdrew from the College Teachers' Union following the failure of a bid by himself and others of like mind to overthrow what he regarded as its Communist-dominated leadership. To academics, the Union had seemed a bold act of solidarity with the workers, and the group of defectors (including Niebuhr) seemed to many to be putting petty bourgeois suspicions ahead of the cause of justice.[40] The incident speaks plainly of Niebuhr's views on American Communism by 1939. Neither Niebuhr nor anyone else cared to deny that the Communists had won their control of the College Teachers' Union on the plain result of a democratic ballot. Niebuhr had simply reached the point, by 1939, where he believed that Communists had become subversive of too much that had to be valued in American life above the privilege of indiscriminate association. Communists, he now felt, should be entirely insulated from cooperation with the liberal community as a whole. In taking this position, Niebuhr was parting company with many of his elders in the radical wing of the Social Gospel.[41]

Interestingly enough, only a year earlier he had figured in a movement to demand the restoration to office of one Simon Gerson, who had been removed as an assistant to the Republican Borough President of Manhattan when it became publicized that Gerson was a Communist Party member and a former correspondent for the *Daily Worker*.[42] Niebuhr's behavior in these two cases (the Gerson case of 1938 and the Teachers' Union case of 1939) is inconsistent. Either the mere fact of Communist membership is subversive of democratic process or it is not; it is hard to see that a Communist in a position of responsibility to an elected legislator is harmless while Communists presiding over a largely ineffectual union are a menace. It is the difference in timing of these two events that explains the difference in attitude. During the months between the Gerson incident (mid-1938) and the Teachers' Union row (early 1939) Niebuhr's attitude toward domestic Communism took on a new hardness. The reasons, however, lie in the realm of international affairs—as we shall shortly be discovering.

In summary it can be said that Niebuhr combined a generous open-mindedness about the Soviet revolution and its accomplishments with a firm concern for civilized values threatened by the same historical force. His cloth did not blind him to the genuine spiritual force that generated much of what was done in the name of irreligion. Nor did an unballasted good-will deprive him of his critical responsibilities as an intellectual. Niebuhr's record on the whole justifies his own observation of 1937: "As Christian socialists ... we are glad that we have religious certainties which absolve us of the responsibility of finding our religious security in the shifting forces of politics."[43]

# RADICAL RELIGION

*We believe that a capitalistic society is
destroying itself and yet that it must be destroyed,
lest it reduce, in the delirium of its disintegration,
our whole civilization to barbarism. . . .
We believe that [a socialist society]
can be established only through a social struggle
and that in that struggle we ought to be
on the side of the working man.*

(FROM NIEBUHR'S FIRST EDITORIAL IN "RADICAL RELIGION,"
FALL, 1935.)

On November 30, 1931, Niebuhr realized an ambition that had
possessed him since his conversion to religious socialism, in the
formation of The Fellowship of Socialist Christians. The model for
the Fellowship was the informal coterie of Christian Socialists of
which Tillich had been a member in Germany. Tillich, indeed, was
to prove one of the mainstays of Niebuhr's new American group as
well, thus providing the Fellowship's claim to lineal succession from
the continental founders now scattered or silenced. This was a
matter of considerable pride to the Fellowship, which liked to think
of itself as speaking for something more than a merely American
religious tradition—a claim which, as our argument so far should
bear out, had considerable merit. This pride reflected itself in the
slighting tone which their journal affected toward the residue of
"naive," "social gospel" thinking in the ranks of American clergy.

The Fellowship was committed to the principle "that a Christian ethic is most adequately expressed and effectively applied in our society in socialist terms"; and it was committed furthermore to "support[ing] the aggressive assertion of the rights of the exploited and disinherited."[1] Following the line of argument which Niebuhr was to develop in his *Reflections* of 1934, the Fellowship declared that it is "not impossible" to ward off a violent class struggle, provided "a constantly increasing number in the privileged groups ... recognize the extent of covert and overt violence inherent in the present order and its maintenance." To improve their own example in this matter, the members (mostly clergymen) pledged themselves to submit to a stiff income tax levied by the Fellowship in support of its activities.[2]

These activities were of two sorts, discussion and direct social action.[3] Members were divided into groups of twelve and urged to meet regularly to discuss ways and means of applying their socialist convictions to their ministry. Annual conferences were held, during which papers were read by members (Niebuhr, Tillich, Eduard Heimann, and Francis Henson were regularly recruited) or by sympathetic outsiders. In the field of direct action, its work was remarkably varied. The Fellowship encouraged its members to test their socialist convictions by such deeds as throwing themselves into labor organization where their parishioners were unorganized and exploited; testing restrictions on civil liberties; and organizing co-operative ventures in areas of agricultural distress. Once a member got himself committed in some such fashion, his cause became a project for the whole of the Fellowship—and the membership levy went up all around. The number of such projects is too numerous to mention. Some were ephemeral; others carried on for many years. The best example of the latter type is the Fellowship's role in direct action in aid of distressed southern farmers. The executive of the Southern Tenant Farmers' Union included members of the F.S.C.[4] The Fellowship threw its support behind Howard Kester's Fellowship of Southern Churchmen,[5] and it adopted a project for re-establishment of tenant farmers who had been victimized by the New Deal's Agricultural Adjustment Program. This project had been begun by Bishop Scarlett and Sherwood Eddy and took the name, Cooperative Farms, Incorporated.[6]

In the earliest months of the Fellowship's existence, Niebuhr and a handful of members visited the scene of labor unrest in Kentucky coal country, to discover the facts and to make them known. This they effectively did—not without some unpleasant brushes with local defenders of established order.[7]

It is interesting that it was these activities undertaken in the ranks of the F.S.C. that first brought Niebuhr to the attention of the press in a serious way. The *New York Times*, which had discovered his newsworthiness when *Moral Man* arrived to disturb the peace of the seminaries,[8] seems then to have assigned a man to keep on top of his speaking dates, and to bring back the most shocking statements.[9] The newly-launched *Newsweek* introduced Niebuhr to its readers in an egregiously inaccurate presentation of April 29, 1933, in which he was made to appear himself the victim of an early round of the class struggle he was now abetting.[10] But, these brief moments of notoriety aside, Niebuhr's influence during the mid-thirties remained confined to the ranks of the radical clergy and a wider circle of readers of his paper, *Radical Religion*.

Founded in the autumn of 1935, *Radical Religion* presented for two decades a lively forum for discussion regarding the proper relationship between Christian faith and socialism. The burden of filling the pages, issue after issue, fell largely upon Niebuhr. In the average issue, one large article, most of the editorials (running, all told, over half-a-dozen pages or more), and several book reviews all were done by Niebuhr. All of this work, it must be remembered, was done in addition to teaching at Union, special addresses and lectures outside Union (including the Gifford Lectures for the University of Edinburgh during 1939), organizational chores in connection with the F.S.C., and its various projects (including Cooperative Farms), the continued output of articles for other periodicals (including articles and book reviews for *Nation*, of which he was now a contributing editor, four books—*Reflections*, 1934, *An Interpretation of Christian Ethics*, 1935, *Beyond Tragedy*, 1937 and *Christianity and Power Politics*, 1940), and numerous pamphlets.

The journal had a distinct editorial "line" which shaped the thinking of almost all of its contributors. Most of its readers probably thought of it as Niebuhr's newsletter. There were occasional contributions by outsiders, some of these in disagreement with one or another aspect of the editor's Christian realism. But the regular contributors (Reinhold Niebuhr, H. R. Niebuhr, Eduard Heimann, Paul Tillich, and Francis Henson), agreed on essentials. Their differences (debated at the Annual Conference of the F.S.C. and in occasional articles) would have seemed to outsiders rather esoteric.[11]

But *Radical Religion* was by no means merely, or even primarily, a "theoretical journal." It was meant to provide its small but loyal audience with practical evidence of the urgency of a program of radical politics, through examination of the events of the day. Niebuhr carried over into *Radical Religion* the scornful assessment of Roosevelt and his New Deal that he had already expressed in the *Christian Century*, in the *World Tomorrow* (before its demise), and elsewhere. Having a regular corner from which to speak his piece gave Niebuhr the opportunity to develop the grounds of his dissatisfaction from issue to issue. The Roosevelt Administration, he said, was "brazenly dishonest" in its handling of the relief situation.[12] A captive of the conservative masters of the Democratic Party, the President had weakly allowed his social legislation to suffer "an ambiguity and uncertainty which could be eliminated in a party more solidly based upon the support of workers and farmers."[13] By the middle of 1938, the Roosevelt Administration had "reached a new low level not only in morale but also in strategy . . ." and was peddling "whirligig reform" to the country.[14] In sum: "his program reveals how impossible it is to heal the ills of modern capitalism within the presuppositions of capitalism itself."[15] This would remain the essence of the indictment against F.D.R. in the eyes of *Radical Religion* until 1938.

As the election of 1936 approached, however, a subtle minor note begins to appear in Niebuhr's assessments of domestic politics. His basic view of Roosevelt did not change, nor did he moderate his scorn for those who would support Roosevelt as the lesser of two evils. But it does begin to seem a consideration to him that a Republican victory (the only possible alternative, after all, to Roosevelt's re-election) would be "a threat." (But, one wonders, a threat to what?—if, as he has been arguing, "capitalism is dying and . . . ought to die," and if fascism is "inevitable?") It must have seemed a small concession to make—but it proved to be the thin edge of the wedge. Somehow, the possibility of Landon in the White House (and it proved to be the most one-sided victory in the history of Presidential elections) unsettled Niebuhr on his prophet's perch.

> It will not be much easier to bear all the soul stirring appeals in behalf of Roosevelt by labor leaders, church leaders, and tired radicals [than it will be to bear the Republican praise of their candidate, Landon]. There will be less dishonesty and just as much confusion in their appeals [for Roosevelt]. Obviously Roosevelt is preferable to the Republican candidate. But it is just as obvious that no real ground has been gained for social justice in his administration. . . . Mr. Roosevelt, goaded by the populist radicalism gathered around the banner of Mr. Lemke, speaks in terms which suggest a determined challenge to reaction; but it is not even certain that he will seek to end the tryanny of the Supreme Court in the event of his re-election.[16]

Henceforth, but very grudgingly, an element of calculation begins to enter into Niebuhr's appraisals of the Administration: it is at least better to have these few crumbs of cheer from Roosevelt than stiff-necked reaction.[17] Sometimes, indeed, Roosevelt acted with a vigor that caught Niebuhr off guard, and compelled him to grudging concessions of admiration. For example: in the Fall of 1936, Niebuhr was reasonably sure that Roosevelt's threats against the Nine Old Men were mere theatrics; by the Spring of 1937, he was embarrassed to find that Roosevelt did indeed mean to have it out with the Court, and was, if anything, acting more drastically than Niebuhr would be willing to do.[18] Still, the most that Niebuhr would concede was that a Roosevelt regime was more easily endured than any imaginable Republican one.[19]

Plainly, the threat of a Republican victory bothered Niebuhr more than it ought to have bothered a consistent socialist. Although he would not confess as much until the end of the decade (in time for Roosevelt's third campaign), Niebuhr's conscience was being affected by the calculation that a vote for Socialist Norman Thomas (the right man in the right party, but without prospect of victory) was a vote taken away from Roosevelt, who "must be given credit for having carried the [Democratic] party much farther to the left than anyone imagined possible."[20] There is nothing unique about Niebuhr's feelings in this situation. Such considerations were persuading many life-long Socialists (like Walter Reuther and Paul Blanshard) to commit themselves to the preservation of the small but real gains for labor rights and social justice accomplished by old-line party figures (F.D.R., LaGuardia in New York City, Lehman in New York State). It was not a happy decision for any of these Socialists, some of whom had been at least as close to Norman Thomas as Niebuhr had ever been. Once under the spell of the personality of a Roosevelt or a LaGuardia, and having experienced the satisfaction of bringing concrete social and economic gains to their unions or their communities, the Reuthers and the Blanshards abandoned their socialism, in all but a sentimental sense; others would abandon it altogether. Niebuhr was clearly beginning to succumb to this logic himself by the end of 1936. But in his case the full logic would not take hold until some time after 1940. The basic reason for Niebuhr's greater reluctance to submit to the logic of pragmatic-liberal politics was intellectual. Having plumbed to the intellectual and moral depth that we have seen to lay his commitment to socialism he would have had to dig to that depth again to re-examine it.

In the meanwhile, Niebuhr kept an anxious watch over the ups-and-downs of Roosevelt's political fortunes. It is a fascinating business to read through Niebuhr's comments on all these events. How determined he was to keep his socialist perspective on the "ambiguous," "futile," "stop-gap," "whirligig" reforms of the Administration; and yet how nervous he was that these small mercies might be swept away by Republican "reaction" and Southern Democratic "treason"!

Despite his reputation as the theologian of gloom, he could be exceedingly optimistic when he wanted to be. Thus, he was inclined to view Roosevelt's increasing difficulties with his own party as a long-range blessing: the conservatives and the liberals would have to abandon their age-old league of opportunism within the Democratic Party, thus setting the stage for a re-alignment of the left-wing in a new farmer-labor party.[21] There would, Niebuhr admitted, be "perils for socialism" in such a strategy, but the Socialist Party had by now become so isolated that it was, in Niebuhr's thinking, duty-bound to bow out of the political arena, becoming a kind of American Fabian Society cheering on a new electoral party having its base in labor. Niebuhr was equally certain, however, that the newly-formed American Labor Party did not fit this bill. His reasons offer interesting corroboration of what we have described in this book as his elitist orientation: "[The A.L.P. is] completely in the hands of the trade unions and offer[s] other radical groups only the alternatives of absorption or support of the labor candidates without a voice in its counsels. A labor party completely dominated by trade union officialdom is dangerous, as British experience has proved. A labor party needs the leavening influence of a radical wing which takes the ultimate goal of a new society seriously and does not get lost in day to day tactics. Therefore a labor party needs the socialist party."[22] Niebuhr's refusal to go over to the A.L.P. was not, *at this point*, owing to its infiltration by Communists. He was aware that the Communists were "too wedded to the necessities of Russian foreign policy"[23] and were therefore not altogether trustworthy; but that consideration did not at this point outweigh the advantages of cooperation within a United Front.

Roosevelt's bold effort in 1938 at purge of some of his party's more notorious reactionaries raised his stock considerably in the pages of *Radical Religion*. For the first time, Niebuhr now let loose the thought that Roosevelt might prove the founder of the new and broader left-wing party. Roosevelt's primary qualification for such a task, it now appeared, was, of all things, political courage!

Mr. Roosevelt [has] finally decided to fight these reactionary influences openly and appeal to the people against them in the primaries.

In the case of several of the primaries in the southern states, Roosevelt made his appeal with the almost certain knowledge that it would not avail to bring the nomination to his candidate....

> There is . . . nothing remotely savoring of dictatorship in these
> presidential appeals. They are remarkably honest appeals for the
> reason that some of them clearly imperil the presidential prestige
> by the certainty of the defeat of the presidential candidates.
>
> The impossibility of ridding the democratic party of its
> dependence upon southern landlordism and northern municipal
> political corruption will probably result in the formation of a new
> party sometime after 1940.[24]

The "purge" proved a monumental fizzle. This defeat, Niebuhr
argued, only improved the prospects for construction of a Rooseveltian Party of the Left, however—Niebuhr's reasoning being that
Roosevelt's failure made Republican victory more likely in 1940; and
the outcome of that event would be a rallying of the left for victory
in 1944.[25] A victory for "Republican reaction" seemed a harsh
prescription to the electoral difficulties of the left; and indeed
Niebuhr must have thought better of it at once, for he never offered
this particular purgative to his readers again. Yet, it seemed so
difficult to keep one's head in the midst of rapidly shifting political
developments. Everything seemed so hopeless and so hopeful at the
same time.

Take the case of the Socialist Party. Its opening to the Left,
following the Militant victories of 1934–35, had left it weaker,
rather than stronger. While Norman Thomas was seeking to make
pacifism the test of Socialist loyalty, the Communist Party was
working to line up all of the Left for automatic support of the
U.S.S.R. in case of war. At the same time, the Socialists' friendship towards Trotskyites was bringing the Socialist Party increasing
criticism from the *Daily Worker*. In return, the Socialist press was
castigating the Communists for their opportunism in courting such
improbable allies as the A.L.P. and Father Divine! The end of the
line was the election of 1936, during which the Communist Party
attempted to lend support to Roosevelt by the tactic of concentrating
all its attacks upon the Republicans, while the Socialist Party cam-
paigned for its own ticket—thus (in the C.P. view) strengthening
Landon against Roosevelt.[26] The poor showing of Norman Thomas
as candidate for Governor of New York in 1938 demonstrated
Niebuhr's argument that it "must resign itself to the role of a
socialistic educational force in the ranks of labor and give up the
ambition of becoming of itself an instrument of political power. If
Socialism comes in this country, a farmer-labor party, gradually
schooled by historical realities to the necessities of socialism, will have
to be the instrument."[27] Yet, as Niebuhr suggested on the same
page, the example of the A.L.P. appeared to demonstrate the pro-

position that unions will not cooperate in any political arm that their own myopic leadership does not dominate. Always the progressive-elitist, Niebuhr expected to have to lead the workers, firmly, but benevolently, toward the socialist state. He had no patience with the notion of a Labor Party in which labor did the leading.

By 1938, therefore, Niebuhr was beginning to talk himself into political limbo. Pragmatic considerations were turning him from the Socialist Party. A vote for the Socialist Party was worse than wasted: it was a gift to the Republicans, to the cause of reaction. But so long as Roosevelt served the interests of the possessing classes, Niebuhr could not support him. Whether Roosevelt's political fortunes waxed or waned, Niebuhr professed to believe that his regime must prove to be a prelude of fascism. Marxist science required this conclusion; and in a world in which all other interpretations of history were being discredited by swiftly moving events, Niebuhr would not let go of the anchor of Marxist determinism.

# AGONIES OF A DYING
# CIVILIZATION

To continue to cling to a Marxist interpretation of events in the mid-1930s required a great deal of faith indeed. Marxist theory taught Niebuhr to expect that increasing economic competition in modern life would issue in class antagonism and eventual civil war. American experience seemed to be falsifying that theory. The American worker was remaining stubbornly resistant to social radicalism despite his increasing impoverishment. Roosevelt, the opportunist-aristocrat, was going from strength to strength, while the cause of socialism seemed not to be gaining at all among the workers.

But if the total Marxist expectation is correct, why should it be necessary for America to run entirely true to Marxist form? In Europe, affairs seemed to be running to the Marxist model; and thus, taking the macrocosmic view, the end of the capitalist order was clearly at hand. The "senility" of western civilization as a whole was declared in "surfeited markets" and "world depression." "The old [order] is literally beyond repair," and is heading for a complete collapse which can no longer be averted.[1]

Niebuhr's precious "time-lag" theory provided sufficient explanation for all that might otherwise seem, from a Marxist point of view, "exceptional" about the American scene. If class consciousness is weak among American workers, so it was among Britishers *fifty years ago*, before Fabian intellectuals entered into their fruitful political pact with the trade unionists. Since European events were in the van and American events in the rear of the historical process, one should reasonably turn to European events for the direction of history.

European events held the key to the future of American politics and society: this was Niebuhr's first rule of political analysis through the 1930s. American events, on their own, made no sense to him. The drift of American politics, indeed, seemed so perverse to Niebuhr's Marxist reckoning, that he found he could only keep his bearings by regular sorties into the problems of German and British politics. Here he found evidence much more congenial to his Marxist world-view.

There is a decided quickening of the pulse to be detected in Niebuhr's writing of the 1920s and the '30s whenever he turned from the American to the European scene. American affairs simply did not have for him the stature of European affairs. More precisely, it was Germany which Niebuhr found very early in his career to be the key to the process. As Germany had been the most conspicuous victim of the self-righteousness of the victorious Allies, so she ought to be looked to as the likely instrument of history's vengeance. (Here, the link with Tillich is evident.) The increasing bitterness of the class struggle in Germany during the twenties and early thirties, and the increasing violence of German politics generally, Niebuhr saw as an omen of what was ahead for all of Western civilization.

Niebuhr's reporting on German developments in the early thirties[2] is remarkably careful, well-documented (by reason of his visits, his reading in German papers, and his growing personal contacts with German clerics and intellectuals); never merely alarmist, but unfailingly realistic. The drive-wheel of German politics, Niebuhr early concluded, was the resentment that all Germans felt against the Allies, and against America in particular. The failure of America to nullify this resentment by a generous policy of debt-liquidations had frustrated attempts of the Weimar leadership to establish Germany on a sound economic footing and to reintroduce her to the community of nations. Worse still: Allied "enslavement" (as he described it) of Germany's economy ruled out the possibility of a test of economic democracy in the one nation which needed socialism most. Germany's capitalists had regained their stranglehold upon the instruments of power, thanks to American connivance.[3] When one got down to examining the social realities beneath the political surface, there was too much similarity between America's situation and Germany's for comfort. It certainly *can* happen here: "[Hitler's] technique proves the power of an adequate symbolism in politics. Let the symbol be at once vivid and vague, as Hitler's symbols were, and it will catch the young idealist, the imperiled industrialist, the bank-rupt storekeeper, the aggrieved ex-soldier and everyone who suffers so much from the slings and arrows of outrageous fortune that he has become willing to fly to others that he knows not of. Roosevelt's 'new deal' belongs in this class of vague symbol."[4] To escape the fate of Germany, American socialists must learn from the errors of German socialists, who had proved "too completely wedded to the parliamentary method," and lost the political initiative to the less scrupulous fascists.[5] A correct socialist strategy would require that the workers' representatives not let parliamentary legality stand in their way once they are within striking distance of power, eschewing "the faulty [German] socialist strategy" in favor of the "correct [German] fascist one (correct in the sense of effective)."[6] Despite the weak-kneed Ramsay MacDonald, British Socialists (Niebuhr predicted) would probably get another chance. German Socialists would not—and at the moment the American picture was running to the German pattern, not the British one.

And so, the Nazis had come to power. In the beginning, Niebuhr was confident that Hitler could not long hold onto power; there would soon be a showdown between the left-wing "populist" forces in the Nazi ranks (as Niebuhr described the followers of Storm-Trooper chief, Roehm) and the industrialists who had taken Hitler into tow. Hitler's bold gamble for permanent control was based upon his conviction that he could neutralize class antagonisms by raucous appeals to national unity, promises of a great imperial future, and, above all, evocation of the memories of Allied cruelties. "Hitlerism," Niebuhr wrote in April, 1933, "is hardly an international danger at the present time," because class antagonism ("the fissure in the body politic," as he put it) went so deep that any attempt to take Ger-many into a war would "immediately be resolved into a class war," and Hitler would thus be destroyed.[7]

It is too easy to say, in retrospect, that this was a bad guess. In view of the stealth and the duplicity which Hitler invested in his purge of his party's left-wing, it is clear enough that Hitler himself took the threat of dissension seriously. In any case, by 1935, the prospect of class-warfare within Germany seemed more remote. Niebuhr was reluctant to admit this for a good few months beyond the purge of 1934. He did not concede that the internal crisis had passed for Hitler until late in 1936. Until that concession was made, Niebuhr continued to hope that there would be a dramatic bursting of the patience of the German workers, which would issue in revolu-tion on the Soviet model. The fact that Hitler had deprived his people of democratic instruments for the expression of their discon-tent would not delay their triumph but would rather hasten it, he was sure. Social antagonism in the Western world generally was now so great that democratic instruments merely obscured social realities under the rhetoric of compromise and accommodation. Delivered of these trappings by Hitler's ruthlessness, German workers now were prepared to face the realities of their exploitation without sentimentality.

The German workers could not be so simply deceived again. Their American counterparts, however, seemed unable to draw the necessary lessons from German experience. Labor leadership was dividing its strength mindlessly, some supporting Socialists, some Democrats, some (like John L. Lewis) Republicans. It was a rare union leader who saw the need for industrial collectivism or, indeed, understood what it meant! As a result, the American petty bourgeoisie are disproportionately powerful, and potential pawns for any would-be fascist leader without the obvious handicaps of a Father Coughlin or a Dr. Townshend. Indeed, "if Senator Long had lived, the peril of American fascism might be an immediate one." In the meanwhile, "Roosevelt claims the allegiance of both workers and lower middle classes for a political program which satisfies both because ultimate issues are postponed." This moment of social peace is likely to be brief, however, for "a general tendency of contraction" appears (in early 1937) about to set in, routing "the present prosperity," leading to disenchantment among Roosevelt's supporters in the ranks of the poor and dramatic fascist advances in time for the election of 1940.[8]

All such stop-gap and "palliative" devices as are employed by Roosevelt would only aggravate social strife in the long run. Class lines must harden as reactionaries on the one side grow impatient with taxation for the meager social services which a demagogue must provide, and as the poor, on the other hand, grow impatient with the inadequacy of New Deal-type solutions to their situation. Thus, Rooseveltism will give way to fascism; and after fascism, the revolution.

British socialists, Niebuhr observed, seemed to have learned the lessons of the German situation correctly, for they were now assuming a more critical attitude regarding the worth of democracy.[9] This was decidedly to the credit of British socialist leaders, and reflected both their own political realism and the great sense of class solidarity that moves the British workingman.

Niebuhr, as he himself admitted, was throughout most of his life an unabashed "anglophile."[10] But at different stages of his career, Niebuhr would find grounds for admiration of Britain in somewhat different circumstances. After 1939, he celebrated the courage and patriotic solidarity that marked Britain's resistance to Hitler. In the post-war years he found occasion for praise in Britain's enlightened program of decolonization, as well as in its domestic welfare program. In the 1920s and 1930s, he was somewhat more selective in his enthusiasm, finding most, if not all, of the fruits of British civilization in the British Labour Party. In the early 1920s, Niebuhr, not yet a socialist but already convinced that the continuance of western civilization required an early satisfaction of the just demands of the working-class by the possessing classes, discovered—or thought he discovered—the secret of social reconciliation in the British political arena. That discovery had moved him to predict that "the Christian political party" that America must have would be like the Labour Party.[11] As Niebuhr read the signs in the wake of his European trip of that year, the British possessing classes, discerning the justness of the demands of the British working-classes, were preparing to allow MacDonald to lead them by peaceful steps to the Socialist state. Things did not work out that way. By 1931, the Tories had taken the Labour leader into the camp of reaction, at the cost of a modest mess of potage; the prospects of a peaceful Socialist victory now seemed more remote than ever. Yet Niebuhr retained his conviction that there was an element of grace operating on the British political scene that made it worthy of the envy of American radicals.

Left-Wing American observers (Niebuhr wrote from England in 1931) were too hard on the British upper classes. A *propos* of the collapse on August 24th of the Labour cabinet (occasioned by an utimatum from financiers that the unemployment benefits be cut by ten percent), Niebuhr wrote: "The fact that a ten per cent cut in such benefits could cause such a crisis in Britain while America will worry through another winter of unemployment without any recognition by the federal government of the nation's responsibility for the misery of the unemployed marks the difference in social conscience between the two nations."[12] The very fact that England had a Socialist party so vital—though not yet strong enough to secure the workers' state—was the true mark of her advance over America. Despite the increase in cynicism in the ranks of Labour, Niebuhr still held out the possibility (so inconsistent a Marxist was he, even in 1931 at the beginning of his Marxist phase), that the forces of reason and conscience could yet bring social peace in England.[13]

"We are the first empire of the world to establish our sway without legions. Our legions are dollars."[14]

American events (we have been arguing) seemed to Niebuhr to be very much in the rear of the historical process. This is not to say, however, that he thought of America as without implication in the sins of recent history. It was characteristic of intellectuals in the 1930s to view Europe as caught in the grip of a death-wish which was none of America's doing.[15] Niebuhr, in refreshing contrast, was unsparing in his reckoning of America's responsibilities for the present state of international affairs. Like all good prophets, he may, in his eagerness to bring contrition to the hearts of his American audience, have over-stated their complicity. But the main themes of his critique proved so compelling that they would ultimately help to work a revolution in the field of theoretical study of American foreign policy. His critique of these years would eventually bear fruit in the school of foreign policy "realism"—the school of Hans Morgenthau, Walter Lippmann, and George F. Kennan—which became the ascendant school in foreign policy discussion by the mid-1940s.

Even during the 1920s when Niebuhr was developing the indictment against American civilization that was preparing him for his commitment to socialism, it had seemed to Niebuhr that the aspect of America's conduct which betrayed her faults most vividly was her foreign policy. That "sentimentality" with which Americans were wont to hide from themselves the cruel facts of economic strife in this world especially colored their consideration of international affairs. The fact of the matter, Niebuhr wrote, was that the international arena was the scene of a ruthless contest for commercial domination. There was no din of battle to call the attention of simple folk; only the muffled fall of dollar bills and the steady music of the stock-tickers. Americans, who had been taught to believe that the ultimate crime was imperialism, prided themselves on their lack of imperial ambition. The proof of their purity, they argued, was in the fact that no American soldiers stood guard over unhappy subjects. But, Niebuhr explained,

> We are living in an economic age, and the significant power is economic rather than military. In moments of crisis the banker may find it necessary to call upon the marines; but the civilized world is fairly well disciplined and permits its life to be ordered and its social and political relationships to be adjusted by the use of economic force without recourse to the more dramatic display of military power.
>
> In such an economic age, it is natural that our nation, the wealthiest in the world, should become the real empire of modern civilization. . . . We are able to dispense with the soldier almost

completely; we use him only in a few undeveloped nations to the south of us.[16]

America's entire foreign policy was thus determined by these two facts: America's character as the ascendant empire of the moment; and the American people's steadfast effort to deny their imperial character before themselves and before the world. The first of these factors drives America to unsleeping conquest of foreign markets for goods and capital, both of which she has in embarrassing excess because she refuses to distribute the products of her wealth equitably at home. Failing to recognize that these activities are more than "merely business," Americans cannot believe that there is anything but love for them in the hearts of Europeans—a love which they have earned by their selfless abstention from the contest for political empire which has brought about all the wars and rumors of wars that bedevil the life of contemporary Europe and Asia. It is more than simply ignorance, however, and the normal human defensiveness that disarms Americans for realistic appraisal of their role in the world. There is, as well, that ancient curse of Puritanism, the "penchant for over-simplifying moral and social problems" which has always obscured the fact of our self-interest: "We make simple moral judgments . . . support them with an enthusiasm which derives from our waning but still influential evangelical piety, and are surprised that our contemporaries will not accept us as the saviors of the world." It is therefore not surprising that "America is at once the most powerful and politically the most ignorant of modern nations."[17]

A good example of these vices at work Niebuhr found in the American policy on the international debt issue during the 1920s and early thirties. It was unrealistic, he argued, to try to apply village-banker's ethics to this issue. The money could not do America any good so long as Europe remained too impoverished to purchase goods from America. It was, he said, "dead capital."[18] This debt-fixation seemed to Niebuhr the perfect symbol of how self-interest, conceived in inadequate or irrelevant terms, defeats the true interests of a nation.

America's policy toward Germany illustrated these same themes. Americans had seized upon "a dogma which emerged out of the hysteria of the World War" in order to fasten a shameful "enslavement" upon Germany, all the while congratulating themselves (on the evidence of their abstention from territorial spoils of 1919) on their charity as conquerors. The ingenious Dawes and Young plans served to tighten the fetters of German enslavement while at the same time closing the door on any prospect for waiver of Allied debts—all of this accomplished behind a smoke-screen of pieties about business ethics, the sanctity of contract, and so on.[19] Americans cannot understand why Europeans do not appreciate these businessmen's sermons with which American diplomats wrap up such negotiations.

> Perhaps [our economic success] was due to the fact, as Spengler suggests, that culture and civilization are incompatible with each other, and that the vast immigrant hordes who came to our shores dissipated their cultural inheritances to such a degree that they could give themselves to the extensive tasks of civilization with complete and fervent devotion. It may be that the modern Russians will become our chief competitors for the same reason, for there a nation has sloughed off the Greek and the European culture forms which were never really indigenous to it, and the result is the same complete obsession with the engineering task which has characterized our life since the Civil War. The Russians, incidentally, show signs of the same political ineptitude and parochialism in manipulating their budding power which we reveal in our developed strength.[20]

It is thus, the beginning of wisdom both in internal and international policy to acknowledge the fact of self-interest lurking behind the protective coloration provided by slogans and even behind honestly-held ideals. This emphasis upon "realism" in Niebuhr's critique of American policies in these years tempts one to suspect that he is working towards a defense of a foreign policy based upon the sort of international realism promulgated by Theodore Roosevelt and much favored at this time by contributors to the *New Republic*. "We cannot very well destroy the economic power of America," he writes: "We would not destroy the unity of our continent, and we will not change the habits and inclinations which have contributed to our prosperity."[21] This declaration—together with the indictment against "sentimentality" as a substitute for policy—disposes the reader to expect a policy centering on the establishment of spheres of influence. But at this point, it is not Theodore Roosevelt who carries the day, but Karl Marx. "When it is remembered that the advantages of empire accrue to a very limited portion of a national population, it is apparent that our real salvation lies in setting that portion of the population which does not benefit from empire against the extension of its power.... It is the historic mission of labor movements in our civilization to be especially critical of national pretensions and imperial ambitions.... [Labor alone can] achieve that attitude of critical detachment which the whole of civilization needs and which is particularly helpful as an antidote to the pride of nations."[22] There is thus no salvation in a policy of national self-assertion. America can only have security by pursuing a policy of self-restraint which is, unhappily, out of line with the character she has shown up to this point. She must renounce her claim to reparations and debts still outstanding. She must abandon her policy of tariff-protection.[23]

But, Niebuhr had already admitted that he could see no prospect of changing "the habits and inclinations which have contributed to our prosperity"—which have, incidentally, prevented the establishment of basic economic democracy in America. It is clear that what Niebuhr was offering was a program which he knew to be without prospect of implementation. The alternative to that program of American self-denial is war. And war there must be. "It is a sad and significant commentary on the Western world that the policies which are most needed to bring convalescence and health to its common life have least chance of general acceptance. Good people everywhere continue to express their abhorrence of war and their desire for peace; yet they refuse to entertain political and economic ideas which have become the *sine qua non* of decent international relations. Everyone wants peace, but there are only a few who are willing to pay the price which peace demands."[24]

As early as 1931, Niebuhr expected international war. The surest omen of the coming of that war, he argued, would be the political collapse of Germany. "Either the German people will be forced into a fascist experiment, with its offer of a military venture as a means of escape from the present servitude, or it will turn communist and seek freedom through an alliance with Russia. In either case . . . the indifference of America to . . . [Germany's economic woes] will clearly be the root of any such eventuality."[25]

There is no question that, at one level of his thinking, at least, Niebuhr desired just this eventuality. It fitted precisely into his anticipation of imminent catastrophe—that expectation which, as we have seen, was one part religious hope and one part Marxist mythology. In the early 1930s, Niebuhr's Marxist commitment appeared to him to require that he expect a calamitous international war in the near future; or to put it more correctly, Marxist mythology seemed to him to strengthen a long-standing conviction, born of religious discontent with the materialism of present civilization, that that civilization was under judgment. His faith in the righteousness of God required him to believe that God would not endure this civilization much longer.

Niebuhr had long since decided the case against pacifism as a method of resolving serious issues of political conflict. He had decided the theological and the moral side of the case as early as *Moral Man* (that is, 1932); a few months later, he decided the matter of associational commitment by withdrawing from the Fellowship of Reconciliation. The same intellectual conversion that brought him to a commitment to Marxism sealed the matter of pacifism as well. While Niebuhr was late to change his mind about the uses and abuses of Marxism, his position in regard to pacifism seems not to have altered in any significant detail since 1932.

Niebuhr had never been a consistent pacifist in any case. Though much tempted by theoretical pacifism (as he was, in certain moods, by other aspects of religious perfectionism), Niebuhr had never been able to still the voice of practical reason within himself. As we noted in the early pages of this essay, Niebuhr was convinced as a young man that the ethics which Jesus taught his disciples were those of non-resistance. He had never changed his position in this matter; the plain reading of the Gospels seemed not to allow any alternative. But from the very beginning, Niebuhr had been disinclined (following the lead of Albert Schweitzer) to believe that the "interim ethics" taught by Jesus could be immediately applied to real political and social situations. After all, the practice of the ethics of non-resistance ended not in historical success but on the cross.[26]

If theoretical pacifism requires a conviction that loving non-resistance is an adequate substitute for force in all aspects of human relations, then Niebuhr was never a pacifist. At the moment of his greatest affection for religious pacifism (at the moment, indeed, when pacifism was most widespread among American clergymen in general), Niebuhr wrote the article (discussed earlier in these pages) in which he denied his right to the title of a Christian because he could not accept the practicability of the ethics of non-resistance.[27] That was during the early 1920s. Niebuhr cannot be found on record at any time in support of anything more absolute than the position that non-violent resistance, and perhaps in certain instances pure non-resistance, might sometimes prove to be the appropriate substitute for the use of force—"appropriate," either because they promise to accomplish the same end as force without increasing the amount of hate already extant in the human situation; or because they promise to accomplish an end that force could not accomplish at all.

The case of international warfare, he felt, obviously came under the second of these two heads. For a "conscientious Christian" he argued, there seemed no "reasonable alternative . . . to a position of unequivocal opposition to all warfare."[28] But if it is indeed "reason" by which we measure the alternatives, one wonders why Niebuhr needed to include the phrase "for a conscientious Christian." When he found the principle to be relevant, he did so, again, on pragmatic grounds. Thus, he defended the program of Gandhi as an appropriate one in *Gandhi's* situation: given the unavailability of military force to Gandhi, the vulnerability of the British to economic coercion, and the relative sensitiveness of the English conscience (particularly, he suggested, the conscience of the British workingman, who shared some of the Indians' own suspicions regarding their common oppressors, the British upper-classes).[29]

Niebuhr was fully aware of how untenable his intellectual position was in this business. It was thus with great relief that he found in the encounter with the new "crisis theology," (which we have already described) the religious answer to this religious problem. With the aid of Barth's formulations, he was able to develop, as the central thesis of his *Moral Man*, the arguments which justified his rejection of pacifism. Because of the gulf that stood between God's purposes and man's, all political programs were equidistant from the perfection of God. Men cannot act without sin. The program of non-resistance was the program which reflected the perfection that God meant men to have but which, because of their "original sin," they do not have. For responsible Christians, who must preserve their own lives and the lives of their families and their nations, and must preserve the relative good against the relatively less good, the ethics or non-resistance are impossible. To claim that they are possible is the gravest sin of all, because it tempts us to pretend that we are God, not men, and thus to act with culpable irresponsibility.[30]

But, while "impossible," the ethics of the Kingdom were nonetheless "relevant."[31] Men will always be men: which is to say, imperfect; and the more prone to sin the more they incline to think of themselves as engaged in programs of perfection. The Kingdom is not something we strive to accomplish by pursuing the ethics which are relevant to it, but something we witness to.

Thus, the same intellectual *tour de force* relieved Niebuhr from the indecision which accompanied his failure to follow the ethics of Jesus ("I am not a Christian!") and committed him to Marxism. It was a paradoxical result; the escape from the burden of religious pacifism freed him for pragmatic consideration of the issues of war and peace; while in the same moment he found himself committed to the service of Marxist ideology. To restate the burden of the previous chapter: Niebuhr was not committed (by the arguments of *Moral Man*) to Marxism itself, but merely to its use. But we have already begun to see how difficult it proved to use that "mythology" without being used by it.

The conventional approach to the problem of the dramatic crisis which Niebuhr underwent at the end of the decade is to show him struggling under a double-yoke of pacifism and Marxist-dogmatism, which he ultimately throws off, to go—finally and forever—under the yoke of pragmatism. The record is clear that Niebuhr's pacifism had long since been forced to go under the yoke of pragmatism. It was his Marxism that refused to be bent—until the eleventh hour.

Niebuhr's great intellectual crisis of 1930–32 thus drove him to a highly uncomfortable corner. He was still "a pacifist of sorts," he argued, but on pragmatic, even utilitarian grounds.[32] He was still a Christian Marxist, on what were for him still higher grounds: namely, that Marxism was truer to objective circumstances than any other ideology and, being *en kairo*, commanded the allegiance of Christians by dint of its compelling "mythology." It was clear from the moment *Moral Man* was struck off that, in any direct collision between the two allegiances, the pacifist allegiance would have to give. And it did.

The occasion for Niebuhr's public abandonment of his pacifist allegiance was provided by (of all people) J. B. Matthews. Matthews was one of the four executive secretaries of the Fellowship of Reconciliation, in addition to being one of the most publicized fire-brands of the non-Communist left. During the early part of 1933, the executive board of the F.O.R. (which was as strongly representative of Socialist feeling as it was of pacifist)[33] was rocked by a debate about the possibility of a conflict arising, in the event of civil war, between pacifist loyalty and loyalty to the cause of the proletariat.[34] J. B. Matthews had occasioned much unhappiness in the ranks of the Fellowship, particularly among those (still the faithful core of the movement) whose roots were firmly in historical Christian pacifism of the Quaker or Mennonite brand. Strident Marxism of Matthews' sort distressed them. Matthews—a one-time lay missionary now turned voluble agnostic—had closed down the worship aspects of the Fellowship's meetings—and had accomplished this with the Devil's own best argument: that it would smooth the way into the ranks of the Fellowship of many thousands of good persons whose pacifism was genuine but not grounded in religious faith. For many, the final straw was J. B.'s recent appointment as Chairman of the U.S. Congress against War and Facism (soon re-named the American League against War and Fascism), the most blatantly pro-Soviet and perhaps the most successful of the many Communist Front apparatuses.

Matthews, who was embarrassingly eager to have the issue out in the open once and for all, prepared a fiery statement which he presented to the Fellowship's annual conference held in October of 1933 at Swarthmore College. Defending Matthews' position at the conference were (among others) Roger Baldwin and Reinhold Niebuhr.[35] Convinced by John Haynes Holmes that this was the hour of decision for disciples of unqualified non-violence, the Fellowship's council decided to dismiss J. B. Matthews (and Howard Kester, the one other member of the four-man executive council who supported Matthews). Niebuhr, a former chairman of the Fellowship and still a member of its council, chose this moment to resign.[36] Without delay, Niebuhr rushed into print with his reasons.[37]

There is a great vigor to these *Christian Century* articles, born, no doubt, of relief. There is, as well, a somewhat strident tone, born of impatience with those who had chosen to cast their lot with the "impossible ideal."

The Fellowship controversy has revealed that there are radical Christians who can no longer express themselves in pacifist terms.

Recognizing, as liberal Christianity does not, that the world of politics is full of demonic forces, we have chosen on the whole to support the devil of vengeance against the devil of hypocrisy. In the day in which we live, a dying social system commits the hypocrisy of hiding its injustices behind the forms of justice, and the victims of injustice express their politics in terms of resentment against this injustice. As Marxians we support this resentment against the hypocrisy.

It is only a Christianity that suffers from modern liberal illusions that has ever believed that the law of love could be made an absolute guide of conduct in social morality and politics. As a Marxian and as a Christian I recognize the tragic character of man's social life, and the inevitability of conflict in it arising from the inability of man ever to bring his egoism completely under the domination of conscience.

As Christians we know that there is a devil in the spirit of vengeance as well as in the spirit of hypocrisy. For that reason we respect those who try to have no traffic with devils at all. We cannot follow them because we believe that consistency would demand flight to the monastery if all the devils of man's collective life were to be avoided. But our traffic with devils may lead to corruption, and the day may come when we will be grateful to those who try to restrain all demons rather than choose between them.[38]

In future, Niebuhr vowed, he would apply strictly pragmatic rule

when tempted by pacifist-absolutist sirens. He had already concluded that he could not participate or urge others to participate in
war between nations. But he believed that the use of force was still
relevant to the more immediate and the more real conflict between
the classes. "We expect no basic economic justice without a destruction of the present disproportion of power and we do not expect the
latter without a social struggle."[39]

PART

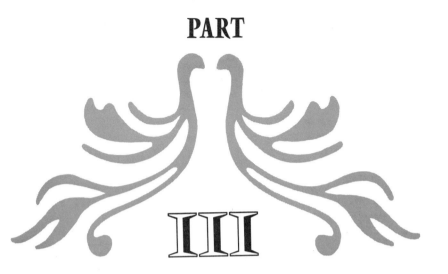

III

# THE THEOLOGIAN OF CRISIS

# HISTORY TAKES ANOTHER PATH

*The kairos which we believed to be at hand*
*was the coming of a new theonomous age,*
*conquering the destructive gap between religion*
*and secular culture.*
*But history took another path. . . .*
*A new element [came] into the picture,*
*the experience of the "end. . . ."*
*We looked at the beginning of the new*
*more than at the end of the old.*
*We did not realize the price that mankind has to pay*
*for the coming of a new theonomy. . . .*
*We did not see the possibility of final catastrophes*
*as the true prophets,*
*the prophets of doom, announced them.*

PAUL TILLICH, 1946[1]

At mid-decade, then, Niebuhr was preaching the inevitability of international war. The signal for catastrophe must be Germany's collapse: the class struggle would erupt and tear down the façade of national unity contrived by the capitalist puppeteers behind Adolf Hitler.

But still there was no news out of Germany of the stirrings which must precede the social revolution. Hitler had suppressed populist discontent in his own ranks, and routed Socialists and Communists. Anyone capable of leading mass opposition to the regime was locked up, exiled, or dead. By November of 1936 Niebuhr was writing of European affairs from the premise that Hitler no longer needed to fear internal overthrow as the result of social discontent.[2] It remained possible, however, that if Hitler should embroil himself in too daring international adventures and should then lead Germany into defeat, his people would rise up and destroy him. Hitler's successes vindicated his conviction that national patriotism was still the irresistible solvent of class loyalties. Even his destruction would then, ironically, be a vindication of him.

Whether he should survive or whether he should be destroyed, Hitler's career had upset the premises upon which Niebuhr had been basing his analysis of politics since his adoption of Marxism. Two forces which Niebuhr had thought to be secondary or dependent forces in collective human psychology were now proving themselves anew to be primary; the one force which he had thought to be primary now revealed itself to be secondary. Hitler's uncomplicated political genius had demonstrated that the force of patriotism and the craving for violence which is in all men are not by-products of something more basic (namely, of economics). People do not love their country or hate their neighbor because of economic circumstance, although these facts have economic implications. What Niebuhr called "the spirit of vengeance," impelling the civilization towards its rendezvous with catastrophe, is not the product of the economic distress of the poor. It is not the product of anything. It is given in human nature. Niebuhr, who prided himself on his recovery of the doctrine of original sin, now began to realize that he had not been radical enough in the application of that discovery.

A conspicuous example of this failure is in Niebuhr's assessment of the anti-Semitism of the Nazi-movement. At first he had regarded anti-Semitism as a marginal aspect of the movement, a transparent device which Hitler exploited to neutralize class division in the hope of strengthening national unity behind himself. "Anti-Semitism," Niebuhr had written, "is, in fact, secondary to the economic aspect of the movement. . . . The really important element in fascism is . . . . its toryism and reaction."[3] Against Niebuhr's expectations, Hitler's use of anti-Semitism increased—and was increasingly applauded. Each indignity offered to the Jews strengthened Hitler's hold upon Germany, and increased his capacity for international mischief. The economic realism which Marx promised would increasingly immunize the proletariat against the infections of patriotism, racism, and other irrational loyalties, simply evaporated. That "attitude of critical detachment" which Niebuhr had so recently declared to be the distinctive virtue of the worker, which made him proof against the "pride of nations," was now nowhere to be found.[4]

The "spirit of vengeance" which he had so recently foreseen as the instrument of judgment upon the old civilization and the awful preparer for the new, might not, after all, be in the keeping of the proletariat. Perhaps history was preparing an awful instrument of judgment upon western civilization, not out of the righteous anger of the oppressed but out of the old forces of tribal pride and racial hatred. The proletarians were rushing to escape the roles cast for them in the rhetoric of Marx and the great deeds of the Soviet revolution, to return to the old familiar roles cast in antediluvian swamps: tribe against tribe, blood against blood.

Ever since 1930, there had been implicit in Niebuhr's writing the assumption that the catastrophe that must come would be a great sifting-time. Out of it there would come, not utopia (this had always been the point of Niebuhr's dissent from Marxist mythology), but the realization of some matchless historical goal, which Niebuhr sometimes described as "social equality," sometimes as "industrial democracy." But Hitler's successes prefigured a hitherto unthinkable scenario: general and universal degradation and possibly chaos.

The "shocked fascination" with which Niebuhr had contemplated the coming "judgment" upon western civilization was rather quickly being drained of its fascination. We now find a new word entering into Niebuhr's descriptions of the things to come: the word, "horror." We find an early hint of this shifting prospect in an article of 1934, "Shall We Seek World Peace or the Peace of America?"[5] Its starting-point is, as always, the newest evidence of German trouble-making on the international scene. Its conclusions imply considerations not hitherto evident in Niebuhr's thought. "There is very little that can be done," he begins, "to stop an international war. What can be done ought to be done, provided it does not increase the risks of spreading the war." It develops, however, that Niebuhr believes that what needs doing should be done by the European powers, and not by the United States of America. For the moment, America should strive to keep clear of international rivalries, while earnestly praying that somehow they can be contained before international war develops, for, "If the next war should become a general conflagration it would result in such widespread destruction that any original reasons and motives for participation would be completely lost in the confusion. There would be neither victors nor vanquished."

Here we have come to a new consideration, the true water-shed

of Niebuhr's thinking, not only about international affairs but about
the world of politics in general.

> While the neutrality of any great power in another conflict will
> not protect the world against the inevitable consequences of a
> general holocaust, it will nevertheless be valuable to preserve
> some islands of sanity in a sea of insanity and a few areas of
> comparative health in a sick world. American neutrality would
> probably help to keep Great Britain out of the war. . . . There is
> therefore every possibility that neither Britain nor America will
> become involved. *It may be that such neutrality will serve to
> fasten the capitalistic system upon these nations for additional
> decades.* But even that result would be preferable to *the general
> destruction of all the physical and moral bases of our present
> civilization, which, whatever its defects, is surely preferable to
> the complete chaos which would result from a world war.*
> [Emphasis added.]

Even as he wrote these words, Niebuhr's *Reflections* were in the
hands of reviewers, who were savoring his description of the coming
class struggle and the happier society that lay beyond it.[6] But in the
article just cited the keynote is one that plays no part whatever in
the rhetoric he developed in his *Reflections*. It is the note of solicitude for what might be lost of present civilization in universal social
upheaval. The lack of this concern in the pages of *Reflections* and
its sudden importance in the periodical pieces which begin with the
one just cited (from early 1934) point to the impact upon Niebuhr's
thinking of the political events which, as we have just seen, most
occupied his attentions in these months: namely, the birth pangs of
the Nazi regime.

It is to be noticed that this new solicitude for the old order did not
take the upper hand all at once. Indeed, for some four years, more or
less, to come, it would remain a wayward sub-theme, subordinate to
the major theme of the sins of capitalistic civilization. But it becomes
increasingly prominent, until by about the end of 1938 it has
become the major theme. This development in Niebuhr's analysis of
international politics parallels the development we have already
noted in his analysis of domestic politics. As the prospect of universal war drove Niebuhr to a sudden and quite un-Marxian solicitude for the values of existing civilization, so the prospect of
Roosevelt's defeat at the polls drove him to calculate what America
stood to lose *in a relative way* if Landon were to win in 1936. The
habit of appealing to relative ends was eventually to become irresistible, and fatal to Niebuhr's Marxism. It is essential that we note that

this new spirit of relativism enters into Niebuhr's analysis of international politics a good two years before we find it in his analysis of domestic politics. This reflects the priority that he invariably gave to European affairs through the mid-thirties.

For the moment, consideration of what civilization stood to lose from international war persuaded Niebuhr that America's proper role was to stand aside. America's entry into international squabbles could not serve the cause of peace. It should be noted, however, that the proper policy for America seems to Niebuhr to depend upon practical considerations, not theoretical ones. His affection for Marxist theory was to prove recalcitrant; but, by 1935, the thin edge of the wedge of pragmatism was firmly in place.

By early 1934, it was beginning to be clear to Niebuhr that the civil war which he had expected to shake and overthrow the fascist regime in Germany might not materialize after all. It thus became possible that Hitler might survive long enough to bring Europe into a war so terrible as to eclipse even the Great War. The success which Japan was experiencing in Manchuria, together with the likelihood that Japan contemplated a revival of her ancient feud with Russia, offered the prospect of a truly global war. Either Germany or Poland seemed to Niebuhr a possible henchman for Japan in an early war of encirclement against Russia.[7] There is no doubt, Niebuhr asserted in 1934, that America ought to favor the cause of Russia in such a conflict. Everything should be done, by diplomatic overtures and the increase of commercial relations, to "[draw] Russia more and more into the circle of mutual relations."[8] Unless such overtures are made, Japan will be encouraged to make her perhaps lethal assault against Soviet Russia, and the great and promising Russian Experiment will be lost to mankind. Failing such a policy of western rapprochement, a more serious and tragic possibility looms: that Russia's "fear psychosis" will grow until present "undoubtedly militaristic" tendencies could tempt Stalin into something like "the Napoleonic venture and the ensuing wars at the beginning of the nineteenth century."[9] But in no case could America serve any good purpose in coming to the aid of Russia directly in the event of her being attacked. America's resources were inadequate to rescue the Soviets; and, in any case, such intervention would merely encourage an extension of the war to other powers, inviting general anarchy.[10] Even in so good a cause as the rescue of socialism, therefore, Niebuhr could not condone American entry into an international war.

But war there must be—though he hoped, at least as late as mid-1934, that both the United States and Britain would stay out. By 1935, however, he was beginning to see reasons why Britain should run the risk of war, while he continued to believe that America should not. He was cheered by early indications that Britain meant to oppose Italy's imperialist assault against Ethiopia. But he refused to applaud—for Britain, he was sure, had not acted from disinterested conscience but rather out of "self-righteousness" and "self-interest."[11] Britain had to resist fascist imperialism at some point, or see her own empire crumble. This need *incidentally* served the hope of world peace, now actively threatened by the fascist powers. Americans should draw comfort from this coincidence of Britain's selfish requirements and the cause of collective security; but they should not applaud either the British or the League. The League is merely an instrument of the imperial will of Britain and of France: "if British interests were not at stake, the League would not act so energetically." In the immediate situation, "the best we can do is to seek the enlargement of American neutrality sanctions." But if it should prove that something more considerable needs doing to dissuade the aggressors, then America will have to stand aside. "The consequences of a world war are too terrible to permit irresponsibility towards any measure calculated to mitigate the international anarchy or postpone international conflict."[12]

By mid-1936, Niebuhr had become convinced that Hitler's behavior was making war all but inevitable:

The German internal situation is a . . . guarantee of the inevitability of war. So precarious is the economic foundation of German rearmament that the Germans are forced to strike before growing economic weakness will negate and vitiate growing military strength.

The whole situation presents Britain with a problem which gives us a vivid illustration of the relativities of politics. Britain would like to stay out of the next war, partly for imperial motives and partly for genuine pacifist motives. But every impulse in that direction tends to strengthen the German military will. . . . If Britain gives her former allies unequivocal support on the other hand she may be able to prevent the war. But of course such a policy risks immediate involvement for the sake of an ultimate prevention of war.[13]

From this point until late 1938, Niebuhr was to write at least one editorial in each issue of *Radical Religion* on this subject of Britain's moral responsibilities in the present hour. The moral was always the same: let's you and him fight! Britain owed it to western civilization to resist fascist aggressions, *now*, before Hitler's strength should become so formidable that the entire collapse of western civilization must be the outcome. In view of the demand he was making, one might expect Niebuhr to be as charitable as possible towards England. In fact, at this hour he had few good words to spare:

> England and France are not angels of light because historical
> destiny forces them to play this role against the Nazi threat of
> anarchy in Europe. *Their* unjust peace [emphasis mine] made
> Germany what she is today. But that does not change the fact
> that German hysteria threatens to engulf the whole continent in
> a great war and may possibly tempt Japan to spread the war in
> Asia. There seems no longer a possibility of avoiding some kind of
> hostilities. . . . The nations which are now trying to act as the
> police court of Europe have done more to create the anarchy than
> the recalcitrant nation which must now be disciplined.
> Nevertheless it is important to preserve some system of collective
> security and prevent militaristic fascism from triumphing in both
> Europe and Asia. Yet even this effort cannot be made without
> running the danger of war.[14]

One must admit that, while there was much that was sound in Niebuhr's descriptions of the international situation in this period ending in the Winter of 1938–39, he was not very helpful when it comes down to recommendations. His judgment was seriously at odds with itself. He was still slowly working off the spell of his Marxist allegiance. The positive, almost exultant tone of his *Reflections* and of the other products of his high-Marxist phase first begins to falter in 1934, under the impact of the bad news from Germany which we have described; with the Presidential election of 1936 (when, as we have seen, Niebuhr was so agitated by what in retrospect appears the fanciful prospect of Republican victory), he is quite plainly shaken. To put it as generously as possible: Niebuhr seemed to be trying too hard to keep his perspective on events that were moving too swiftly. Nothing that he had learned from his European travels in the past prepared him for the barbarity of fascism and its international recklessness. There seemed no fixed points left anywhere on the horizon. Even the sturdy common sense and the spirit of wholesome compromise which had made Britain seem to him an island of grace in a graceless world now seemed to be evaporating. If he frequently fled to the shelter of Marxist rhetoric, it was not that the Marxist world-view still seemed as real to him as before, but rather that the rest of the world was becoming increasingly unreal. It is a curious and uneven record that he leaves in his writings of these years. One is tempted, again and again, to declare that at last one has found the decisive turning-away from Marxist ideology, only to discover, when one turns the page, that he is ringing the changes again.

The most interesting aspect of Niebuhr's crisis of political conscience in these years (from about mid-1934 to 1939) is that it had nothing to do with any sudden disenchantment regarding Soviet diplomacy. His analysis of the role of "religious" enthusiasm in the psychology of Communists had, from the beginning, prepared him for the discovery, just now beginning to impress itself upon so many American intellectuals, of the cynicism of the Soviets and their international supporters. Rumors of Soviet duplicity in the struggle to save the Republican government in Spain from Franco and his fascist henchmen did not cause him any surprise. Nor did it yet cause him to conclude, as he *later* would, that Communists were altogether to be shunned in anti-fascist causes; he was still a qualified believer in the United Front.[15] Unlike many of his fellow-liberals, he was prepared to learn that the Russian leadership was decimating its own ranks in bizarre heresy trials.[16] However, the news (or rumors) out of Russia gave Niebuhr occasion to express somewhat kindlier thoughts about democracy itself, which were to become more and more characteristic of him. "The whole of contemporary Russian history proves the tremendous value of democracy in any change toward a socialized society. This is not an easy task because the democratic process tends to break down in the crisis in which the new society comes to birth.... The knowledge of this fact does not invalidate the genuine achievements of a socialized society in Russia nor does it prove that the hazards of a new birth for society are reasons for not desiring it."[17]

How difficult it was becoming to keep a Marxist perspective on events! This new solicitude for "the value of democracy" is out of character with Niebuhr's frequent warnings against "the rhetoric of parliamentarianism." But, would there not be a great deal more than "parliamentarianism" exposed "to the hazards of birth ... of a new society?" By the Fall of 1937, we find Niebuhr speaking in rather more homely terms: his subject is the recent aerial bombings that have been part of the war of Japanese against Chinese and Spaniard against Spaniard. Perhaps, he writes, the scenes of "horror" that have been enacted in these wars "will increase the determination of European peoples and statesmen to avoid the next war." But, suppose they do not; suppose that Hitler is not moved by such things?

It is difficult to see how the war can be avoided without yielding to those nations which are ready to use any instrument for the attainment of their end and the governments of which are sufficiently desperate to adopt the terrible motto: "After us, the deluge." At the moment the possibility of a continent dominated by the fascism of Germany and Italy is actually more immediate than the prospect of a European war. Whether the one prospect is preferable to the other is one of those questions for which there is no convincing answer. In some moments of reflection anything would seem preferable to the realities of warfare in a technical civilization. On the other hand the corruption of culture and the oppression of the people which may result from the tyranny of a triumphant fascism may prompt a new Patrick Henry to arise in Europe with the slogan, "Give me liberty or give me death."[18]

Why does not such a Patrick Henry emerge?

Why are the democratic nations so completely impotent before the continued aggression of the fascist power? The answer is fairly simple. The democratic nations are also the great capitalist nations. They have the economic power to stop the fascist nations by the simple use of economic pressure. But this economic power is devoted to the cause of capitalism rather than the cause of democracy. The capitalist democracies do not like fascism but they like socialism and communism less. The class interests of the financial oligarchies in every capitalist democracy are incompatible with the interest of the nations which they represent. This is the real cause of the duplicity and deviousness of British foreign policy.[19]

The two articles just cited mark a significant departure in Niebuhr's use of language. The cause of fascism is now opposed, not to the cause of the proletariat, but to the cause of "democracy." "Democracy" has everything to lose from the triumph of fascism, and everything to gain from its containment. If the leaders of the governing parties of Britain and France had the interests of "democracy" at heart, they would contain, and then crush, "fascism." That they do not betrays their hatred for "democracy" and their basic sympathy with "fascism." Though disappointed in the working-class of Germany for their betrayal of their fellow-workers in the international struggle, Niebuhr was still able to wield the Marxist bludgeon a little longer from the other end: if the workers have forgotten their need for solidarity, the capitalists have not forgotten theirs.

There now follows one of the most wayward periods in Niebuhr's career as a political analyst. If ever a man suffered the torments of ambivalence, it was Niebuhr in these months (1938–1940). As western civilization went into its penultimate testing-hour, all the political actors in whom Niebuhr had expected to find the wisdom and the moral strength demanded by the times chose to bury their heads in the sands of sentimentalism or dogmatism. When, at last, a courageous and realistic voice was heard, it spoke with the accents of the British ruling class; it was the voice of a Tory politician, Winston Churchill, whom Niebuhr had always considered the most benighted, the most "frenzied" and "cynical" of all Britain's imperialists.[20] For several months after Munich, however, there was little ground for thinking that Churchill was more than an isolated exception. By and large, the ruling classes and the middle-classes were running true to form, wanting to avoid war (which would be harmful to the regular processes of profit-making), but lacking the courage to offer resistance to the fascists' military adventuring, which alone could prevent that war. Whenever a politician of the ruling party showed something other than the instincts of the counting-house, it was a reversion to the sentimental pieties which these same merchants once learned in their Sunday Schools. Both types of wisdom, which together exhaust the range of moral philosophy in the bourgeois world, played into the hands of ruthless dictators.[21]

For a while, it had seemed to Niebuhr that the British Socialists would prove to have the courage and the wisdom that the situation needed.[22] But as the crisis worsened, both British and French Socialists scrambled for cover. By mid-1939, there seemed not to be a single figure of strength in the socialist leadership in either country. At the same time, the circle of conservative realists led by Churchill seemed to be expanding. But their pleas for resistance to Nazi aggressions were wasted upon the generality of their fellow-Britishers. "Munich," Niebuhr discovered, "was possible because the man in the street felt it to be just that the Sudeten Germans should be incorporated into the Reich. . . . The British people are a collective Hamlet, and conscience has made cowards of them all."[23]

It was becoming increasingly clear to Niebuhr that Marxism was not the source of realism that it advertised itself to be. He had been lulled by "Marxist science" into the expectation that the German working-class, strengthened against the appeals of the slogans and the false idealism of "patriotism," would overthrow Hitler at the first opportunity. There had now been numerous such opportunities, and Hitler was firmly entrenched in the affections of the German people. As the awful truth of Hitler's strength became inescapable,

Niebuhr had transferred his hope for the rescue of civilization to the British working-class. He had (as we have seen) always looked upon the leaders of British labor as the supreme realists of the international Socialist movement. Again his faith in the realism of the working-class was to be betrayed. If Munich had been "primarily the work of the British ruling classes," it was equally true that the public as a whole had cheered the deed loudly, and that Labour had been able to offer no alternative policy. The Labour Party was, indeed, "completely lacking in resolution ... and ... in any great quality of statesmanship."[24]

Writing from England in the lull between the rape of Czechoslovakia and the invasion of Poland, a much-chastened Niebuhr confessed that he now wanted to be counted out of the ranks of "those who see politics in purely economic terms." For firsthand observation was now strengthening the impression that had been forming in his mind for some months: that "the most effective opposition to Chamberlain has come not from labor but from clearer eyed imperialists like Churchill."[25]

Chapter

11

# WHAT SHOULD AMERICA DO?

The preceding pages should make it clear that Niebuhr had never been tempted to think of America's future as self-contained. In this, he provides a refreshing contrast to the better-known liberal-isolationists who thought from America outward. He was never tempted by the notion that America might serve some uniquely useful function in a world somehow made more responsive to her peaceful example by the catharsis of a European war (which was the approach which appealed to liberal isolationists like Charles Beard).[1] Niebuhr's political thinking remained within the universalist mould that had been set for him back at the beginning of the decade by his conversion to Marxist socialism under the impact of Tillich's religious message. Niebuhr's uniquely internationalist vision was the supreme gift of his Marxism which had conditioned him to think in macrocosmic terms. His disappointment in the failure of American politics to conform to Marxist models had encouraged his interest in European affairs, wherein, as he had at first believed, he would find the true drift of history. It was European developments which aroused his concern about the scope of the universal catastrophe that Marxism had promised. And this, in turn, as we have seen, was undoing his commitment to Marxism.

A close examination of Niebuhr's thoughts on the various crises in international affairs, from Manchuria to Munich, reveals that Niebuhr never held anything like a neutralist's view of America's proper role. It was never for him a matter of involvement or non-involvement of America in the plight of the world. America was inexorably involved by dint of her long course of economic imperialism; she could not revoke that involvement. The debacle of order in the western world would carry America into ruin as well. Until about the middle of 1937, he doubted that America could do anything to avert the debacle of western civilization. The situation might still be manageable, provided that a resolute Britain and France, acting in enlightened self-interest, resisted fascist aggression. But for America to involve herself would only compound the hazards, tempting the aggressors to expand the theaters of war beyond the point where any combination of forces could contain it.[2]

As the decade wore on, however, Niebuhr's growing appreciation of the horror that would accompany the debacle of western civilization made him increasingly alert to possibilities for initiative on America's part. Thus, against the background of Japan's assault upon China over the Marco Polo Bridge (July, 1937), Niebuhr fretted about the effect that the Neutrality laws of 1935 were having in restricting America's freedom to distinguish between aggressors and victims in international affairs. "Mandatory neutrality legislation," he concluded, "means complete irresponsibility toward every possible aggression in the world."[3] Still, Niebuhr opposed American military aid to China, while professing to believe that America could somehow help in "averting the struggle or affecting the outcome." As he shrewdly guessed,[4] the Roosevelt Administration was preparing to turn all of the ambiguities in the Neutrality Acts to account in order to aid China. As the Japanese thought it served their best interest not to declare war upon the Chinese, Roosevelt was able to cheer the Chinese on with modest help that was disallowed, under the Neutrality Acts, where an acknowledged state of war existed. This, and other bits of *realpolitik* which the Roosevelt Administration was to display in its conduct of foreign policy under the watchful eye of an isolationist Congress, served to increase Niebuhr's respect for the government as the months proceeded. Step by step, Niebuhr came to see larger and larger contributions that America might make to the preservation of peace, until, imperceptibly, he had worked himself into a case for all-out aid to the anti-Fascist cause.

There is no dramatic turning-point to be found. But somewhere between the summer of 1938 and the end of 1939 Niebuhr passed the boundary line between merely token or "nuisance" involvement and interventionism. As late as mid-1938, he firmly opposed all preparations for war. "It is perfectly clear," he wrote in his paper during that summer before Munich, "that the British Tories will not accept the German challenge until imperial interests are directly imperilled. When that happens they will fight for 'democracy' and not before. Naturally they will then call upon us to come to the support of democracy. . . . Let us hope when the time comes that those of us who believe in the principle of collective security will not allow ourselves to be fooled by pure imperialism hiding behind the façade of collective security for democracy."[5] With this conviction before him, Niebuhr addressed himself to the task of discouraging preparations for war among Americans. The villains in the piece were various and ill-assorted war-mongers. The arguments of all must be met. The most attractive of these sirens (for Niebuhr's audience) were those who argued the need to save the Soviet Experiment as a worthy *casus belli*. "We have strong doubts about the wholesomeness of politics in Russia. We are not willing to see young Americans die to protect Stalin's type of dictatorship from Hitler's type of dictatorship."[6] Then there were the supporters of the Administration's argument that preparation for war was the soundest method for discouraging aggression by outsiders, and hence of avoiding war. On this score, Niebuhr inclined at first to the thesis of the Nye Committee, that it was preparation for war which brought about American involvement the last time around.

"The billion dollar defense budget of the Roosevelt administration cries to heaven as the worst piece of militarism in modern history. All the reactionary forces which have been crying for a balanced budget raise not a word of protest against this supplementary budget for which no taxation provisions are made.... Our nation like England is drifting into the worst possible foreign policy. We refuse to use the non-military pressures which we have to stop the fascist nations and then build up huge armaments to fight them when they have grown strong enough to throw down the gauntlet."[7]

In these last words, the secret spring of Niebuhr's reluctance for military preparation is revealed. To be in the camp of military preparedness is to be in impossible company for a Socialist. The same people who oppose the taking of American diplomatic initiatives against Fascist aggression are proposing unilateral American rearmament: businessmen, who want to use American strength only when it can advance the economic frontiers of America. They are secretly envious of Britain's commercial empire, and likewise sympathetic to fascism. They are the same people who oppose expenditure of public money to provide jobs for the poor. The real sticking-point was, thus, not any theoretical commitment against involvement in war. That had long since been a closed issue, as Niebuhr repeats in every issue of his paper. But Niebuhr could not shake off the suspicion that to prepare for war was to run the risk of being used by capitalists in a bid to destroy democracy and institute fascism.

Gradually, however, the issue was being redefined by circumstance: "If a society which has possibilities of a development toward greater justice can not be defended against a society in which the concept of justice has been swallowed up in the ideal of power, then fascism must ultimately triumph over democracy."[8] Thus, responsibility toward humanity required that America do whatever would most likely ward off international catastrophe. The question of actually declaring war against the aggressors and taking to the battlefields was no longer the heart of the matter. While American leaders could not risk involving America formally as a partner of the Allies until American security was clearly affected—"America," he wrote, "is still suffering from having been drawn into the world war beyond the obvious necessities of national defense"[9]—the important thing was that America be prepared for war if necessary. He quoted with approval the dictum of Lewis Mumford: "At the moment war became an absolute evil to most men, it became an absolute good for the new barbarians."[10]

These considerations brought Niebuhr at the same hour to the great parting-of-the-political-ways. We have already noted early signs of grudging admiration for Roosevelt's foreign policy: "Whatever may be his lack in not taking the country into his confidence completely enough and in playing the game with a little too much cuteness, he has anticipated the perils in which we now stand more clearly than anyone else. In fact there are few among us who did not make unjustified criticism of his preparedness program."[11] In May of 1940, Niebuhr resigned from the Socialist Party.[12] The decision for Roosevelt was encouraged by what he now regarded as the irresponsible behavior of Norman Thomas and the Socialist Party. Thomas had made himself one of the key figures of the neutrality movement, and had succeeded in bringing the majority of his party with him.[13] No longer a believer in absolute pacifism, Thomas argued for non-involvement in terms of a remarkably Marxist complexion—"remarkable," that is, in view of Thomas's reputation as the least doctrinaire of American socialists. What annoyed Niebuhr, mainly, was Thomas's practice of trying to broaden the appeal of his isolationist arguments by dilating upon the three-thousand-miles-of-ocean which assured America's immunity from the infection of this war. This seemed to Niebuhr like playing both sides of the street. If this was an evil war, precipitated by capitalists and fascists for their own ends, as Thomas sought to show, then the arguments regarding America's geographical security were irrelevant. Thomas thought he had jumped the hurdle of theoretical pacifism when he abandoned his specifically religious commitment to it. But, Niebuhr charged, he persisted in seeing contemporary affairs in the class-struggle context which had become irrelevant at this moment of life-or-death for civilization as a whole. And that obstinacy (required by his commitment to Marxist doctrine) had betrayed him into the very perfectionist-pacifist rhetoric that he thought he had abandoned when he abandoned orthodox religion!

Thus, Thomas's position seemed to Niebuhr to be both idealistic and cynical at the same time. Ironically, Niebuhr argued, "[Thomas's] type of idealistic isolationism plays into the hands of reactionary appeasement."[14] Taking as evidence a *Fortune* poll of mid-1940 which showed (he said) that "48 per cent of our big business men are appeasers at heart," he concluded that Thomas was making himself an unwitting cat's-paw of his own declared enemies, the capitalists.[15] It would be ironic indeed if the efforts of the Socialist Party to keep America out of war had the effect of strengthening the hand of American plutocrats in *their* deepest ambition, which was to come to terms with Nazism with a view to an agreement on economic spheres of interest to follow the defeat of the British Empire.[16]

Despite the bitterness of the attacks which each published upon the positions of the other, their friendship survived while other Socialists parted in rancor which was never subdued in some hearts.[17] Until their last days they were still debating with one another, and before one another's congregations so to speak, the positions they took in 1940–41. From the moment of their first verbal set-to, Niebuhr was acknowledged to be the principal antagonist of the isolationist policy of the Socialist Party. His arguments took many a socialist out of the Party—as we shall see.[18]

"It is not a great compliment to this nation that there is no decent alternative to the Roosevelt policy, nor yet a person besides himself to carry on his own policy. But these are the facts."[19] With this left-handed compliment, Niebuhr sought to prepare his readers to follow him into the camp of Franklin Roosevelt. He did not attempt to make the decision seem more palatable than it was. It was a painful duty:

> Whatever liberal front the Republican candidate may give the ticket [as, for instance, if Dewey should be nominated] the forces behind the Republican ticket will stand not only for reaction but for ignorant and dangerous reaction. They will seek to destroy

the Wagner act, the social security legislation of the Roosevelt administration, the freedom of labor to organize and the relief of the unemployed. . . . There is no one of sufficient stature to bear the mantle of Roosevelt and win the election. Only he can overcome the treason which all the reactionary bourbons of the south will engage in. . . . All this means that Roosevelt, despite anti-third term tradition, is the only hope of maintaining the real gains which have been made in the past years of the depression.[20]

Then, with Roosevelt's re-election, Niebuhr let up this great shout of relief: "Despite the ambiguities of Rooseveltian liberalism the re-election of the president was a heartening revelation of the ability of democracy to arrive at a right decision in a crisis.

"No election in our history has validated the principle of universal suffrage more than this one. The 'good' people and the 'wise' people, the intellectually respectable, the 'leaders' voted generally for Willkie. . . . [Roosevelt was elected] by the wisdom which resides in hungry stomachs and anxious hearts."[21]

Defending their support of Roosevelt and their abandonment of the Socialist Party, would, Niebuhr knew, put quite a strain upon the socialist consciences of the members of his Fellowship. To meet this dilemma, Niebuhr offered a homely parable.[22] Suppose a man comes down with a disease (economic depression). There is a cure extant (socialism), but the relatives refuse to let the proponents of that medicine near the patient. They decide to put their trust in a sympathetic and genial G.P. who has discovered "medicine which wards off dissolution without giving the patient health." Other doctors, glib of bearing but inwardly vicious and stupid, are competing for the favor of the relatives, with the argument that "the patient could be restored to health if only all medicine were cut off and he were sent to bed." If the relatives succumb to the arguments of these latter "quacks," the "palliatives" being adminstered by Dr. Roosevelt will cease, and the patient will surely "die." This presents us socialists with "an interesting moral problem": should the genial pill-doctor be defended, or should socialists join with the vicious "quacks" in the effort to get him removed from the sick-room? "It is practically imperative that such a defense be made. . . . The Rooseveltian doctors are quacks only in the sense that they hold out the prospect of an ultimate recovery which lies completely beyond the potency of their medicine. This quackery must be recognized and exposed. . . . [But, so long as socialists are being kept from the bedside anyway,] the Rooseveltian program deserves qualified support wherever it is under attack from reactionary critics."

Yet, there was a time when Niebuhr believed that the patient "ought to die!"[23] Now he was playing a quite different tune. Reviewing a book written by "one of [Roosevelt's] most potent brain trusters" in defense of New Deal economics, Niebuhr commented in 1939: "Socialists would have to be pure catastrophists, looking forward to general breakdown, if they did not prefer such an attempt as Mr. Ezekiel describes, to the alternative of further crises and the threat of a fascist escape from the crisis."[24] There was a time when Niebuhr himself had been just such a "pure catastrophist," standing (as Arthur Schlesinger describes him) in "shocked fascination [before] ..; the possibility of some basic turn, some drastic judgment in history." There was, Niebuhr now appreciated—as the dimensions of the coming catastrophe began to become clear to him during 1939—not a little of morbidity in that fascination for catastrophe. As the true face of catastrophe became clear to him, Niebuhr realized that the only *dependable* outcome must be new horrors of mass destruction and perhaps a reversion to barbarism in the sequel. To talk of gains for socialism in such a context was not merely irrelevant, but an ultimate blasphemy. In *Moral Man* Niebuhr had endorsed Marxism as a reliable anchor of historical realism, appointed in the hour of Western civilization's penultimate trial to secure believers against the expectations that history would not fulfill—principally, the expectation of human altruism (the besetting illusion of liberalism). But there was in Marx's expectation of a changed human nature *beyond* the revolution a sturdy and irreducible optimism more dangerous than the pale optimism of liberals. In his *Moral Man*, Niebuhr had noted this optimistic vein in the Marxist structure, observing that it could encourage delusions of self-righteousness, and tempt Marxists into tactical errors. But, for all his protesting, he had succumbed to it himself. For the sake of the promise of a just social order around the next bend, he had cheered on the forces of "vengeance" which would bring on the next war, accomplishing the death of capitalism. He had concocted a tendentious theory, whereby the "liberal" virtues of detached goodwill would survive the social catastrophe which was being generated by a "vengeance" much tougher than liberalism's powers of accommodation. But when the scope of the coming destruction began to be made clear to him—in the bombings of Manchuria, in the tribal madness of Nazism, in Hitler's intimidations of German Jewry—the scales fell from his eyes.

If the resistance of the old civilization was going to be so vigorous, social justice could only be had over the dead bodies of us all. It was the socialist who would have to give ground—to yield the immediate accomplishment of social justice for the sake of the preservation of humanity itself.

*Thus, the capitalist order must be rescued.* Socialists must not deceive themselves that the majority of capitalists have changed their basic sympathies. But the emergence of a realistic and patriotic minority in the ranks of Tory leadership had exposed the fallacy of Marx's class analysis, and given to socialists the opportunity to tap the deeper spring of patriotism which still continued in most hearts. Never mind the fact that Marx taught that patriotism was the most vicious of all the forces of inertia! Events have proved that life is more complicated than Marx knew. Already the revival of patriotism had cleared the ground upon which the proletariat and the middle-classes can stand together in the defense of civilization. There could be no hope of a society of improved justice, if civilization itself were to go under.

It was no longer thinkable that international war could be transformed by the alchemy of class struggle into a prelude to universal social justice. The democracies, he was confident, would win, because "the coerced unity, the cynical opportunism, the military strength bought at the price of economic weakness, of the fascist powers will be no match for the democracies in the end."[25] How potent these *unnamed* virtues of democracy must be, to be more than a match for fascism! The dramatic change of emphasis is to be found in Niebuhr's expectations for western civilization beyond the war: "Fascism as a system will undoubtedly be destroyed in the course of the war. The democratic powers will be greatly altered. Some slight social gains may be made. But the possibility of establishing a decent socialist society is very dim indeed. That belongs to the ultimate and not the immediate possibilities of a new Europe."[26]

*Chapter*

# CHRISTIANITY AND CRISIS

Thus, Niebuhr supported and voted for Franklin Roosevelt for the first time in 1940. He still reckoned himself a socialist.[1] But it was becoming increasingly uncomfortable for him, in view of the overriding urgency of the issue of war and peace, to remain in the Party. Through his organization of the Keep America out of War Congress, Norman Thomas was seeking to commit Socialists irretrievably to practical isolationism.[2] At its convention in Washington in April, 1940, the Party voted for total repudiation of U.S. assistance to the Allies. (The vote was recorded as 159 to 28.)[3] The decision was a bold one to take at this hour, when the political tides were beginning to move unmistakably against the isolationists. And, once taken, it seemed to inspire the leadership to a display of its authority over the ranks that hardly seemed justified after so many years of internal indiscipline, failing confidence and electoral disaster. A few days after the convention, the following letter went out from Irving Barshop, Executive Secretary of the Socialist Party of America, to "Dear Comrade Niebuhr":

> May I call attention to the fact that you are serving as a sponsor on the Committee to Defend America by Aiding the Allies, the position of which is contrary to the Socialist Party position on war. As you know, members of the Socialist party, in line with the Party policy, conform with the Party position in their public political actions. I am interested in getting your reaction on this matter. As you know, Party discipline demands conformance to Party policies.[4]

That, apparently, is what did it:

> Dear Mr. Barshop:
> You may count this as my resignation from the Socialist Party.
> I have no intention of conforming to the discipline of the Party
> on the question of American responsibility in Europe. The
> position has become an intolerable one for me.[5]

When Norman Thomas sought and obtained a hearing before the Senate Foreign Affairs Committee considering the Lend-Lease proposal, a group of prominent ex-Socialists, with Niebuhr at their head, issued a strongly-worded statement demanding equal time.[6] A few days later, Niebuhr appeared before the Committee, at the personal urging of Senator James Byrnes.[7]

There was no doubt that Niebuhr was going to be (as Thomas later put it) "a great help to F.D.R."[8] But he was not so eager to be helpful that he would abandon his critical responsibility. While insisting that America must fulfill her "obligations to a civilization of which it is a part," and roundly condemning the testimony of Thomas that "the present struggle in Europe is ... merely a clash between rival imperialisms,"[9] he would not hew to the line taken by other pro-Administration witnesses—namely, that Lend-Lease would make involvement in war less likely. Instead, he warned that "nations which try to eliminate every risk of war with too great caution may face the horrors of war the more certainly."[10]

There were giants in those days in the Senate—and unquestionably some of the most formidable were arrayed against the Bill. Hiram Johnson of California, apparently hopeful of getting another Administration witness to commit the usual double-talk, wanted to know if the Bill "will keep us out of war?"[11] This was one witness who refused to promise that result. The Senator wanted to draw the conclusion that the prospect of war obviously "held no terrors" for the witness. But Niebuhr was not so easily dismounted: "I do not see how any human being could be without a terror of war. I think we all have to face this proposition, whether a war is the worst terror we can conceive, and I am frank to say that I am not certain that it is, and if I were certain that it was I do not see how I could assume any responsible attitude toward any political question, because there is no political question that does not have to face ultimately the possibility of war, if we decide there are some things we want to maintain at all costs."[12]

While Niebuhr insisted that he was appearing before the Senate Committee only as an interested citizen, and not as the spokesman for any party or element within the nation, the nature of the

arguments presented by him suggests that he had been recruited by
the Administration to present a challenge to two principal groups:
the Socialists, and the ideological pacifists.[13] As for the first, the
miserable showing of the Socialist Party in the campaign of 1940
(fewer than a hundred thousand votes in the whole nation)[14] indicated that its influence was not likely to be decisive in the inter-
ventionist debate. Pacifist (or, more generally, pseudo-pacifist) expressions, however, were gaining currency even in secular-liberal
circles, as isolationists of varying sorts groped for arguments. Thus,
Niebuhr threw himself immediately and energetically into the cause
of defense of the Allies.

As Niebuhr saw it, the bond that drew socialists and pacifists
together was the conviction "that nothing is at stake in the present
European struggle."[15] As an ex-pacifist and ex-Socialist, Niebuhr
believed he understood the attractiveness of this delusion, and he
thus appointed himself the task of giving the issue of the struggle
against Nazism a meaning for these two groups. Within the so-
called William Allen White Committee (properly, "The Committee
to Defend America by Aiding the Allies"), the American Friends of
German Freedom, the Inter-Faith Committee for Aid to the Democracies, and the Union for Democratic Action, Niebuhr rehearsed
the arguments which we have seen him developing for the small
family of faithful who read his *Radical Religion*.[16]

But this was not enough. Pacifism's greatest strength continued
to be among the clergy—and it would not do simply to hope that
the arguments which he propounded before the large and variegated
audiences provided him by the William Allen White Committee
would meet the needs of the perplexed clergyman. The most important non-denominational paper, the *Christian Century*, was becoming more explicitly pacifist with every issue; and, with a vigorous
parting blast ("To Prevent the Triumph of an Intolerable Tyranny,"
December 18, 1940), Niebuhr left the *Christian Century* taking
some of the clientele with him.[17] He had for some months been preparing the readers of *Radical Religion* for the parting-of-the-ways.[18]

As a respected voice in the church, and as a one-time proponent
of religious pacifism, Niebuhr felt a special responsibility to preach
against the dogma of Christian pacifism in an hour when its counsels
could encourage the triumph of the "intolerable tyranny" of Hitler.
Niebuhr's production of anti-pacifist pieces had increased steadily
since Munich.[19] But these articles and pamphlets were not enough.
Events moved too swiftly. To be able to exercise an effective influence on the thinking of the American clergy (and through them,
upon their congregations) he had to be able to present his arguments
against the background of the day's news. *Radical Religion*, a

quarterly, could not do this job. Thirteen issues of the *Christian Century* would pass the desk of a subscribing clergyman before Niebuhr could say his piece again to that portion of the same audience which read his *Radical Religion*. Thus, Niebuhr decided to launch yet another journal—a bi-weekly, appropriately titled, *Christianity and Crisis*.[20]

*Christianity and Crisis* would eventually prove to be a highly effective and influential voice of the Protestant social conscience in our time. By 1966, it had a circulation of about seventeen thousand, mainly clergymen, but also including a large number of laymen who placed some stock in its careful assessments of current social and political issues. In the beginning, however, this small (usually eight-page) journal dealt so single-mindedly with the one great issue of intervention, that one would have been justified in predicting that it would vanish from the scene with the coming of the war.

In the beginning the paper was dedicated wholly to representation of the Allied cause.[21] In the ten months between its first issue (February 10, 1941) and the first issues to appear after Pearl Harbor, there is no development of views to be traced. The very first of Niebuhr's signed articles[22] declares the thesis: "That there are historic situations in which refusal to defend the inheritance of civilization, however imperfect, against tyranny and aggression may result in consequences even worse than war"; and that many clergymen are tempted to this refusal by a dangerous "Christian perfectionism which is too easily compounded with an irresponsible and selfish nationalism." To those whose doubts derive from Marx, he announced:

> We believe the task of defending the rich inheritance of our
> civilization to be an imperative one, however much we might
> desire that our social system were more worthy of defense. . . .
> We do not find it particularly impressive to celebrate one's
> sensitive conscience by enlarging upon all the well-known evils of
> our Western world and equating them with the evils of the
> totalitarian systems. . . . Nazi tyranny intends to annihilate the
> Jewish race, to subject the nations of Europe to the dominion of
> a "master" race, to extirpate the Christian religion, to annul the
> liberties and legal standards that are the priceless heritage of
> ages of Christian and humanistic culture, to make truth the
> prostitute of political power, to seek world dominion through its
> satraps and allies, and generally to destroy the very fabric of our
> Western civilization.

The short pieces in *Christianity and Crisis* of this year have an intensity about them, a fervor of expression that is not to be found in any previous or later product of Niebuhr's pen. For example, this expression of the stakes involved in the present crisis:

> Christians are aware that they are living at one of the turning points of human history. Because they know what the works of God look like through their faith that in Jesus Christ the Word of God became flesh and dwelt among us, they are capable of recognizing the works of the Devil when these appear. They know that in Hitler and in the society the Nazis have organized we face an incarnation of evil more diabolical than anything mankind has yet experienced. Here is a corruption of civilization which has sworn to destroy our civilization—a civilization which, with all its imperfections, tolerated the Christian faith and was slowly but surely responding to the demands of the Christian ethic.[23]

In keeping with the testimony he had made before the Senate Committee, Niebuhr refused to promise that the program of "all measures short of war" which he was advocating improved America's chances of remaining out of the war. His record on this matter (for the year 1941, at least) is much more creditable than that of any other supporter of the Roosevelt program of the same stature. Thus, he had no need to retract anything when war was thrust upon Americans by Pearl Harbor: in this event (to use the language of an article in *Christianity and Society*)[24] history simply "overtook" America. America's abstention from the responsibilities of collective security over the decade since Manchuria, he was now convinced, had made this outcome inevitable: "There is no escape from our moral responsibility and no evasion of our duty toward our neighbors in the community of nations. We are not the only nation which has had to learn that lesson. We are only the last to learn it."[25]

As relations with Morrison and *Christian Century* were turning sour, Niebuhr was giving more of his attention to the readers of the *Nation*. Since 1934, he had been in steady service as a book reviewer —his specialities being books on the theoretical aspects of liberalism, and socialism,[26] on communism,[27] on the new isolationists,[28] and a variety of religious themes.[29] In 1936, he became a contributing editor. This step was a logical one (though it would add further to the burden of work that was causing increasing concern to his family and friends). The thesis has already been offered in these pages that Niebuhr, in effect, created a constituency of his own through his early writing in the small-circulation journals for radical churchmen, which the liberal journals (the *New Republic* and the *Nation*) found it necessary to co-opt. As the editorial line of the *Christian Century* became uncongenial to his own Christian realism, Niebuhr began to depend more and more upon the two liberal journals as outlets. In consequence, his articles in these journals came more and more to take on the tone of the pieces that he had been writing for the *Christian Century*. Even the titles began to take on the ring of sermon topics. The suddenly drastic character of world affairs was making the tone and style of "the American Amos" as appropriate now for the "secular" audience as for the clientele of the *Christian Century*. It is not without significance that so many of that large company of middle-aged liberals of the 1950s, who were the hard-core of the Niebuhr enthusiasts in the "Vital Center" (the contemporaries, that is, of Arthur Schlesinger, Jr., and Hubert Humphrey, for instance) developed their enthusiasm for Niebuhr at this juncture, when "the Crisis" dominated everything else on the political horizon. It was a moment for a preacher with a pen.

Though *Radical Religion* provided him the forum he had so long wanted in which to preach to the Protestant clergy his brand of "Christian realism," and though the *Nation* served as an adequate soapbox for his pitch to the liberal intellectuals, Niebuhr was for a long while to remain politically homeless. He had written off the Socialist Party by 1940 because of its commitment to isolationism. Yet the corruption and reaction of powerful elements of the Democratic Party prevented him from taking shelter under that ample roof. The American Labor Party he rejected absolutely, originally (as we have seen) because of its domination by trade-union leaders, but increasingly because of its evident subservience to Communist leadership.[30] The party he wanted was one which would bridge the gap between liberal intellectuals (whose votes were now scattered three ways: Democrat-New Deal, A.L.P., and Socialist) and· those trade-union liberals who had supported the A.L.P. because they wished to re-elect Roosevelt, but who had become wary of Communist gains in their ranks.

Characteristically, Niebuhr did not wait for someone else to do the job that needed doing. He himself sounded out the key people meeting the description just given. Mainly, they were disenchanted socialists, people who had signed the manifesto against Norman Thomas of January. Some came out of the ranks of Niebuhr's supporters in the Teacher's Union battle of a few months earlier. Others were trade-union figures (such as Murray Gross, of the ILGWU) who knew and respected Niebuhr as a veteran of Socialist politics. Out of these soundings came the Union for Democratic Action.[31]

U.D.A. was not a political party, though it aspired to be the nucleus around which a left-wing party of modified socialist principles might emerge. (As we shall soon see, such a party did eventually result.) It described its main work as "educational." It sought to influence opinion in the circles from which it drew its leadership mainly in three directions: towards acceptance of all aid short of war in support of the Allies (and, after Pearl Harbor, towards wholehearted support of the nation's military effort); towards democratic left-wing unity in demanding the preservation and extension of all the social gains made by the New Deal; and thirdly, towards insulation of the Communists from cooperation with left-wing politics. Its technique was basically simple: it boiled down to getting into the papers as often as possible, and on every available pretext, with some declaration in support of these ends.

It is impossible to gauge the influence of this effort with any precision. Only the *New York Times* gave much space to its unremitting flood of press releases. The President was certainly made aware of it, however; several members of his official family paid it the respect of appearing at its programs—as did Mrs. Roosevelt.[32] Though it claimed members in twenty-seven states, practically all of its activities were confined to New York State. In any case, the U.D.A.'s activities were vigorous enough to attract the attention of the Dies Committee[33] whose confusion was by now so compounded by all its bad guesses in recent months, that it persisted in believing that Niebuhr's organization was a political ally of the A.L.P.[34]

Probaby, U.D.A.'s greatest significance for the political historian is in its development of techniques of applying pressures upon politicians through the stirring up of debate on public issues. These techniques (which included, for example, the dissemination of box-score "ratings" for all legislators on crucial issues)[35] were a permanent bequest to citizen politics in America. The principal beneficiaries were its two lineal successors, the Liberal Party and the Americans for Democratic Action.[36]

It was the U.D.A. which spearheaded the effort to strengthen the non-communist elements in the A.L.P. by way of primary contests during 1942.[37] The failure of this attempt led to the exodus of "right-wing" members from the A.L.P. (men like David Dubinsky and Alex Rose) and made possible the formation of the Liberal Party.[38] Here again, Niebuhr's position was pivotal; he was both the principal leader of U.D.A. and a member of the National Political Action Committee of the C.I.O., the other major sponsor of the party.[39] Adolf Berle, Jr., who played a powerful role in these organizations, regarded their primary accomplishments as two-fold: they established a working alliance between New York intellectuals and liberal-minded labor leaders, often functioning as a decisive make-weight factor in New York politics as late as 1970 (in the re-election of Mayor Lindsay;) and they isolated Communist forces from the democratic left, probably forever. Both of these accomplishments, at least in New York State itself, Berle regarded as "direct achievements" of Reinhold Niebuhr.[40]

The strongest indication of Niebuhr's almost charismatic function in these circles is that when he began to curtail his work for U.D.A., in view of his new responsibilities as Vice-President of the Liberal Party, U.D.A. almost immediately began to wither on the vine. It was then that other hands took up the task of creating a more broadly-based successor movement, called Americans for Democratic Action.[41] A.D.A. carried the techniques perfected by Niebuhr's U.D.A. into the national arena with a greater success than Niebuhr had ever had. Niebuhr presided over the formation of A.D.A. in January of 1947, and was its Vice-President.[42] But the limited energies left to him after a series of small strokes that began in 1952 never allowed him to be as active in as many capacities as, in his vigorous fifties, he had been for U.D.A.

All of this—the lectures, the books, the political activity—is a matter of public record. Yet there was an incredible amount of activity as well below the surface of public notice. Of Niebuhr's many unpublicized involvements during these years, it is safe to say that probably none but a few friends—perhaps no one but his wife —knew of them all. Simply establishing a retrospective inventory of them all—as we can now do, with reasonable thoroughness, by means of Niebuhr's papers at the Library of Congress—is an exhausting chore.

The reader is asked to recall our earlier discussion of Niebuhr's labors for the Delta Cooperative, which continued into the early forties. Add to that his service on the executives of several committees drawing public attention to the large issues raised by the war and which would continue into the years of peace: the American Friends of German Freedom, the American Friends of Captive Nations, the American Association for a Democratic

Germany, the American Committee for Christian Refugees, the American Christian Palestine Committee, The World Council of Churches' Commission on a Just and Durable Peace, the Committee for Cultural Freedom, the Resettlement Campaign for Exiled Professionals, and many others.[43]

In addition, Niebuhr was contributing to the war efforts of the Roosevelt Administration in a number of ways. This work began with his appointment to a committee of three which was to attempt to clarify for the President and his Cabinet the implications of the policy forecast by the President in his "Four Freedoms" speech of January, 1941. He made trips to the camps in England to report to the Government on troop morale and discipline. He served the State Department as an adviser on the German domestic situation, drawing for these purposes on his continuing contact with figures in the anti-Nazi underground of Germany.[44]

Of his many unpublicized labors, one seems especially worth recalling: that is, his activity on behalf of refugees from Hitlerism and the European wars. Niebuhr was a major figure in this fascinating story.[45] His connections with the German academic community (particularly with the theologians) went back to the early thirties (as we have seen). During the decade, increasing numbers of these sought escape from Hitler's Germany—and after 1940, from Vichy France—by appealing for sponsorship by American citizens as immigrants to the U.S. under clause 4d of the National Origins Act (1917), which allowed the granting of non-quota immigrant visas to clergymen, to teachers in higher education with assured positions in the U.S.—and to their families.[46] Niebuhr was, in effect, a broker between his large acquaintanceship in the academic community and these desperate Europeans. It would require a very hard heart, indeed, to read without emotion the large files that contain the remains of Niebuhr's correspondence during the thirties and early forties with European seekers of sponsors, with American clergy and academics who were candidates for sponsorship, with colleges and theological seminaries for the necessary jobs (in a time when these were scarce enough for Americans), with State Department officials, and with all and sundry of his American acquaintances for money. It began with Paul Tillich (as we have seen) in 1933. In 1935 Niebuhr met in Europe[47] a key figure of the exiled German Social Democrats —Karl Frank (alias, Paul Hagen), leader of the *Neu Beginnen* (New Beginning), the younger element of German Socialists who repudiated the leadership claimed by the survivors of the Social Democratic Executive of 1933 (the Sopade Bureau, as they were called).[48] Through an American organization called Friends of German Freedom and a British organization called the Academic Assistance

Council (under Leo Szilard),[49] and, after the capitulation of France, through the Emergency Rescue Committee,[50] Hagen was able to keep American academics interested in the fate of the anti-Hitler opposition in Europe. Unhappily, Hagen did not have the unqualified admiration of all exiles from Nazism. The bitter political quarreling on the German left that had originally made possible Hitler's internal successes continued into the *diaspora*; in fact the factions became more irreconcilable than ever.[51] The campaign to discredit Paul Hagen threatened again and again to jeopardize Niebuhr's vital work of rescue; and many hours went into the writing of letters to sponsors of his work who were being unsettled by the whispering campaign against Hagen.[52] A good case could be made that only Niebuhr had the required combination of qualifications (stature in the American intellectual community, friends in the State Department, and credibility among the German exiles of the Left) to have kept this work going. What can be said without cavil is that many of Laura Fermi's "Illustrious Immigrants" owe their lives to Reinhold Niebuhr.

Niebuhr has made out of dialectical theology something quite new, something genuinely American, while translating its concepts from the theological language into that of the philosophy of culture and social criticism, and kindling them with his prophetic spirit.[53] (Emil Brunner, 1956)

One almost hesitates to turn (as we must now do) from this description of political and other activities to remind the reader that our subject's *principal* preoccupation was not in these areas at all, but still where it had always been—in the teaching and writing of applied theology. In fact (though the reader will be forgiven an immediate reaction of disbelief), it was in these same incredibly active months that Niebuhr planned, developed, and published his most important theological work—undoubtedly the most influential theological work written in this century by an American.[54]

The book was prepared under almost irresistibly symbolic circumstances. In the spring of 1939, as war clouds gathered over Europe, Niebuhr flew to Edinburgh, Scotland, to deliver the first part of a two-part series of lectures for the prestigious Gifford lectureship; and in the Fall, after Great Britain had gone to war and as America's long agony of watchfulness began, he returned to deliver the second part, with the sound of falling bombs *literally* accompanying his words at times.[55]

Why should Britain need the ministry of an American theologian at this hour—and, especially, why should she need the "theologian of gloom" the celebrated re-discoverer of "original sin"—the one whom Archbishop Temple had greeted some years earlier with the words: "At last, I have met the disturber of my peace"?[56] Were not German bombs disturbing enough? And if one does have to hire an American theologian, shouldn't his theme be more modest than this one—"The Nature and Destiny of Man"?

Matching the ambition of the title is the range of scholarly reference. Many claim to find this book a difficult one. The basic problem seems to be with what one might call its texture. There are so very many threads of argument, each one leading through several chapters of intellectual history, compacted of scores (it seems) of the proper names and references to the works of theologians and philosophers—and all woven so tightly that one is compelled to stop regularly to recover one's bearings. But the arguments of this book —*if they impress one at all on first reading*, become more compelling with each subsequent reading. And with each reading one gains confidence in the solidity of the vast sub-structure of scholarly reference which makes this one of the most ambitious essays of our time into the history of western thought.

The speed of the composition of *Nature and Destiny* is remarkable by any standard. But it must be appreciated that Niebuhr had been rehearsing the argument of this book, and gathering the documentation for over a decade. One can follow the progress of this work through several of its earlier pre-figurations as the lecture-notes which have been preserved in his "Papers."[57] The earliest lectures are virtual scripts—clumsily typed drafts for some of the Edinburgh themes. Here in these early notes we can watch him doing the exercises, the scales, that set the technique that underlies the virtuoso performance which is the *Nature and Destiny of Man*. Each subsequent series of lecture-preparations gets slimmer, as the lecturer's improving grasp of the subject-matter permits a greater degree of emancipation from prepared text. New proper names appear, and new texts to illustrate the argument. If *Nature and Destiny* is "dense" to some, it is the density of compactness, not of opacity. "The Crisis" is pressing in upon himself and his audience, and he must go immediately to the heart of his argument. Later on (God willing!) he could return to some of this same ground, and develop all the sub-arguments, and offer more and better illustrations.[58]

For assessment of the theological worth of this book we will leave the reader to the theologians.[59] We must, however, say a certain amount here about the *sorts of argument* that it contains—and this for several reasons germane to the purpose of this present book. The principal of these reasons is that this book completed Niebuhr's elevation to the ranks of the very few most widely-read and discussed of Protestant thinkers. Emil Brunner is quite right in arguing that the distinguishing feature of Niebuhr's accomplishment—and, at the same time, the feature which most surely identifies him as an *American* theologian—is his success in bringing about a confrontation of European theology with secular thought. "With him," Brunner writes, "theology broke into the world.... Reinhold Niebuhr has realized, as no one else has, what I have been postulating for decades but could not accomplish to any degree in an atmosphere [that is, the atmosphere of continental, academic life] ruled by abstract dogmatism: namely, theology in conversation with the leading intellects of the age."[60] Despite the insistence of many theologians that Niebuhr is in fact dependent upon an unacknowledged ontology,[61] or (a variation of the same charge), that he is in fact preaching natural theology in the guise of revealed theology,[62] it seems to most critics that Niebuhr has been faithful to the main lines of argument of the "crisis theologians." (Certainly Brunner had no doubts about this.)[63]

To appreciate the point that Brunner is making about Niebuhr requires a brief *excursus* into the life-and-times of the German theologians in the nineteen-thirties. And again our starting-point is Karl Barth. In 1933, when Barth was a professor of theology in Bonn, the new regime of Adolf Hitler was able to badger and persuade a majority of the leaders of the Lutheran Church to restructure the Church as the "Evangelical Church of the German Nation," and to issue statements asserting the complementarity of Nazi doctrine and Lutheran theology.[64] The gist of their discovery was this: "A mighty national movement has captured and exalted our German nation.... God has given us this—to him be the glory.... We take our stand upon the ground of positive Christianity.... We see in race, folk and nation orders of existence granted and entrusted to us by God. God's law for us is that we look to the preservation of these orders."[65] It was Barth who took up the challenge of providing the theological counter-argument to the argument (which a majority saw as having the authority of Luther behind it)[66] of the Nazis. ("I am withstanding a theology that is today seeking refuge in National-Socialism," Barth insisted, "not the National-Socialist ordering of state and society.")[67] Imitating the Reformers of the sixteenth century, Barth and his followers produced "confessional" statements, to be signed by as many as would have the courage to do so and then thrown in the face of the blasphemers.

The principal of these confessional statements was written single-handedly by Barth, and is remembered as the Barmen Declaration of the Confessing Church (May 31, 1934).[68] The gist of this Confession is in these words: "We reject the false doctrine that the Church can and must acknowledge as a source of its proclamation, beside and in addition to this one word of God, other events, powers, forms, and truths as the revelation of God."[69]

This may seem a rather mild and even a vague declaration. But, as Barth later pointed out: "If you bear in mind that these words were written in the world of Hitler, Göring and Goebbels, and whatever the rest of them were called, it can be claimed that at least it was made clear that the attitude of Christianity to the State was rather different from that trumpeted abroad by the Nazis."[70]

Barth believed that the incorrect political position of the "German Christians" derived from a theological error: namely, the resort to "natural theology." William Nicholls explains Barth's logic in these words:

From his earliest days Barth had affirmed a sharp distinction between the Gospel and human culture even if that culture took a lofty religious and moral form. He had opposed every kind of synthesis between Gospel and other spiritual forces, every kind of "Christianity and . . ." programme. . . . The programme of the German Christians seemed to be proving this up to the hilt. The choice between Jesus Christ as the Word of God, and Jesus Christ *and* some kind of human religious insight was proving to be identical with the choice between Jesus Christ alone, and ultimate loyalty to the nation and Führer. As the further events of the thirties and forties unrolled, culminating in the horrors of the concentration camps, and the martyrdom of many Christians who defended the Jews or opposed the regime of Hitler, Barth had only too much reason to believe that his original conviction, however polemically expressed, had always been correct.[71]

When Emil Brunner came out, about this time, with a book (*Natur und Gnade* [*Nature and Grace*], 1934) arguing (somewhat ambivalently) in favor of finding a place for natural theology alongside revealed theology, Barth reacted immediately with an incredibly bitter book with the straightforward title, *Nein!* ("No!"). Its message is very simple: any traffic with revealed theology is traffic with the Devil![72]

Anyone not brought up in the German Lutheran tradition (and

thus not subject to the spell of Luther's thorny doctrine of the two realms) can only with great difficulty think himself into this bitter dogmatic debate—let alone know with confidence what side he should be cheering for from time to time. Perhaps our "pragmatic" conditioning makes it difficult for us to see where "theology" ends and mere "politics" begins in these debates. We read, for instance, that Barth, in his *Theologische Existenz heute* (June, 1933), was urging theologians to eschew all political work and political comment for the sake of the purity of their theology: "Friends, let us think both spiritually, and consequently realistically.... [Let us speak] only [of] theology, now as previously, and as if nothing had happened."[73] And then we are told that "he was the only German professor of theology who refused to take the state employee's oath of loyalty to the Führer without any qualification, and therefore lost his teaching post and was ultimately forced to leave Germany in 1935."[74] (Barth actually attempted to return to Germany to preach thereafter, only to be arrested and deported!)[75] Elsewhere we read that Dietrich Bonhoeffer, one of the pillars of the Confessing Church, and protégé of Barth himself, somehow managed to combine allegiance to the Confessing position, with these views (from a document entitled, "The Church and the Jewish Question," dating from April or May of 1933):

> Without a doubt, the Church of the Reformation has no right to address the state directly in its specifically political actions. It has neither to praise nor to censure the laws of the state, but must affirm God's order of preservation in a Godless world; it has to recognize the state's ordinances, good or bad as they appear from a humanitarian point of view.... Without doubt the Jewish question is one of the historical problems which our state must deal with, and without doubt the state is justified in adopting new methods here.... The true Church of Christ, however... will never intervene in the state in such a way as to criticize its history-making actions, from the standpoint of some humanitarian ideal.[76]

...and we are obliged to wonder whether the Barthian position doesn't let in by the back door what it so noisily and so righteously orders out the front.[77]

"The Church," Bonhoeffer believed, "has to recognize the state's ordinances, good or bad as they *appear to be* from a *humanitarian point of view*"! But then follows this curious and unexpected line of logic (in a passage excised from our earlier quotation, but following immediately upon the phrase, "from a humanitarian point of view"): "and to understand that they [i.e., the state's ordinances] are based on the sustaining will of God amidst the chaotic godlessness of the world. This view [i.e., the Church's proper view] of the state's action . . . *is far removed from any form of moralism . . . and is distinct from humanitarianism* of any shade through the radical nature of the standpoint of the Law. . . . It remains the concern of humanitarian associations and individual Christians *who feel themselves called to the task* to remind the state of *the moral side* of any of its measures, i.e., on occasions to accuse the state of offences against *morality*."[78]

The passages and phrases to which I have added emphasis offer us, I believe, the key to the ethical dilemma of the Barthians. There is, apparently, some source of "moralism" ("morality," "humanitarianism") apart from the Gospel. This is the domain of natural wisdom (including the law)—and is presumably within the purview of what is called "natural theology." About matters coming within these areas—"historical questions" (like "the Jewish Question")—the church is properly silent—though "*individual Christians who feel themselves called to the task*" may well want to speak up!

How tortured this argument is! The whole point seems to be that without the insights of secular wisdom ("humanitarianism," "moralism") the state *must sin*. Yet having an attitude towards "the moral side" of the state's actions is optional to the Christian. ("Individual Christians [may] feel themselves called to the task"; but then again they may not!)

Again, Barth's own political behavior is the best key to this dilemma. Eventually he realized that Nazism was an absolute threat to *civilized values* (as Niebuhr had done)—and (characteristically) threw himself energetically into the cause of urging resistance to Hitler's plans for conquest of his neighbors. Realizing the potential of his leadership among European churchmen, he directed fiery public letters to the Czech churches, calling upon them to defend themselves against Hitler—to "fight and suffer for all of us."[79] Similar *bulla* went out in the next few months to the churches in France and in England.[80] ("We count on you," he wrote to the French, "that you will not leave us in the lurch"!)[81] In 1942, Barth was writing to American churchmen with the same message:

> [The War is a] particularly visible form of the judgment of God upon mankind . . . . Over against this judgment of God, there are no degrees of guilt. . . . [But] *this* group of nations (the United Nations today) has on the whole remained more righteous than *that* one (the Axis coalition). . . . The more readily we realize and admit that we all stand equally under God's judgment in this war,

that this war in itself can assume the character of a serious
"police action," which, while bringing unavoidable suffering over
all, may be a defense of the righteous state, and the less that we
(who are in similar need of God's forgiveness) concentrate the
war effort on any single guilty person or nation, the more
cold-bloodedly and energetically will the war be waged, for then
and only then, will we have a good conscience in this hard and
terrible business.[82]

"A good conscience"! Reinhold Niebuhr saw the paradox immediately: this courageous and correct *political* action nonetheless
"discredits Barth's [own] theological emphasis: he had spent all his
energies to prove that it is impossible to mix political judgments
with the unconditional demands of the gospel.... We agree neither
with Barth's previous separation of the gospel from fateful political
and historical decisions ... nor yet with his present [1938] identification of the Czech soldiers with the liberty of the Church of
Christ."[83] When, in late 1938, Barth published a public letter, and
then a pamphlet, both directed to German Christians and urging
them to oppose their Nazi government,[84] Niebuhr wrote for the
readers of his *Radical Religion* an article which deserves quotation at
some length, since it draws together so thoroughly all the themes of
Niebuhr's dissent from the political implications of Barthianism:

> The Nazi press has published it [Barth's public letter] widely to
> prove that Barth's opposition to it was informed by political
> animus rather than religious scruples from the very beginning.
> More interesting still, Barth has published a pamphlet on "The
> Church and the Political Question of Today" in which he
> elaborates systematic conclusions from the position he took in the
> Czech crisis.
>     The pamphlet is important because it really brings to an end
> what has been known as Barthianism; for Barthianism in its pure
> form declared political questions to be irrelevant to the gospel.
> Barth conceded that Christians must indeed make choices between
> political alternatives, and that his own common sense judgments
> were on the whole socialistic, but he did not relate these decisions
> with the *content* of the gospel, which is solely a declaration of the
> mercy of God to men who are and remain sinners, whatever side
> of a political controversy they may choose.
>     These are exactly the principles for which we as Christian
> Socialists have stood, though of course we would extend the
> range of political judgments beyond those envisaged by Barth.
> We have insisted that we have no right to declare that only

socialistic political convictions are compatible with Christian faith
but that we have both the right and the duty to insist that they
are binding upon us and that they are organically related to our
Christian faith; and that we have the right and the duty to
challenge those who do not agree with us to validate their political
convictions in the light of their faith. The Church must not be
a mere forum of diverse political opinions. It is important that
those who speak from within the church should speak in terms
of their faith. It is also important that our convictions should not
be bound by any official position of the church, but that they
should be bound by a common faith.

    If Barth had arrived at his present convictions ten years earlier
the history of central Europe might be different, considering how
powerful his influence was in accentuating those tendencies of
Lutheranism which make it politically neutral.[85]

Will Herberg, an admiring critic of Barth, gives the game away
when he concludes a brief account of Barth's political adventures
into political leadership with the comment: "In this *indirect* way, a
Barthian social philosophy has emerged, and this theologian, *who
abjures apologetics* and desires nothing but to expound the Word of
God, has been *compelled by circumstances* to propound views on
society and the state that make him into one of the most influential
social thinkers of our time."[86] It is difficult to think of any significant "social thinker" of the present or past who became that as a
result of being "compelled by circumstances"—that is, who thought
of politics as being (as Barth himself speaks of it) characterized by a
pervasive "monotony," as "fundamentally uninteresting."[87] And
there is really no reason to make any exception of Barth; for there
is little evidence anywhere that anyone other than Will Herberg
regards him as "one of the most influential social thinkers of our
time." Barth's own theology, which includes his anathema against
taking political affairs "seriously," disqualified him from the outset for the title of "a social thinker." For Niebuhr, the case is quite
different.

    We are here in the difficult realm of Christian ethics. But surely,
as Niebuhr has pointed out in these two articles, the same dilemma
applies for Christians to all questions touching upon the relationship
between the two spheres of "revelation" and secular wisdom. It
should be clear from the context we have just provided how bold a
thing it is from the point of view of dialectical theology that
Niebuhr has done in his *Nature and Destiny of Man*. Niebuhr
plunges into the whole realm of secular thought where the contin-
nental theologians could at most (like Brunner) dip in a cautious toe

to test the temperature. Because of his relative insulation from the academic infighting of continental scholarship, Niebuhr never succumbed to the line of absolute hostility to secular thought which was the pride of the continental masters. He was able to avail himself of Brunner's own work in developing an adequate "anthropology" (i.e., a doctrine of Man's nature) out of the basic insights of "crisis theology"—and to carry even further than Brunner dared the task of presenting that anthropology as a corrective to what he called the "inadequate anthropology" of the modern mind.

Niebuhr placed a high estimation upon common grace. Replying many years later to the criticism of his historical theory by the Barthian philosopher Karl Löwith, he put the issue in these words: "I know that Christ is the 'light that shineth in darkness.' The question between us is how absolute the darkness is."[88] Thus, he was able to give to "crisis theology" an apologetic force that its founder (Barth) claimed was hostile to its nature—but without which it was doomed to become at best irrelevant to political life, and at worst accessory to the worst political crimes the world had ever seen.

Barthians saw the Gospel as something that astonished and affronted all culture. Niebuhr saw it in a more truly dialectical sense as something that could both astonish and affront secular culture (being "foolishness to the Greeks") and yet fulfill the hidden expectations of secular culture. Essential to Niebuhr's entire argument in the *Nature and Destiny of Man* is the belief that the meaning of Christian anthropology *at some point* can only be appreciated when we are confronting it with one or all of the rival anthropologies. He has been attacked from one side with the charge that his allegiance to the "Biblical view of man" in fact overcomes his receptiveness to secular thought;[89] and from the other with the charge that his real allegiance is to the works of "reason," with the appeal to "God-talk" being essentially arbitrary, selective and un-Biblical.[90] All that we can suggest in these pages is that the reader must satisfy himself by his own reading of the *Nature and Destiny of Man*, about the degree of Niebuhr's success in his ambitious undertaking of confronting secular wisdom with the Gospel and the Gospel with secular wisdom to the improvement of both theology and philosophy. The argument of *Nature and Destiny* is far too complex to be reduced to a précis of a few pages (though I have begun the project a dozen times, and rejected it finally as fatuous). Those who are persuaded of Niebuhr's success as a mediator between theology and secular thought will endorse Brunner's appraisal: "In [Niebuhr's] hands the new theological concepts were used to throw a light upon the spiritual and social framework of modern civilization and lay bare its fundamental flaws and errors. . . . Thus he makes clear the essence of both the present-day world and the Christian faith. With him theology broke into the world."[91] Those (like Kenneth Hamilton) who are not persuaded of Niebuhr's success will at least be obliged to conclude as Hamilton has done, that Niebuhr belongs legitimately in the company of those "neo-supernaturalist" theologians (Barth, Brunner, Bultmann and the others) who "appealed to what was permanent in classic Christianity over against every interpretation that could urge only its topicality. None did so to a further extent, or more convincingly than did Niebuhr. . . . Perhaps the sense of being liberated from the compulsory modernity of liberalism so as to be able to rejoin the long tradition of Christian thinking was the greatest blessing which Niebuhr's writings brought to his readers."[92]

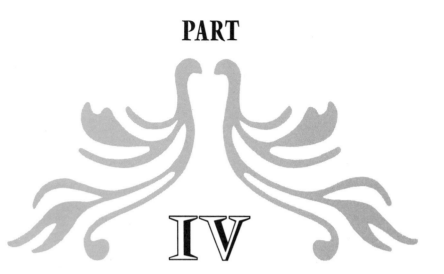

PART

IV

# THE THEOLOGIAN OF THE VITAL CENTER

*Chapter*

# 13

# BEYOND SOCIALISM

### A Vindication of Democracy

Pearl Harbor had a cathartic effect on the American psyche. It wonderfully resolved the debate about America's policy toward the belligerents in the global conflict of course, by lifting the United States bodily into one of the camps. But besides clarifying the immediate issues, it transposed the public philosophy into a robust and affirmative mode.

Not the least of the consequences of the great ongoing debate about neutrality during the 1930s was that it had seemed to cast its shadow of negativism upon every feature of the intellectual landscape. In the field of history, for example, it inspired not one but several revisionist forays into the archives for new interpretations of the motives of the great actors of the past—whose total effect was greatly to dampen the instinct to celebrate the past or the present of America. Similarly, a negative tone was dominant in academic and popular discussion of political and economic institutions. This habit of negativism had earlier roots—for example, in the historical research of Beard and Pratt. It seems, however, that it was the great debate attending the passage of the Neutrality Acts that brought these nay-saying modes into general currency. At the heart of the argument of the isolationists was a great warning against badly-invested enthusiasm. Enthusiasm—for institutions, ideals, traditions —was the meat that the Woodrow Wilsons of this world would feed us on; restraint and calculation were the virtues preached by the isolationists. The tone of their arguments set the style for discussion of public issues, past and present, in the best intellectual circles in the years prior to Pearl Harbor. And, needless to say, the effect was encouraged by the grimness of the economic scene.

Pearl Harbor suddenly set the *Zeitgeist* in motion in the opposite direction. The merest sampling of the non-fiction best sellers of 1942–46 should satisfy anyone as to the strikingly affirmative tone that suddenly appeared. (The effect was helped, not hindered, by the government regulations which restricted the quality and quantity of paper that might be used, but fixed a cartoon-Minuteman on the frontispiece of every book, to make the point about the spirit of national sacrifice that was making it all worthwhile.) The history-writing of the 1940s was marked by an affirmative, patriotic spirit which was in strong contrast to that which characterized the books of the 30s. Books on political and economic themes spoke positively now of the present, and especially of the future performance of American institutions. As for the war and the cause it embodied, the magic word was Democracy.

Reinhold Niebuhr found himself unable to get onto this band-wagon. He was still enough of a Marxist at least to believe that the political, as well as the economic, cultural and other institutions operative in western democracies, worked preponderantly to the advantage of the minority who controlled preponderant power (the capitalists); and that the habit of singing the praises of Democracy in chorus before breakfast, lunch and dinner in time of war, could dangerously dull the critical faculty of workers and even of intellectuals, disqualifying them for the real struggle for redistribution of economic advantages which must come after the peace. In the present mood of celebration of Democracy, church leaders as well as politicians were coming perilously close to the idolatry of identifying the cause of Democracy with the cause of God. As a believer in what he called "the radical openness of history," Niebuhr could not accept the corollary to this sanctification of Democracy—namely that God would not permit Democracy (His cause) to fail. Both privately[1] and in print,[2] Niebuhr insisted on facing up to the possibility of an Axis triumph. (That consideration immediately sets him apart from virtually the entire company of preachers in time of war, and from the purveyors of the official government litany on the same theme.) But, should God see fit to sustain us (despite the shameful lateness of our responding to our obligations), we had better have in readiness for the peace a more realistic framework for future statesmanship than this manic glorification of our existing institutions and of the national virtues reflected by them.

The lines of this argument culminate in *The Children of Light and the Children of Darkness* (1944).[3] The text for its ingenious thesis derives from the Gospel of Luke, 16:8: "for the children of this world are in their generation wiser than the children of light." The argument can be condensed thus: The traditional defense of democracy as a system of government has come out of "liberal culture," which is to say out of that dominant modern philosophy (against which *The Nature and Destiny of Man* was written) whose principal features are its optimism (about human nature), its "excessive individualism" and its idealism (that is, its easy "confidence...in the possibility of achieving an easy resolution of the tension and conflict between self-interest and the general interest" (page 2). Since the possessing classes in this civilization have a stake in maintaining the credibility of this incredible philosophy, we must admit that Democracy is, to some degree, "a bourgeois ideology" (page 1). Nonetheless, there are some "permanently valid elements" in Democracy, viewed both as an ideal and as an existing institution. The first step in the direction of separating what is permanently valid from what is "ephemeral" or historically conditioned, is to recover a more realistic conception of both the limitations and the possibilities of human nature. This is very difficult to do, since most of us are biased either in the direction of "cynicism" or in the direction of "idealism" when it comes to our assessment of our fellows. Historically, one or the other bias dominates the political philosophy elaborated in any given epoch by the intellectuals and expropriated (in defense of existing regimes) by the statesmen. In the most recent chapter, it is the idealistic bias that has prevailed. "Modern democratic civilization is, in short, sentimental rather than cynical" (p. 11). Our civilization has been built, not by children of darkness but by foolish children of light (p. 10). We can therefore expect that in the post-war world both official ideology and the mainstream of intellectual discussion will obscure the hard realities which continue as obstacles to the reconciliation of man to man at the level of national life and at the level of international competition.

To a degree, Marxism will be of assistance here. As against the predominant capitalist philosophy, it offers a measure of realism (p. 31). But the cynicism of the Marxists is selective and partial. Put aside the immediate programmatic side of Marxism and you find in Marxist millennialism the same heresy about the perfectibility of human nature that informs all of truly modern thought. For, "Marxism was also convinced that after the triumph of the lower classes of society, a new society would emerge in which exactly that kind of harmony between all social forces would be established, which Adam Smith had regarded as a possibility for any kind of society...(pp. 31–32). The charge that this is a creed of moral cynicism cannot be justified. . . . The Marxists, too, are children of light" (p. 32).

It is not that either the cynics (the children of darkness) or the idealists (the children of light) are right about human nature. The human situation is so complex that neither is entirely right—or wrong. It is rather that, against the prevailing *consensus* on the subject of man's nature, a realistic alternative will have to be one that has some place in it for the *fact* of original sin. For instance: on the matter of the individual's place in society, the bourgeois democrat sees no conflict in theory between the needs of the individual and the claims of society *in the present state of things* because he denies any sort of transcendent goal to man's striving, and can easily imagine the individual being satisfied at every point of his need by wise governance deriving from democratically chosen leaders; similarly, *in the future (post-revolutionary) state of things*, the Marxist envisages an identical state of affairs. Once one introduces the thought that an individual's vision properly transcends this world and what it can provide, the fallacy that makes possible both bourgeois complacency and Marxist millennialism is exposed.

Among the practical lessons that Niebuhr draws are these:

(1) "Bourgeois civilization is in process of disintegration" (p. 5). Its ideology is therefore highly suspect, and should be confronted with the charges laid against it by its only serious challenger, Marxism.

(2) "There is . . . a serious gulf between the social function of modern property and the emphasis upon its 'private' character in legal tradition and social thought" (p. 99). Marxist theory, "emphasizing the social character of industrial property is closer to the truth than the bourgeois creed which insists on its individual character" (p. 104).

(3) However: while "the logic of history [is] behind proposals for socialization, the logic is not unambiguous" (p. 117). The record of bourgeois government in recent times is by no means as black as Marxists have painted it. "Every modern democratic society has been prompted, both by its natural necessities and by the prompting of the voting power of the workers, to redress economic inequalities through the use of political power. This process has invalidated the Marxist thesis that the state is merely the executive committee of the possessing classes" (p. 104).

(4) A gradual, step-by-step approach is required. "Since there are no forms of the socialization of property which do not contain some peril of compounding economic and political power, a wise community will walk warily and test the effect of each new adventure [in socialization] before further adventures. There must, in other words, be a continuous debate on the property question in a demo-

cratic society and a continuing adjustment to new developments" (p. 117).

(5) In America, we are further behind than are the Europeans in applying the valid side of Marxism to the criticism and reform of our life. We are held back by "the anachronism of a too dogmatic and consistent liberalism and individualism. This is a consequence of the fact that the wealth, security and vast expanse of America gave bourgeois illusions a greater force in the United States than any other nation" (p. 105).

(6) "We must therefore expect more social friction and convulsion in the settlement of this issue than in Britain" (p. 105).

Years later, Niebuhr told an academic interviewer that this book, *The Children of Light and the Children of Darkness*, is "'about the U.D.A.' in a general sense."[4] The approach that Niebuhr takes (in what might be called the *practical* sections of the book) to the challenge of Marxist Socialism is one that would suit the political style of most members of his U.D.A. These were ex-Socialists for the most part, now ardent New Dealers, newly converted (like Niebuhr) to a more appreciative view of those American political institutions which had brought about the leadership of the President whom they had latterly despised. It is a moot point, however, whether the practical arguments of this book follow from the theological ones. It must be said that within the pages of this one book alone, it cannot be seen that they do. But this small book is really a kind of codicil to *The Nature and Destiny of Man*, applying the thought of the main text to specific issues that have been especially pressing. In other words, Niebuhr's ambivalent assessment of democracy; his endorsement of a more limited and critical application of Marxism to social theory; the arguments for a mixed (part capitalist, part socialist) economy; and the rest of the programmatic contents, *do* follow from the main line of Niebuhr's thought. There is no way in the world of persuading someone that this is so, if he has read both books and finds himself unpersuaded; but proponents of the thesis of the *integrity* of Niebuhr's thought have at least the obligation to insist that the two books be confronted before critics leap to the conclusion that the political theory and the theology are separable.

The point is, of course, that large numbers of admirers of Niebuhr's political leadership did read this small book—in many ways, his most approachable book—at the time; and, finding that it provided enough theoretical help to meet their own needs as moderate-socialists and enough of a practical programme to meet their needs as New Dealers, ran off with it into the arenas of political argument persuaded that the whole of Niebuhr's doctrine of man was now at their command. The woods are full of "Freudians" who once read

*Civilization and Its Discontents*, and of "Niebuhrian realists" who once read *The Children of Light and the Children of Darkness*. There was, for some time, and in the most improbable circles, something of a vogue for "original sin," as the ultimate argument-stopper against conservatives on one side and socialists on the other. The fault is not really Niebuhr's. We shall return to this theme later: but, for the record, here is where we find the beginnings of that vein of adulterated Niebuhrism that will soon be running through the work of political commentators and (with great effect) through a considerable sampling of government propaganda. Niebuhr does not say in this book that the practical attitudes he is taking on political matters do follow necessarily from Christian premises. He offers us a mere glance at his version of the Christian premises—and then a lengthy elaboration of his political attitudes. For him, the connection is necessary. For those who have read *and assented to* the argument of *The Nature and Destiny of Man* the connection is also necessary. Within the pages of *The Children of Light and the Children of Darkness*, the connection is not necessary —even (it must be said with all respect to the large numbers of those who read the book at the time) if one reads the book and *thinks* the connection is made. The most important premises of the Christian faith are left out of that book. There is, after all, good reason for leaving them out of a book that is about something else; and they *are* clearly presented in Niebuhr's earlier books (especially, *The Nature and Destiny of Man*).

With this book, the returns are at last all in on his long and ambivalent affair with Marxism. Its arguments exactly fitted what would be the policies over the next twenty years of Niebuhr's political comrades in the U.D.A., the Liberal Party, and A.D.A.[5] Like the others in this company, he would show an increasing interest in problems of international relations as the years went by, and by 1947 would be treating domestic affairs largely in afterthoughts, in-and-around the edges of his increasingly excited discussion of world affairs.

In addition to providing, in articles and books, a much-needed critique and vindication of democratic institutions, Niebuhr was busy with practical politics. We have already seen how he contributed to the formation of the Liberal Party, a device for keeping New Deal politicians on a larboard track. In a real sense, the formation of the Liberal Party enfranchised many thousands of intellectuals of Niebuhr's stripe, whose ballots for Socialist candidates of the previous decade had been mere gestures of protest, without effect in the choice of legislators. As a halfway house to the New Deal establishment, the Liberal Party was a place from which one could continue to view government critically while feeling that one was using one's ballot effectively and responsibly. Niebuhr's continuing distaste for the Democratic Party always colored his judgment of F.D.R. during his lifetime.[6] To the readers of the *New Republic*.[7] early in 1944, he put the case for Roosevelt so coolly that one wonders why he bothered to make any case at all.

> If Roosevelt is nominated and elected again (by the help of
> reactionary Democrats who will oppose his program as soon as
> the election is past), we shall have a very tired and ambiguous
> "New Deal" in 1944–48 and it will almost certainly usher in a
> period of terrible reaction in '48. . . . . If [the Republicans]
> nominate Willkie one choice will be as good as another, even
> though Willkie will probably try to sell us a "pig in a poke" on
> domestic policy. His election would have the advantages of (1)
> taking the idea of America's responsible relation to the World out
> of party politics; (2) avoiding a worse reaction in 1948; and (3)
> encouraging a new party alignment which would be arrested by
> a Democratic victory.
>     On the other hand a Willkie victory might produce an even
> more reactionary Congress than Democratic victory. If such a
> choice confronts us, we had better center on the congressional
> contexts, all the more so because recent experience proves the
> danger of relying on the presidency too absolutely for democratic
> advance.

But Niebuhr must have realized that the Republicans would not go back to Willkie; and when they passed him by for Dewey, they provided Niebuhr and other Liberals the excuse they were doubtless hoping to have for their support of Roosevelt: if the Liberals could not warm to the Democratic Party, they certainly could not hope for anything from the Republicans. In view of what is now known of Roosevelt's secret approaches to Willkie in the Fall of 1944, looking to collaboration in the realignment of the two-party system on a strict reformist/conservative polarity,[8] it is interesting that Niebuhr raised this very possibility in print in August of 1944.[9] But, while Niebuhr conceded Roosevelt's "tactical skill amounting to genius" in welding labor to his cause without really having earned this support in the legislative arena and while still retaining the loyalty of southern conservatives, he doubted that F.D.R. had the stature for so heroic a realignment of party forces as the times called for. "There are undeniable elements of greatness in this man. But nothing will avail to maintain his political authority after the conclusion of the war. His various reluctant supporters are bound to fall out amongst themselves between the end of the war and the end of the fourth term; and even Roosevelt's political dexterity will not be able to cope with the anticipated frictions. The fact is that his uncanny dexterity would long since have been subject to the law of diminishing returns had not the war intervened."[10]

A significant clue to Niebuhr's political mind at this time is to be seen in the fact that when Niebuhr turned from the more-or-less disinterested constituency to whom the words just cited were addressed (the readers of the British paper, the *Spectator*) to the readers of the official paper of the American Socialists (the *Call*), he put the case for Roosevelt in stronger terms. Thus, in reply to an open letter from Norman Thomas, appealing for his return to support of the Socialist Party in the election of 1944, Niebuhr publicly burned behind him the bridges leading back to the Socialist Party:

> The Union for Democratic Action contends that Americans
> cannot afford the luxury of a gesture toward a perfect program,
> while real issues are being decided on a much more modest
> scale. . . . Since the American people in the years immediately
> ahead, must not return to the mad Republican cycle of doom and
> depression, and since they will not advance to the Socialist
> Commonwealth, the realistic choice is a continuation of the
> present Administration in office, with a determination to push it
> forward along the paths of domestic reform and of genuine
> international organization.[11]

Still, it cannot be said that Niebuhr ever went gladly into political combat for Franklin Roosevelt during his lifetime. Nothing in the substantial body of commentary written by Niebuhr during Roosevelt's lifetime prepares us for the adulation that was the keynote of Niebuhr's ultimate assessment of F.D.R.:

> The New Deal era of our history [he wrote in 1963] radically
> altered the social climate and the political policy of the nation,
> bringing it abreast of all modern nations who had come to terms
> with the moral necessities of modern industrialism. It was
> achieved because a statesmanship in the proportion of genius,
> particularly in the art of pragmatic adaptation of old and partly
> contradictory principles to a new situation, was at the helm of
> the national government.

Roosevelt's political skill was apparent not only in working out a pragmatic *modus vivendi* between the traditional liberalism and the pressing necessities of a national government, dealing with a crisis of national dimensions, but also in using present emergencies to build a political structure which would be adequate for the future.[12]

There is a pattern of increasing complacency about domestic affairs traceable in the Niebuhr canon from 1945 onward to at least the eve of his death. If Roosevelt's stature as a statesman grew in Niebuhr's estimation only in retrospect, Harry Truman's grew steadily during his tenure in the Presidency, so that by the end of his Presidency he seemed to Niebuhr to stand on a par as a keeper of the social peace with the Roosevelt of Niebuhr's recollection. There is a fairly general consensus among historians nowadays that Truman received much more indulgence from his supporters of the liberal-intellectual community than his practical accomplishments seem to entitle him to—certainly more, considering the discrepancy between their performances, than Franklin Roosevelt himself seemed to garner in at least the last years of his life. The reason for this seems to be that the elements with which Niebuhr was allied politically now had a lien upon the Democratic Party, as they did not as late as 1944, through the A.D.A. (essentially the result of a pact between labor's political-action organization and formerly independent intellectuals of the U.D.A. sort).[13] It is not clear whether Niebuhr played any part in the A.D.A.'s pre-convention (1948) campaign to dump Truman for Eisenhower (or, *pis aller*, for Justice Douglas).[14] In any case, when the conventions were over, the A.D.A. wheeled briskly into line behind Truman, and turned the best energies of all its intellectuals to the manufacturing of rhapsodies about the fighting game-cock from Missouri, and variations on that theme.[15] From this there eventually grew the all-forgiving and unmistakably patronizing treatment of Truman which remained canonical in the history textbooks until the current season of revisionism.

Niebuhr's political attitudes were typical of the A.D.A. element in those years. He regarded Truman as the President "who saved himself from defeat [in 1948] by embracing the cause of the common man more unambiguously than Roosevelt did."[16] Niebuhr was apparently persuaded that the future of social and economic reform was now permanently secured. His complacency shows itself in his conviction that organized labor, by becoming a countervailing element in the political scales against business, had accomplished the fundamental redress of social power that secured the future of reform. This faith had become an essential feature of his argument for the abandonment of socialism in favor of "pragmatism." As late as 1957, Niebuhr could write that "the organized power of labor has come more to increase the health of both our economic and political life than any other factor. . . . It is a New Deal achievement that the two great giants (big business and big labor) are fairly evenly balanced. That solves the over-all problem of justice."[17]

Niebuhr's reputation as a political commentator will always remain colored by the fact that he became a fixture of the liberal establishment in days when men of a reformist bent were, for the most part, genuinely persuaded that problems of social policy were settled in principle in America. Retrospectively, their complacency is difficult to credit, and impossible to excuse. In Niebuhr's case, this lapse is doubly problematical, for it implicated him in the pro-pounding of a variant on that heresy of American exceptionalism which he so vigorously condemned in old-line liberal-idealists. Like the others in this company, Niebuhr would be accused by the generation coming of political age in the 1960s of muting discussion of domestic issues because of his fixation with America's role in world affairs. The historians of that generation would be presenting the argument that there was something bogus about the treatment by these "liberals" of domestic affairs—that their social programs were always expendable—and *were*, in fact, expended callously in campaigns to secure the lines of "the non-Communist left" on the foreign-policy front.

An article from the middle years of the Truman Administration serves as well as any to make the point of complacency on domestic matters:

In America no full-fledged Marxist movement has ever developed. If the lack of one retarded the political development of the working classes here, it also freed American labor from many Marxist illusions which European labor parties carry as so much excess baggage. The highly pragmatic and not very consistent policies of the New Deal first showed the American people how to use political power for correcting economic abuses. But the election of 1948 was more instructive than anything which happened in the Roosevelt era. For here a candidate seemingly doomed to defeat saved himself by embracing the cause of the common man more unambiguously than Roosevelt ever did.

The highly pragmatic type of progressive democracy developing in America, which is condemned by the reactionaries, as a halfway house to communism and criticized even by British Socialists as lacking in dogmatic rigor may prove better able to preserve democratic justice in a technical society than any of the alternatives of right or left. This can be our answer to Europeans who criticize the ambiguities of our political life.[18]

Is it necessary to make the point that the incumbent Truman Administration, for all of its "embracing of the cause of the common man," would finish out its days with virtually nothing of its Fair Deal program accomplished? And that it was to be followed by the Eisenhower Administration?

Yet, Niebuhr's thoughts on the future of social and economic reform in the 1940s and 1950s are worth returning to. Those who still count themselves as democratic socialists will resent Niebuhr's frequent abuse of the good name of socialism—as, for instance, when he writes (1955) that socialism, "in its traditional form [is] a spent force in current history."[19] Yet, if one will examine the specifics of his views on economic policy, one will find that he had not really budged an inch to the right of the formulation which he made in *The Children of Light* regarding the crucial matter of the right of the community to deal with the claims of private property. In private discussion, he was willing to admit that it was mainly the label that he refused; it was just too inconvenient to go on calling oneself a "socialist" when so many irrelevant and time-wasting arguments could be avoided by avoiding the label.[20] Toward this end, he organized all of his friends for a campaign for stripping the word "socialist" from everything that belonged to them and to which they belonged. Thus, the Fellowship of Socialist Christians became "Frontier Fellowship"[21]—hardly a triumph of imagination!

It is instructive to compare Niebuhr's handling of this problem of semantics with the disposition finally arrived at by his long-standing colleague in the A.D.A., John Kenneth Galbraith. Their positions on economic policy at every stage of the progress from wartime to the end of the sixties were identical—and this, in large part, because Niebuhr had great confidence in Galbraith's descriptions of the economic situation and depended upon him (as did the A.D.A. generally through the fifties and sixties) for policy expression in these matters. By 1970 Galbraith was insisting that the logic of the political hour now required the Democratic Party to declare itself *socialist*: "The Democratic Party must henceforth use the word *socialism*. It describes what is needed."[22]

But the problem of labels is only symptomatic. The deeper failing of Niebuhr's commentary on social and economic problems during the 40s and 50s is the scarcely disguised assumption that problems were solved in principle. Perhaps it was, as the younger critics affirm, a failure of nerve that caused that generation to settle the accounts so quickly on planning for domestic reform. Perhaps it *was* the case that they *preferred* to believe that domestic issues were "tolerably solved" in principle, because their best energies were expended in issues of foreign policy—and especially, of course, the great central issue of Soviet Communism. Most of that generation who lived to be active in the politics of the 1960s had to recant a portion of their earlier anti-Sovietism, as the price of reinstatement in the left. And all of them, when they returned in their writing to serious re-examination of the need for domestic reforms, would find that they had to make up for a great many years of neglect of such areas as racial inequality, urban decay, poverty, and the other issues which are now being found to be essential to the achievement of that social peace which Niebuhr had envisioned when he spoke of the counter-vailing force of labor and business as guaranteeing the solution of "the over-all problem of justice." For Niebuhr, it would be too late in the day for reinstatement on the left—though that is where his heart was until the end. The frailty of his health in the sixties excluded any opportunity for more than a few gestures of revision of his long-published opinions. The basic arguments of *The Children of Light* must stand as the most complete statement of his mature position on matters of economic and social reform.

*Chapter*

## 14

# TOWARD A JUST
# AND DURABLE PEACE

*It now appears that, though we have learned*
*many things about the character of life*
*and history from this war,*
*the nations are not likely to learn enough*
*to build a secure peace. (1943)*[1]

Discussion of Niebuhr's attitudes toward the problems of post-war policy for the U.S. should begin with a recapitulation of the story of his rather unique relationship to the "other Germany" that the public—and to a large degree, the government—had lost sight of. We have spoken of his close collaboration with exiled anti-Nazi political leaders in rescue and relief work. These contacts, of course, lived in fear of Allied vindictiveness. Echoing their fears, Niebuhr spoke out against the senselessness of Allied reprisal bombing of German cities, against what became known as the "Morgenthau Plan" for the "pastoralizing" of Germany, and against the adoption of the unconditional surrender policy.[2] These views put him in the minority corner; but as regards America's German policy he had always been in that corner:

> Yesterday we had to stand against the sentimentalists who
> declared that we had no right to resist Nazi tyranny because we
> were also guilty. They did not know that common guilt is a
> perennial fact in history, which does not annul our responsibility
> to strive for relative justice. Today we must resist the pharisees
> who imagine that our impending victory is the proof and the

validation of our virtue. Yesterday the sentimentalists falsely regarded the humility that men ought to have in God's sight as a reason for being humble in the sight of the Nazis. Today the self-righteous Philistines will seek falsely to play the part of God and try to summon the defeated foes to a judgement in which they are not involved. ... No matter how we turn this problem or from what angle we approach it, it becomes apparent that the punishment of a guilty and defeated nation is a very subordinate problem in reconstituting our world. If we become obsessed with it, it will prevent us from accomplishing our real task.[3]

Very much in Niebuhr's mind as he wrote of these matters was the fate of German Christians of the "Confessing Church" whose defiance of the "German Church" of the Nazis had been inspired by the preaching of Karl Barth and his disciples, and whose leaders were now languishing in Hitler's prisons. Some (like Dietrich Bonhoeffer) lent themselves in various capacities to active plotting against the regime, and would pay with their lives. Niebuhr's associations with many of these men were close and of long standing. He had tried, and failed, to dissuade Bonhoeffer from returning to Germany from his leave of absence in New York in July of 1939.[4] He was kept informed of Bonhoeffer's arrest, incarceration, and execution, through correspondence with Dietrich's twin sister and her husband in England.[5] Because of Niebuhr's intimate association with this circle of Confessing Christians, he was frequently called upon to explain and defend their behavior to officialdom and to the American public during the war and for many years after. For the sad truth of the matter is that few Americans were disposed to credit the possibility of such a degree of resistance among Germans to Hitlerism.[6] The fact that this spirit of revanchism towards Germany could preoccupy American hearts while one or another doctrine of "world community" captivated their minds, is perhaps the best revelation of how unprepared people were for the responsibilities that lay ahead.

The principal features of Niebuhr's vision for the post-war world appear as early as the latter months of 1942; and there is no real development to speak of until after the Potsdam conference.[7] In an article of October, 1942,[8] Niebuhr anticipated a debate developing between spokesmen of two contrary dispositions as Americans contemplate their future in world affairs. The "idealistic" (he also calls it the "rationalistic") disposition is inspired by the prospect of new beginnings after the war. "[Idealists] are inclined to view history from the standpoint of the moral and social imperatives that a rational analysis of a situation generates"—denying significance to the workings of human habit or weakness. As a result, people of this disposition are insisting that because *logic* and disinterested *moral* argument point to the necessity of a federation of the nations of the world, it is as good as accomplished. When the immediate diplomatic aftermath of the war fails to produce this arrangement, full-blown and viable, these same idealists will be quick with conspiratorial explanations for this failure. Thus, the present mood of "idealism" will beget a generation of cynics—unless we have the foresight *now* to temper our expectations with "realism."

The "realist" is less sanguine about the possibility of breaking the hold of the past upon the present. Even if he admits (as Niebuhr says he must) that the time has come for *attempting to implement* the long-cherished dream of a world community, he is more respectful than the idealist of "the stubborn inertia of human history." Realists are bothered by the fact that current idealistic talk "either disregard[s] the problem of power entirely, or ... project[s] some central pool of power without asking what tributaries are to fill the pool."

In 1942, Niebuhr's vision of the world community partook much more of the spirit of Theodore Roosevelt than of that of Woodrow Wilson (the inspirer of his earliest views on world affairs). Like Theodore Roosevelt, Niebuhr argues that there will only be as much international justice as the estate of international order makes possible; and *that* consideration must determine the matter of precedence.[9] "Order will have to be maintained for some time to come by the organization of preponderant power.... Power and responsibility must be made commensurate in the new world order, in a way the League of Nations was unable to accomplish."[10] "Constitutional arrangements [within the U.N.] that allowed smaller nations to determine policies which they lacked the power to implement, could become as fruitful a source of anarchy as unchecked dominant power could become a new source of tyranny."[11]

The youthful Wilsonian had matured into a rather hard-boiled Rooseveltian. It was a fairly characteristic pilgrimage for men of his generation. But where Niebuhr's record as a commentator on international affairs differs from that of the majority of his contemporary liberals is that he did *not*, between abandoning Wilsonism and taking up Rooseveltism, pass through the slough of isolationism. He is no less an internationalist in both phases. His faithfulness to the internationalist perspective was owing to two influences: firstly, his strong sense of community with European Christians (stemming originally from his spiritual indebtedness to the continental theologians, and secured by the manifold personal contacts with German churchmen and the anti-Nazi resistance); and secondly, his Marxism. While the latter of these influences was, by the forties, rather attenuated, certain habits of mind inculcated during the years of his more fervent advocacy of Marxism, remained with him forever. The chief of these was the habit of thinking of historical developments in global, never parochial, terms.

Niebuhr saw the leaders of the U.S.S.R. and the U.S. faced with a simple pair of alternatives: they might assume responsibility for a double hegemony of political authority in the world community; or they might invite the other nations of the world to assume an equal voice with their own in the future business of the United Nations. The second alternative led, he was sure, to anarchy. The price of rejecting the diplomacy based on the equality of sovereign nations must be some default on the rhetoric of wartime collaboration; but the price must be paid, and the outrage of all the other powers endured, if necessary.

Always the Anglophile, Niebuhr toyed for a while with a case for some sort of supportive role for Britain in these global politics. But his argument is vague at best, and dubious where it is not vague—turning on the assumption that Britain's leaders are specially expert in the arts of persuasion, and might thus, in the closed councils of the Big Powers, prove from time to time honest brokers between the Two.[12] But this notion was abandoned by Niebuhr in the summer of 1945—not coincidentally at the time that the British people abandoned Winston Churchill. Niebuhr stood in some awe of Churchill, the foe of "appeasement," while he had never forgiven the Labour leadership for their ineffectiveness in the face of Nazism. As for the other "Powers" (let alone, the lesser Allies), they must decide which of the two "hegemonous powers" has their best interest at heart, and line up accordingly.

But for Niebuhr, it was by no means a foregone conclusion that the United States would accept the responsibilities of world hegemony. In his articles of the years 1942–1945, Niebuhr speaks frequently of the temptation to "isolationism" as the obstacle to America's assumption of her proper responsibility for "internationalism." This is a very misleading nomenclature. In fairness to Niebuhr, it should be pointed out that he was more or less stuck with the familiar nomenclature of academic and journalistic discussion of foreign policy in the United States, according to which the chapter of busy intervention in the economic life of the whole world by American businessmen of the 1920s is called "isolationism," and the chapter of close collaboration with a constellation of Allies in a common political and military purpose during the Great War and the Second World War is called "internationalism." Perhaps the posture of the American people in the 1920s should be called "unilateral internationalism," and the other sort should be called "collaborative internationalism." Historians of the "revisionist" persuasion are agreed that there never was any possibility of America's retreating into isolationism, properly so-called, after the Second World War—and they depend upon this surely unexceptionable point to discredit Niebuhr and other "realists" of the time: their point being that "isolationism" had been a bogey employed to scare internationalists of all sorts, by the trick of compensation, into support of a policy of intrusion into the local affairs of every other nation and neighborhood in the world—and, in particular, into the local affairs of the Soviet Union and Central Europe.

But if one examines the substance of Niebuhr's argument, one discovers that he never pretended for a moment that Americans would willfully retract their attentions to within their own boundaries. On the contrary, he wrote in 1943: "Our greatest peril today is not the temptation to a complete withdrawal from world responsibility.... It is more likely that we will combine the impulse to dominate the world, to which we will be prompted by our undoubted power, with the impulse toward withdrawal, to which we are prompted by our comparative geographical security.... [We] have just enough power to make the policy of seeking security by an unmutual expression of power seem plausible."[13]

Niebuhr's concern was that America should have the grace—and the *realism*—to mix some "mutuality" (as he called it) into her internationalism. It is perfectly clear that when he spoke of the temptation to "isolationism" he meant the temptation to what I have called "unilateral internationalism."

If *isolationism*, properly so-called, was not in the cards, unilateral internationalism was very much so in the mid-nineteen-forties. The business community, as Niebuhr foresaw, hoped to set the style for the post-war internationalism. According to this model (whose most articulate proponent was Senator Taft of Ohio), the Government of the United States would keep itself unencumbered by diplomatic and military alliances, free-lancing its peace-keeping responsibilities by means, primarily, of a powerful all-ocean navy and a greatly enlarged air force, recalling all ground forces to within the American continent (what Taft called, "Fortress America").[14] It is true (as the revisionists argue) that the international ambitions of American businessmen had been greatly stimulated by the opportunities afforded in the post-war situation (the collapse of Japan's empire, the incapacity of European industry, the re-opening of the Far East and Middle East as the result of the crippling of the imperial systems of England, France and Holland). But the policy of military and diplomatic collaboration with a re-shuffled constellation of "Free World Allies" was not the fruit of those commercial ambitions. After all, a government as powerful as the American government was at the war's end could more effectively have run errands for the American business community *outside* of the constraints of the mutual security arrangements that that government did, in fact, begin to devise after the summer of 1945—as Taft, the ideologue of free enterprise capitalism, pointed out at the time.

Taft's alternative to the policy of collaborative internationalism, Niebuhr called by the name "isolationist imperialism."[15] Like Taft, Niebuhr expected the Soviet Union to show itself in an aggressively imperialist mood after the defeat of Germany; but he drew quite opposite conclusions from this expectation. Whereas Taft would use the probability of Soviet imperialism as justification for getting out of the way, and avoiding an inevitable clash on Russia's chosen ground, Niebuhr saw an obligation to sustain, with the threat of armed force if necessary, the independence of Western Europe. His arguments paralleled those made by Walter Lippmann in that same year (1943) in his widely read U.S. *Foreign Policy: Shield of the Republic*. There must be a new level of European unity—for their sakes as well as ours (the argument runs). We cannot permit the expected spirit of anti-German revanchism to stand in the way of an early reintegration of Germany into the political and economic life of Western Europe. We will have to defy the Europeans' fixation on outmoded political sovereignties and outmoded economic institutions in leading Western Europe towards realization of an early political and economic union. They must be "persuaded and forced [*sic!*] into a council of Europe."[16]

This leads Niebuhr to consideration of the basis for America's leadership. In part, he argues, her claim will be based upon her ostensible strength. But ultimately it will be based upon a moral claim. And the fortunate part—and here Niebuhr's argument takes a remarkable and unexpected twist—is that the moral claim is based upon a spiritual reality:

> Only those who have no sense of the profundities of history would deny that various nations and classes, various social groups and races are at various times placed in such a position that a special measure of divine mission in history falls upon them. In that sense God has chosen us in this fateful period of world history.

The world requires a wider degree of community. It must escape international anarchy or perish.

It so happens that the combined power of the British Empire and the United States is at present greater than any other power. It is also true that the political forms in which these nations move and the moral and political ideals that are woven into the texture of their history are less incompatible with international justice than any other previous power of history.[17]

Here, in this article of late 1943, is the first unambiguous appearance of a line of thought which will figure centrally in two short books of Niebuhr's later years dealing with the meaning of American history: *The Irony of American History* (1954) and *A Nation So Conceived* (1963). (We shall be giving extended consideration to the arguments of those books in Chapter Sixteen.) In this essay of 1943, as in a more developed manner in the later books, Niebuhr introduces the notion of America's "election," in the biblical sense. It is a notion that elicits little sympathy among intellectuals at any time and surely less sympathy now, in the 1970s, than when Niebuhr announced it. Critics of Niebuhr's part in the formulation of American attitudes toward foreign policy matters in the 1940s and 1950s are right in seizing upon this notion as the wellspring of his faith in America's essential benignancy in world affairs.

Unfortunately, Niebuhr's panic at the prospect of America withdrawing into unilateral isolationism hobbled his critical vision in regard to the American historical record. He seems to have felt that the only requirement of the hour was to prepare Americans for the exercise of leadership by overcoming what he saw as an ingrained and hereditary reluctance to use power. He seems to have felt that, given this ingrained reluctance, it was more than adequate precaution against the misuse of power to enter occasional portentous warnings against the "moral ambiguity of power" as an instrument of national purpose. A characteristic formulation ran along these lines: "It is not possible to build a community without the manipulation of power and ... it is not possible to use power and remain completely 'pure'."[18] *The lesson about the moral ambiguity of the uses of power remained subordinated until the mid-1960s to the lesson about the necessity of resort to power.*

Although Niebuhr's later observations on American history show some revision of his views, it must be said that even then he suffered obviously from what Arthur Koestler once called the "selective amnesia" that patriots are inclined to display towards their nation's history. It is not necessary to embrace the more hysterical manifestations of current revisionism to conclude that Niebuhr was astonishingly naive about such themes as America's nineteenth- and twentieth-century dealings with her American neighbors. He was still enough of a Marxist to be able to detect the hand of the businessman behind the impulse to imperialism that showed itself from time to time: as, for example, in his original inclination to explain the political success of General Eisenhower in 1952 as being "significantly engineered by eminent proconsuls of the budding American imperium, partly drawn from the Army and partly from business."[19] He saw the problem of keeping the American impulse to power within controllable limits as basically a problem of keeping the business community at a distance from the seats of power— agreeing, therein, with a crucial theme in the historiography of Arthur Schlesinger, Jr. But he did not see that the impulse to imperialism was in the character of the people, and nurtured by historical experience. He was, to that extent, a populist in his historical outlook.

Indeed, so great was his confidence in the innocency of the American people of imperialistic impulse that he would be arguing in the late fifties that American intellectuals and academics should be *consciously* inculcating in the popular mind habits of thought conducive to a more assertive role in world affairs: "A change in our public policy which [would give] moral and political legitimacy to the exercise of our 'imperialist' power, despite the historic roots of our anti-imperialism, is a desperate necessity for our nation, to which both the academic and journalistic guides of the public conscience must contribute."[20]

In the Kennedy years, his enthusiasm for a policy of explicit political imperialism reached its peak:

> We have a strong anti-imperialist tradition and yet are an imperial power, or are a hegemonic power possessing resources of imperial dimensions.... [Our anti-imperialistic tradition] does make for a certain hesitancy in exercising the responsibilities of our imperial power, since we fear that we may violate the cardinal principle of liberalism, the "self determination of nations." We cannot afford such hesitancy, even in a world in which the weak nations are as preoccupied with anti-imperialistic slogans as we are. If the social conditions of our client nations— whether in South Vietnam, South Korea, or, possibly, Saudi Arabia—are the kind which invite Communist infiltration, we must exercise the responsibilities of our power to correct them, even if such a policy can be effective only if the power is exercised with a minimal affront to the dignity of sovereign nations.[21]

His faith that the American people as a whole were innocent of the experience of having imposed their will on others explains why he so often preferred to see the American rather than some other European presence in situations where there were special temptations to the greedy or the vicious. He would, for example, show a most unseemly enthusiasm through the mid-fifties for getting the French out of Indo-China and the Americans in. "We are certainly more disinterested than the French in desiring only the health of the new nation [South Vietnam], and its sufficient strength to ward off the communist peril from the north. Perhaps we have done well enough to give us a better reputation in Asia as a political, rather than a military power."[22] Only much later (beginning in 1965), would he realize that there was something in America's history (and therefore in her character) that might specially *disqualify* her for certain historical tasks.

Niebuhr's furious display of energy on behalf of the Lend-Lease Bill had brought him to the attention of the Roosevelt Administration early in 1941. By his own recollection, his first contact with the Administration came about when Roosevelt appointed him to a committee (whose other members included Archibald MacLeish, Max Lerner and E. B. White) whose job was to prepare a position paper clarifying for the President the implications of the policy already forecast by the President in his "Four Freedoms" speech of January, 1941.[23] This proved the first of a series of advisory services that Niebuhr rendered for the Roosevelt and later the Truman Administrations. He made trips to the camps in England to report on troop morale and discipline.[24] During the war he served the War Department as an adviser on the German domestic situation, depending for his reports on his continuing contacts with figures in the anti-Nazi underground in Germany and France. While it is impossible to measure his influence here, his voice was certainly heard on the side (the then minority side) of a moderate policy toward the defeated Germany—against the Morgenthau plan, for example, which Roosevelt seemed at first to be enthusiastic about, but was eventually persuaded to abandon. In 1946, Niebuhr was sent to Germany as a member of the "U.S. Education Mission" to help in the formulation of a policy for securing the transfer of the educational establishment of Germany to reliable hands.[25] A substantial correspondence in the Niebuhr Papers between Niebuhr and the State and War Departments[26] indicates that Niebuhr was a considerable authority on the American side in certifying the trust-worthiness of the candidates clamoring to replace the Nazi leadership in the educational establishment, especially in the universities. As further evidence of Niebuhr's new favor in the eyes of government, the War Department was soon spending modest quantities of the taxpayers' money making reprint editions of Niebuhr's works available to German readers as part of its "Reorientation Program in Occupied Territories."[27] From time to time Niebuhr made other contributions on request of the State Department, to its propaganda services abroad,[28] and for a while he attended monthly meetings of George Kennan's Policy Planning Staff.[29]

During the immediate post-war months, many of Niebuhr's former colleagues in the political wars were developing the convic-tion that the State Department was veering to the right. In the liberal magazines and in numberless books published between 1945 and 1947, the argument was that Roosevelt's policy of friendly collaboration with the Soviet Union had been swiftly sabotaged after his death by the men who controlled the flow of information and ideas to the inexperienced Harry Truman. Though none of these authors (to my knowledge) mentioned Reinhold Niebuhr in this connection (since his role in policy-making was, after all, peripheral, and in any case not much publicized), it is worth noting one recurring *motif* in this argument (and in the argument of the later "Cold War Revisionists"): namely the matter of the unseemly haste allegedly shown by the State and War Departments in returning the reins of power in West Germany to Germans, and the suspiciously careless screening of the anti-Nazi credentials of these restored authorities.

Niebuhr's name does, however, begin to figure prominently in these debates in the liberal and radical camps following the publica-tion (October 21, 1946) of the first of two articles which he wrote for *Life* magazine.[30] In his later memoirs,[31] Whittaker Chambers claimed responsibility for the sharp change in editorial policy toward the Soviet Union and for the celebration of Reinhold Niebuhr as America's pre-eminent philosopher, both of which occurred in the pages of *Time* and *Life* magazines during 1946 when Chambers was the Senior Editor. (Reinhold Niebuhr was chosen for the "cover treatment" in the twenty-fifth anniversary issue of *Time* (April 29, 1946), the author of the unsigned feature article being Whittaker Chambers himself.) At least one of the Cold War Revisionists agrees with Chambers' estimate of the impact of Niebuhr's 1946 article from Germany. This is Walter LaFeber, who describes (in his *America, Russia and the Cold War*) the opening up of the "[Henry] Wallace-Niebuhr division" in the ranks of American liberals during

1945–47. Niebuhr, "the most formative contemporary influence on American liberalism," gave systematic formulation, LaFeber argues, to "the ideological assumptions" which underlay the philosophy of liberal cold-warriors.[32]

When Secretary of State Byrnes made the speech in Stuttgart (September 6, 1946) which declared his Government's disillusionment with the efforts at peaceful collaboration with Stalin in the affairs of Germany and Eastern Europe and projected the possibility of a new policy built upon American sponsorship of a restored German state in the Western portions,[33] he triggered the debate with Henry Wallace that led to Wallace's removal from Truman's Cabinet and Wallace's emergence, during 1947–48 at the head of those Americans who accused the Truman Adminstration of betraying Roosevelt's dreams for peace.[34] Niebuhr had seen and heard Byrnes deliver the speech in Stuttgart. In what was probably the most widely read article he ever wrote, he announced his support of the Adminstration's tougher new policy: "As one who belongs, broadly speaking, to Henry Wallace's school of thought in domestic politics, I should like to challenge Wallace's foreign politics as announced in his recent attack on Secretary Byrnes' policy toward Russia.... Europe's democratic forces are behind Byrnes and not Wallace.... For it is in resistance to Soviet expansion that all noncommunist Europeans, whether of left or right, see the only real hope of peace.... Russian truculence cannot be mitigated by further concessions. Russia hopes to conquer the whole of Europe strategically and ideologically."[35]

This article (whose argument was reinforced two years later in the article, "For Peace We Must Risk War," *Life*, September 20, 1948) established Niebuhr's reputation as the leader of the anti-Communist and anti-Soviet element among American "liberals." His responses to all of the major foreign policy initiatives of the Truman Administration—the Truman Doctrine, the Marshall Plan, the Berlin airlift, the Korean intervention, the establishment of N.A.T.O.—were carefully attended to by the audience on his side of what LaFeber calls the "Wallace-Niebuhr" division. His interpretation of these events conformed in all essentials to the main lines of the Truman Administration's description of world realities.

Walter LaFeber has noted a distinct "change of tone" entering Niebuhr's commentary on American foreign policy over the year 1951–52: a preoccupation with the "limitations of power" contrasting strongly with the call to arms of the two *Life* articles.[36] LeFeber exaggerates the contrast between the two moods. But there is certainly a shift in emphasis along that line; and LaFeber is no doubt correct in arguing that it owed much to the realization being forced upon all Americans in those days by the Korean War, that the keeping of the peace would increasingly involve them in Asia. LaFeber points to a similarity in the arguments of Niebuhr (drawn principally from his *Irony of American History* of 1952) with those of Hans Morgenthau (drawn from his *In Defense of the National Interest* of 1951). In Europe, providing resistance to communism meant giving assistance to the defenders of our common civilization, upholding the real will of a majority in their struggle to frustrate what Hans Morgenthau called the "phoney revolutions" stage-managed by Stalin to give justification to simple territorial covetousness; in Asia, both Americans and Russians were on alien ground.[37]

Comparison of Morgenthau (the principal architect of the "new realism" in American theory of international relations) and Niebuhr is fruitful to a point, but beyond that point misleading. Morgenthau and Niebuhr were in ostensible agreement in 1952 in stressing the primacy of Europe for American policy, and in basing the case for that primacy upon the fact of a shared culture and kindred constitutional systems. Secondly: they agreed in the argument that America's ability to achieve peace in distant parts of the world was ultimately limited by the degree of soundness of the political regimes she supported. The political ecology of the situation being what it then was, it would appear, therefore, that outside of Europe, America could expect to work her will for peace only in alliance with those relatively few regimes that had benefited from generations of tutelage under benign (invariably British, or, in the case of the Philippines, *American*) imperial masters. Elsewhere, the fruits of imperialism had been social, racial, and economic upheaval: "genuine" revolutionary situations, upon which Communist propaganda could feed and, for a while at least, make political hay. But Morgenthau, unlike Niebuhr, expected the Soviet Union to gain little or nothing *permanent* from whatever propaganda forays she undertook in these areas (China, South-East Asia, the Near and Middle East, Africa and Latin America). *Realistically*, Morgenthau calculated that these potential Soviet clients would soon weary of the Soviet's heavy-handed solicitations; historical-geographical enmities (as in the case of China), or political frictions deriving from great cultural differences (as between the Moslem faith and Soviet atheism would increasingly come into play—and the Soviets would find themselves back at the starting-line with the Americans in the race for friends and influence in the Third World. And history has largely borne out Morgenthau's logic.

There is ample evidence in Niebuhr's commentary on world politics (down, at least, to the mid-sixties) that he did not really grasp this point nor its obverse side: namely "the end of the bipolarity centered in Washington and Moscow." Or perhaps he thought of this outcome as being so remote as to be useful only as a sort of "eschatological argument." Or perhaps it was not a case of his not *expecting* the end of the Washington/Moscow bipolarity, but rather of his not really wanting it! It seemed to fit the logic of history that America and Russia should at this hour be stalking one another around the world. Tocqueville had predicted it. Its apocalyptic fitness seemed to captivate Niebuhr.

Well before the end of the forties, a noticeable hardening of the categories had overtaken Niebuhr's commentary on world affairs. The "realist" was, on the One Great Issue, perilously close to becoming a Cold War ideologue. It is true that Niebuhr, when his attention was on issues of political and military policy, liked to employ the sort of "realistic," no-nonsense, hard-boiled, "secular" logic that Morgenthau was making mandatory for political theorists. Thus, he echoed Morgenthau in making the case, in terms of geopolitics, against getting bogged down in war on the Asian mainland on behalf of regimes only superficially westernized and really lacking in true authority with their own people. But there is a most significant inconsistency in his use of this logic. In fact, he was frequently tempted to see in the very weakness of certain Third World political regimes an opportunity for initiative on the part of the United States. In the early fifties he was talking about opportunities for extending American "tutelage" to certain promising but politically fragile Third World regimes. By the late fifties, he was talking less ambiguously about them as "clients."

The fact is that he could not come to terms *intellectually* with what Morgenthau saw as the end of "bi-polarity." A clue to this is in his recurring use of the notion of "the nuclear umbrella"—a theme that approaches obsession with him in the early sixties. The metaphor was invented by him as a way of wringing some positive element of hope out of the grave concern that everyone felt in those days about the possibility of nuclear annihilation. The point of departure is the argument that because only the two great powers had the capacity to launch a war ending in nuclear annihilation, they must learn to respond circumspectly to one another's diplomatic or military initiatives. By stages, this developed into the argument that the habit of such circumspect behavior *had* developed —as was allegedly demonstrated by the Soviet Union's backing-off from confrontation over Berlin in 1948, over Suez in 1956, over Cuba in 1961 and 1962; and by America's corresponding restraint over Hungary (in 1956), over the Chinese off-shore islands (in 1954–55).—and so on. By stages, this grew into the explicit argument that the bipolar nuclear standoff was underwriting the peace of the future.

By way of illustration: in an article of 1959,[38] wherein he is making the case that the Soviet Union has great advantages over the U.S. in the "ideological struggle" for the allegiance of Third World regimes, Niebuhr unexpectedly veers away from the apparent logical outcome (namely, that the United States should get out of, or at least greatly reduce her commitments in the Third World) with the statement: "Since the struggle is not purely ideological we can feel secure for some time under the umbrella of an atomic stalemate" —which, being translated and considered in the context of the whole article, means that the United States can to a large degree defy Soviet ambitions, and the logic of history, precisely because of the theoretical possibility of nuclear holocaust. Or again (from an interview in *Harper's*, December, 1960): "The only chance that I see of survival is a gradual growth of community across the chasm of this international enmity, under the umbrella of a nuclear fear— rather than any provisional disarmament set-up."[39] Or again (from an article of 1962):

On the one hand, the precarious peace of the world is threatened by the possibility of a nuclear catastrophe, which may always occur by technical or political miscalculation or misadventure. On the other hand, the peace is preserved because, for the first time in history, both contestants possess nuclear destructive power of such magnitude that the party which initiates the ultimate conflict is bound to be met with a retaliatory strike which may well be more destructive than the sum-total of all the wars of history. The peace secured by this "balance of terror" is obviously dependent upon a fairly stable balance, despite the fact that each side is bound to increase its advantages in this or that category of nuclear weapons or means of delivery or to redress any real or imagined disadvantage in each category. This "arms race" is pregnant with its own dangers, which ought to be and will be discussed by competent authorities. It will not be discussed within the limits of this chapter, both because of the author's lack of technical competence and because of the conviction that the balance of terror gives us, ironically enough, a precarious peace, which is bound to shift the problem of the prospects of peace to the political sphere.[40]

It should be noted how the argument about "the nuclear umbrella" has become an argument against taking disarmament seriously. "Terror" has become, willy-nilly, a necessary component in the basically benign, but in any case *inevitable* continuance of America's role as a "hegemonic power"! In painful truth, the "nuclear umbrella" had become, by the 1960s, an ever-available red-herring to be dragged across the path whenever Niebuhr began to feel too uneasy about the shape of politics-to-come.

That it served this purpose in the arena of domestic as well as international politics is evident, for example, in an article, "Revolution in an Open Society," of 1963. Here Niebuhr has been speaking appreciatively of the accomplishments of Martin Luther King; but, feeling (correctly, no doubt) that there is harm to be done in overlooking the great cultural and political obstacles that stand in the way of the accomplishment of complete desegregation, he concludes, without any preparatory discussion at all of international issues, with the staggering *non-sequitur*: "We will have the tension of the integration struggle with us as long as we live in the precarious peace of the nuclear dilemma."[41]

By way of empirical support for the bipolar logic in which his international theorizing was set, he came back again and again through the 1950s and early 1960s to the fact of monopoly of nuclear weapons enjoyed by the two super-powers; and when that monopoly was undone, to the alleged uniqueness of the U.S. and the Soviet Union in having enough nuclear might and deliverance-capability to deal pre-emptive strikes against any one nation (including each other). He was astonishingly late (given his lavish attention to the theme of the "limits of Power") to recognize how irrelevant such brobdingnagian might is, for example, in situations of guerrilla warfare. It is difficult to follow Niebuhr's logic that nuclear standoff would increase the authority of the super-powers and the dependence of lesser powers upon them; the record is clear that as confidence has grown (rightly or wrongly) that the U.S. and the U.S.S.R. dare not push one another to the brink, the lesser powers have become increasingly obstreperous.

An article dating from the early months of Kennedy's Presidency[42] reveals how far he had advanced from the logic of limited involvement in the Third World to a position of political imperialism. From a familiar starting-point—that "Western democracy is an ultimate political ideal which requires greater political skill, cultural adequacy and a more fortunate balance of social forces than are available for many non-European or, more accurately, non-technical nations"— he develops the argument that we should define more modestly than we have done hitherto our hopes for the "non-technical nations."

Thus, the goal of "establishing freedom" is simply too remote a goal to deal realistically with (though it remains "the ultimate goal"). We should settle instead for the goal of "stability." "[We must] cease defining our cause, too simply as the cause of 'freedom,' when the political task is always to make freedom serve the justice and stability of the community. It [that is, this revision of our expectations] might make us more tolerant of military dictatorship." So far, Niebuhr has carried us no further than the logic of the Truman Doctrine ("The Government of Greece is not perfect"). But the degradation of the "polarized" logic of the post-war realists is completed in what follows: "Dangerous as they are, they [military dictatorships] are at least reversible and Communist dictatorship, supported by a religio-political dogma, is irreversible." (Significantly, Niebuhr offers us no examples of the alleged reversibility of military dictatorships.) Once the implementation of "freedom" for "non-technical nations" is postponed to the millennium, practicality can thus claim its proper place:

> An honest acknowledgement of the ultimacy of our democratic ideals and of their immediate irrelevance will certainly prevent us from debasing democracy into a competitive utopian creed with Communism. . . . If we are generous enough in our sympathies for all types of political regimes, except those which combine pretensions of omniscience with pretensions of omnipotence, we may become in time a truly global movement, rather than a conventicle of European liberal democrats. Our policies would still be tough; but they would be flexible enough to accommodate the various levels of cultural and economic and political civilization with which we must deal as an imperialistic nation, as one of the two imperial nations who now bestride this narrow world and hold the fate of mankind in their hands.

For "regimes which combine pretensions of omniscience with pretensions of omnipotence" we are meant to read "Communist regimes"—as is clear from the argument of the article as a whole. The regime of Kwame Nkruma (which in its own weird and wonderful way *surely* combined pretensions of omniscience with pretensions of omnipotence), Niebuhr explicitly reckons as an eligible (because non-Communist) client-state.[43]

Not coincidentally, Niebuhr's enthusiasm for the pursuit of an imperialistic policy was at its height during John F. Kennedy's brief Presidency. He was infatuated with Kennedy's performance and (sad to relate) much too much influenced by the assurances of Kennedy's intellectual courtiers (many of whom, like Arthur Schlesinger, had been Niebuhr's close political allies for many years). Even his literary style—always (for better or for worse) impervious up till now to transient modes of journalistic style—began to be affected, taking on something of the bargain-counter-Hemingway bathos that Theodore Sorensen and Arthur Schlesinger had made part of the New Frontier style. An article, "A Tentative Assessment,"[44] written in the immediate aftermath of the assassination, bears the significant subtitle, "Royalty and Politics," and rings all of the changes on the central themes of the Camelot myth: that "style" generates program; that the essential qualification for creativity in foreign policy is "toughness," and that its rewards are "stature" and "prestige." Niebuhr had no difficulty in supporting the whole of Kennedy's foreign policy, without significant qualification. This was because Niebuhr and Kennedy saw world affairs from the same ideological perspective. Niebuhr, like Kennedy, had hit upon the theme of "complacency" as the best stick to beat the Republican record with, during the early weeks of the political season of 1960. He anticipated one of Kennedy's issues (the "missile gap") as early as February, 1960; there is, he wrote, "a frightening complacency" rampant in the land: "More interested in a balanced budget than in technical advancement, we have allowed a nation which we complacently regarded as backward to establish superiority over us in ballistic and missile achievement. As a result, we shall be really insecure for at least the next five years."[45] Kennedy's own expansions upon this theme encouraged Niebuhr's inclination to Churchillianism. Thus, when President Kennedy went to the people on television to announce preparations for a confrontation with the Russians over Berlin ("as Americans know from our history on our own old frontier, gun battles are caused by outlaws, and not by officers of the peace")—preparations which included a massive dispatch of troops to Europe, provocative "tests" of U.S. rights of access to Berlin by land, and a crash program of public and private "fallout shelter" construction—Niebuhr applauded the performance as a legitimate, indeed an *obligatory* defense of national "prestige." "['Prestige'] holds a central place among components of political authority.... Both sides are really aware, or should be, that the prestige advantages are with Communism in Asia and Africa and with democracy on the European continent.... Berlin is clearly the apex of the pyramid of prestige which is our stake in Western Europe. If we yield on Berlin, even Germany—as Adenauer hints— may be tempted to neutralism."[46] (In fairness, we should note Niebuhr's recommendation that the United States prepare the way for negotiations a little more imaginatively, by abandoning "the shibboleth of German reunification"—something which, he said, the

West Germans cannot do, because of emotionalism attaching to the issue in Germany.) His support for the perilous Cuban blockade of 1962 was similarly eager and equally unqualified.[47]

Niebuhr's commitment to the basic conceptions of the Cold War view of international realities was as inflexible as at the time when he was writing foreign policy statements for a newly-launched A.D.A. It was a case-hardened tool of interpretation, hardly touched by the realities of spectacular discord within the Communist world; indifferent to considerations of the relatively humane accomplishments of Communist regimes ("relative," that is, to the performance of so many of those "non-ideological military regimes" which by his own increasingly eccentric canons of "realism" should be America's client-allies in the cause of freedom). At the root of this fixation was his patriotic ambition for America's success in the world—a success to be reckoned in terms of the ever-increasing effectiveness of her writ throughout the "non-technical world." It is clear that he could not envisage aggrandizement of America without diminishment of Russia. In plain language (from which Niebuhr himself, in the Kennedy years at least, did not flinch), this required a conscious unapologizing policy of *imperialism*. No more than Woodrow Wilson was Niebuhr able to avoid the hazards for the soul of faith in the ultimate benignancy of America's imperialism. Niebuhr was fond of quoting John Adams' famous dictum on the subject: "Power always thinks it has a great soul and vast views beyond the comprehension of the weak, and that it is doing God's service when it is violating all His laws."[48] Yet his own case for America's empire among "the weak" of the Third World was based on nothing else than his confidence in the vast views beyond their comprehension, which America's exceptional accomplishments in the realms of political and social democracy provided her.

His interpretations of the circumstances that made the United States a "hegemonous power" had more and more taken on an ideological coloration. So had his interpretation of the circumstances that had put the U.S.S.R. in the same situation. In 1943, when he was making the case for cooperation with the U.S.S.R. in keeping peace in the post-war world, he spoke hopefully of "ironing out our ideological differences"—which was possible, he argued, "if we assume that neither side has the complete answer to the vexatious problems of social and political justice."[49] He had made a point, in those days, of insisting upon the distinction between Nazism and Communism: "though Communism uses dictatorship brutally, it does not exalt it as an end in itself.... Its moral cynicism is only provisional, and it is never morally nihilistic, as the Nazis are."[50] He was ready to praise Russian achievements in the realm of social reform, and, in fact, to allow that there was something unique in that record—something worth emulating. "We have, on the whole, more liberty and less equality than Russia has. Russia has less liberty and more equality. Whether democracy should be defined primarily in terms of liberty or of equality is a source of unending debate."[51] Thus, out of a thesis and an antithesis reared on the ground of the ancient debate about the relative place of liberty and equality in human society, there might, hypothetically, come a great and creative synthesis. But the Communist alternative was to sink steadily in Niebuhr's estimation. It became less and less a case of thesis and antithesis, and more and more a case of Gog and Magog. Thus, as early as 1950 we read: "What is good in the Russian civilization as for instance its original passion for justice, is embodied in the Western tradition also, and informs the life of many of our allies. We are more likely to appropriate it from our allies than from our foes. ['*Our foes!*'] A cold war does not dispose nations to exchange their spiritual treasures. . . . We could not learn much from the Russians even if they had something to teach us."[52]

Whereas he had once believed that "Russia as a nation is not aggressive," that "Stalin has proved again and again that the instincts and responsibilities of a Russian statesman dominate his thought and lead to a subordination of the purer Communist faith"[53] (a judgment which, for the time, surely errs on the side of naivety, he became increasingly persuaded after 1946 that Russia was *nothing but* a disturber of world peace, incapable of, because uninterested in, constructive cooperation. He ignored or denied virtually all of the evidence of restrained and of constructive work that most "realists" saw in the ambiguous statesmanship of Nikita Khrushchev. Even his staunchest defenders are obliged to concede (with John C. Bennett) that, "Perhaps the deepest problem [with Niebuhr's political thought as a whole] is what is to be said to a generation [that is, the generation coming of age in the 1960s] that has never shared the optimistic illusions over which Niebuhr won so many victories . . . [for] the very success of Niebuhr's polemics leaves a need for hope and morale for people more tempted by despair than by false optimism."[54]

Niebuhr was a much more passionate anti-Communist than Morgenthau or, for that matter, than most of the so-called "realists" (for example, George Kennan). He saw the Soviet hand everywhere. He saw phoney revolutions where a realist might have been expected to see real ones—as, for example, in South Vietnam, where he could see nothing more than Communist manipulation behind the Buddhist opponents of the Diem regime.[55] Niebuhr's increasing cynicism in regard to the Soviet Union paradoxically reinforced his reluctance to abandon the "bi-polar" view of things—the worthiness of America's purposes growing, by a trick of perspective, with the diminishing worthiness of the Soviet Union's purposes. The effects on his own political judgments were at least fourfold: (1) he *invariably* over-estimated the effectiveness of the Soviet presence in all of the "genuinely revolutionary" situations in the Third World: in China, in Indochina, in Indonesia, in Egypt, in Guatemala, in Cuba, in Santa Domingo, in the Congo; (2) he *invariably* over-estimated the effectiveness of the U.S. presence in the bailiwicks of her client governments in the Third World (demonstrating a particular naivety in regard to the effectiveness of the Alliance for Progress program);[56] (3) he *almost invariably* concurred in the State Department's estimation of the degree of popular legitimacy of the various constituent elements within the individual states of the Third World—which amounts to saying that he consistently devalued the popular legitimacy of revolutionary forces in the Third World; (4) his confidence in the prospects for orderly and humane government in the Third World declined steadily. All of these cold war-ideological assumptions are manifest in the pages of the book, *The Democratic Experience*, which he co-authored with Paul E. Sigmund in 1969, to serve as a sort of theoretical guide to contemporary international relations.

*Chapter*

## 15

# THE USES AND ABUSES OF REINHOLD NIEBUHR

Inevitably, Niebuhr's heedless expenditure of his energies in meeting the demands of "the Crisis" brought on a physical crisis of his own.[1] There had been plenty of warnings. He had suffered seasonal visitations of nervous fatigue in the early spring of each year at least since 1939. Without warning he would be beset by anxiety—for instance, when he was in airplanes[2]—severe headaches, and depression would set in—and he would be "no good" for days on end. Then, when the seizure had passed, rather than curtail his workload in response to the clear message of the attack, he would resume his sixteen or seventeen hour workdays to make up for lost time. The pattern continued through the war years. Then, in February of 1952, he suffered the first of a series of strokes.[3] His workday was henceforth drastically curtailed.

For the student of Niebuhr's lifework, the job now begins to take on more manageable proportions. Whereas he is bound to feel that he has up till now been trying to sort out the record of four or five men's work, now quite abruptly, the pace of production slows down. For a year or so beginning in mid-1955, something like the old stride seemed to resume—but it didn't last,[4] and there is a steady decline of the quantity of his production until the end.

But while the quantity of the work declines—and while much of the fire of the earlier writings is gone, there are some marginal gains. Niebuhr could not now *afford* the lengthy digressions that often threatened the structure of his early books. What might have been accomplished by occasional self-restraint, was now accomplished by harsh circumstance. With no more than three hours of work permitted to him in a day (the norm, evidently, for the last two decades following the first stroke) he was driven to a new economy in the definition of his themes and the elaboration of his arguments.

The Self and the Dramas of History (1955) is almost entirely lacking in the intellectual verve that his readers had come to expect. But it is of value for the evidence it gives of Niebuhr's late-developing concern for the mystery of human individuality—a theme subordinated hitherto in his preoccupation with the problem of man in society. It shows the effects of much reading (since the time when Nature and Destiny was being written) in Freudian and other psychology and in the Christian existentialists. The Structure of Nations and Empires (1959), Man's Nature and His Communities (1965), and The Democratic Experience (co-authored with Paul E. Sigmund in 1969), offer some elaboration of the arguments about the possibilities and the limitations of human community, with some interesting adjustments in language (less use of theological terms, greater recourse to the technical language of the political theorists), but only a modest reassessment of his own political theory (roughly speaking, in the direction of a slightly greater optimism). With the exception of two remarkable short books on the meaning of American history (The Irony of American History, 1952 and A Nation So Conceived, co-authored with Alan Heimert in 1963— about which, more in Chapter Sixteen), his later books do not substantially add to his intellectual stature. Though some of Niebuhr's admirers would vigorously disagree,[5] I believe it must be said that Niebuhr's books since Faith and History (1949) (to which we shall be turning in Chapter Sixteen) are all seriously flawed. They promise much more than he had the strength to deliver. It does not seem probable that a new generation of Niebuhr enthusiasts will be recruited by these books. Enthusiasm for Niebuhr's later books seems confined mainly to older readers who are able to provide, out of their familiarity with the early books, the ingredients missing in the later ones. When all is said and done, the genius of Niebuhr's early work was a function of his inordinate energy. When the reserves were gone, the distinctive genius went with them.

Ironically, his later books received far greater attention from the book reviewers than did his earlier ones. Assignments for review of his books now went to senior academics in the learned journals, and to celebrities in the larger-circulation journals.[6] He had become an intellectual monument. His comments on forthcoming books were eagerly sought by publishers for use on their dust jackets. And the mass-circulation magazines were now approaching him for articles.

Apart from the two articles done for Life magazine on the theme of the need for an American policy for the defense of Europe, Niebuhr's articles in the mass-circulation journals added nothing to his accomplishment as a writer, though they did add to his celebrity. But Niebuhr had never sought celebrity; and even a cursory examination of any of these articles will convince anyone that Niebuhr was unwilling to temper or adulterate his message, and unable to manage the more agreeable literary style of such widely-read Christian apologists as C. S. Lewis. He was not "above" popular preaching; he was just not equipped for it. If Niebuhr failed to impress the readers of *Saturday Evening Post* or *Vogue*[7] as a religious spokesman, it was not because he was indifferent to the religious needs of the masses or scornful of their intellectual capacities. On the contrary: he had tried to make the grade for several months from late 1946 to late 1948 when he undertook a syndicated column whose purpose was to suggest to newspaper readers some of the implications of current events from a Christian perspective. The column, though not a complete washout, never did well enough to satisfy its promoters at Religious News Services, and was abandoned.[8] Though parishioners of Niebuhr's days at Bethel Evangelical long recalled his preaching with affection and admiration, it is plain that Niebuhr could not achieve the popular touch with his pen.

Despite his illness, Niebuhr continued to contribute regularly to the liberal journals of opinion, and he continued his contributions to *Christianity and Crisis* (although he resigned as Co-Chairman of the Editorial Board in March, 1966).[9] He concluded his relationship with the *Nation* in April of 1951, joining with some other regular contributors in a protest against what they claimed was the pro-Soviet line of the editor, Alvarez del Vayo.[10] Henceforth, his articles on political affairs went usually to the *New Leader*, which had begun to take in more writers of the A.D.A. persuasion as the Wallace-ite heresy infected (or so they saw it) the older liberal publications. The *New Leader*, however, never did enjoy either the circulation or the prestige of either the *Nation* or the *New Republic*, so that Niebuhr suffered a distinct diminishment of his old clientele. Even among those who supported Niebuhr's position vis-à-vis Communism and the Soviet Union, there was the feeling that Niebuhr was cutting far too many of his ties with his natural allies—that, with a little more forebearance he could have waited out the momentary differences with friends on the left, and thus secured his standing with the old clientele towards the day when his realism on the subject of Russia should have become respectable in the ranks of the democratic left. As things stood, the impression was getting abroad that Niebuhr had changed his philosophical colors (which he emphatically had not), and his books and "sayings" were being selectively raided by spokesmen of the so-called New Conservatism. Many of his old friends were urging him to disown such "false disciples" (as, for example, Will Herberg, William Buckley, and Whittaker Chambers) by softening the anti-Communism in his arguments—for it was this one element of his rhetoric that those men seized upon as the keystone of his philosophy.

An anguished letter from a veteran disciple (occasioned by the *Time* cover story of 1946 and the article written for *Life*) will serve for illustration: "You write about our cultural sickness. And yet you let yourself get all tied up with one of the more insidious carriers of the disease germ—the Luce chain. . . . You and men of your kidney might have helped a whole lot, a couple of years ago, in keeping the old PAC's from falling as much as they did under the semi-domination of the Communists. But so many of you fell out that finally there wasn't any support left for those of us who tried to stand by."[11] There were many such murmurings: that Niebuhr's increasingly strident anti-Communism entailed the suspicion of seeking "respectability"; that respectability would dull the prophetic edge; that the strain of feature-writing for *Life, Saturday Evening Post, Vogue,* and that ilk would only accomplish a vulgarization of Niebuhr's gospel. True: Niebuhr's message is a difficult one, stressing the paradoxical over the plain, stressing the fact of alienation over promises of reconciliation, urgent about the perennial weaknesses of man and dubious about the plain business of progress. There is too much that can be cheaply appropriated for the purposes of such ideologists as Henry Luce (the patriotic booster) and Will Herberg (the systematic anti-utopian). Yet there was more than a trace of cultic possessiveness in these protests from the faithful. While (as already hinted) there is reason to doubt Niebuhr's success as a preacher in the company of the readers of *The Saturday Evening Post,* it has always been the business of the preacher to preach in whatever pulpit is open to him.

In the company just considered, Reinhold Niebuhr certainly had nothing like the success in convicting his hearers that, say, Norman Vincent Peale has had. But what of the intellectuals in the Congregation? Here Niebuhr's influence is undoubtedly great and genuine. Yet here too the question of its abuse arises. Niebuhr's largest appeal was to those who belong to what Arthur Schlesinger called the "Vital Center" of American politics—the ex-socialist, reformist, gradualist school of political amateurs. The fact that Reinhold Niebuhr had been in the thirties so outspoken a Socialist and the fact that he had subsequently become convinced that there were in socialist utopianism great hazards to the reason and soul, and had decided thereupon to translate (for himself at least) the vision of the cooperative commonwealth to some ultimate dispensation—this was powerful grist for the mills of pragmatic liberals. But the principal value that Niebuhr's career and thought had for them was in his use of theological language to justify his abandonment of the socialist vision and his embracing of the pragmatic program. It had all been, he was now convinced, a case of "Providence dissolving the conflicting dogmas of right and left into a creative synthesis."[12]

Even those of Niebuhr's political co-workers who were without theological commitment—and perhaps especially these—found it irresistible to borrow the ultimate sanctions that Niebuhr's formulation provides, thus gaining benefit of clergy, as it were, for their politics of complacency. In the opinion of many, Niebuhr has been misappropriated in far too many of these operations, and is made to appear to be providing what Morton White has called "the ontological argument for A.D.A."[13] It is, indeed, often an appalling descent from the religious sensitivity with which Niebuhr expresses the dilemmas of politics to the palpable and clumsy appropriations of so many of his disciples.

There is a tantalizing passage in Victor Lasky's once best-selling hatchet-biography of John F. Kennedy, purporting to describe how the Liberal Party of New York cleansed itself in 1960 of the concern it had about its candidate's Roman Catholic allegiance. The story (attributed by Lasky to "a private source") is that the Party "assigned Reinhold Niebuhr to question Senator Kennedy in depth, and that eminent divine reported back to David Dubinsky and other troubled Seventh Avenue theologians that the would-be Presidential candidate had satisfied his Protestant doubts."[14] No substantiation for the story appears elsewhere in the now-mountainous Kennedy literature. But then, the story of the laying-on of hands by Simeon may, after all, be apocryphal without being the less essential. Lasky's anecdote captures the whole of what Richard Rovere implied when he identified Reinhold Niebuhr as "the Establishment theologian."[15]

As another example (better documented) we have the accolade delivered by the then Vice-President of the United States at a banquet (February, 1966) honoring the twenty-fifth anniversary of Niebuhr's journal, *Christianity and Crisis*. Reinhold Niebuhr, Vice-President Humphrey declared, was the inspiration "to a whole generation of us as we came out of the Great Depression." "We knew there were urgent demands of social justice that required direct action and idealism. At the same time, we learned that politics was complicated and many-sided, that life just wasn't that simple. Dr. Niebuhr was the man more than any other who put these two things together, and showed how they are both connected with religious faith. Yes, he helped us to see that politicians and theologians had a mutual interest in sin in the world."[16]

The editors of *Christianity and Crisis* themselves report that Mr. Humphrey's declaration of discipleship to Reinhold Niebuhr was met by his audience with some incredulity, coming as it did as the preface to a full-blooded defense of the Administration's Vietnam policy, to which *Christianity and Crisis*, under Niebuhr's leadership, was adamantly opposed.[17] One wonders what it must do to the equilibrium of a sensitive man to wake up each day to a new declaration of discipleship from yet another such unlikely source. One can box the political compass with such declarations: from Martin Luther King, through George Kennan, Adlai Stevenson II, Arthur Schlesinger, Jr., through McGeorge Bundy, to William Buckley and his theologian-in-residence, Will Herberg. Thus, President Johnson, who for his own spiritual counsel preferred the services of Billy Graham, saw to it that his campaign managers bought up job-lots of *Christianity and Crisis* for distribution to Protestant clergymen when that paper came out mildly for him (and vehemently against Barry Goldwater) in October, 1964.[18]

Without doubt, the most disturbing example I have encountered of the abuse of Niebuhr's eminence is a document produced by Bertram Wolfe of the Ideological Advisory Staff of the U.S. Department of State entitled *Ideological Special No. 256*, a shamelessly distorted presentation of arguments culled from Niebuhr's books to illustrate the "demonic" character of communism and the specially Christian credentials of American democracy.[19] But it was ever thus with philosophers and their despoilers. Niebuhr himself struggled against this one-sided expropriation of his theology in conversation, in letters, and in books. But, unhappily, his energies during the last two decades of his life were severely drained by strokes, and the interpreters of Niebuhr were able to outshout him.

Niebuhr's rise to the eminence of a national intellectual monument in the 1950s coincided with a quite remarkable campaign among academic political philosophers and foreign policy commentators for a reorientation of America's attitudes in foreign policy—a movement generally referred to as "the new realism," and with which we associate the names of Hans Morgenthau, Kenneth W. Thompson, George Kennan, Walter Lippmann and Robert E. Osgood. It would be futile to attempt to separate cause and effect here. Niebuhr had to some degree prepared the minds of many intellectuals and policy-makers with arguments and with language, both of which proved appropriate to the preparation of the case for "realism" in political theory. Some of those who now found Niebuhr's arguments and language so *useful* (to put the minimum estimate on the operation) allowed themseves to recollect a long-standing acquaintance with Niebuhr's writings. Now that Niebuhr was shaping up as the pre-eminent American thinker of the hour, it would be a sure admission of obtuseness to acknowledge that one had not discovered Niebuhr before Henry Luce or the State Department.

It is best to be skeptical about the possibilities of demonstrating with any accuracy the actual weight that an intellectual carries in the temples of decision-making, especially when the authority of the intellectual in question is mediated by brokers of his thoughts operating in the field of applied politics. Yet, Niebuhr's pre-eminence as a moulder of the logic of the "new realism" is insisted upon with equal energy by his critics and his defenders. Of the former, Walter LaFeber (in his *America, Russia and the Cold War*, 1967) has gone farthest in the work of actually trying to fit Niebuhr's published word into the record of Cold War apologetics. In LaFeber's book (as we have already seen), Niebuhr appears as the archetypical liberal Cold Warrior. LeFeber describes the political options available to "liberals" in the mid-forties in terms of a "[Henry] Wallace-Niebuhr" polarity[20]—Niebuhr ("the most formative contemporary influence on American liberals") providing the "theological assumptions [necessary for full-blooded] support of the Cold War," as well as the institutional machinery (U.D.A./A.D.A.) which worked the will of his clientele in the political arena.[21] He provided the earliest formulation of the argument for reinstating Germany in the western community (the vital keystone of the Acheson-Grand Design, and the one item which recurringly proved to be the largest obstacle to entente between the U.S. and the U.S.S.R. right through the Kennedy years). "A change of tone," discoverable as early as 1952 in his declining enthusiasm for Germany and in his new concern over the prospect of over-involvement in Asia, and resulting in the new theme of "the hazards of power," comes too late. Niebuhr's continuing irrationality on the subject of Soviet imperialism and his contempt for neutralism puts him "in basic agreement with Dulles' views" throughout the fifties and with Kennedy's during his Presidency.[22]

LaFeber's description of Niebuhr's lock-step conformity with official Cold War policy requires a certain gift of selectivity in quotation from Niebuhr's published word. But no less gifted are those of his apologists (notably, Ronald H. Stone) who have undertaken to prove a case for Niebuhr's exceptional independence of judgment on American foreign policy in the same two decades (1945–65). Niebuhr's opposition to the Vietnam war was rather late in developing. Niebuhr was originally enthusiastic (as we have seen) for the United States to replace France as the mainstay of the Diem regime in South Vietnam, and for reasons that differed not a jot from those unsuccessfully argued for by Secretary Dulles before President Eisenhower. All of the damage that the Vietnam intervention has since done to America's prestige in the world and to her internal peace derives from the pursuit of a policy based upon propositions inherent in Niebuhr's misjudgment about the workings of "international communism" in Vietnam and elsewhere, and the even more terrible misjudgment about what America ought to do to set things right. And it seems incontrovertible that if the prestige of the "bi-polar," Cold War logic persisted in the company of the intellectuals who served the Administrations of Presidents Kennedy and Johnson so much longer than objective reality seemed to justify, this was in part at least an ironical testimony to the intellectual father of the "new realists"—Reinhold Niebuhr.

# THE GOSPEL AND THE INCREDIBILITIES OF HISTORY

*Man is primarily a historical creature. . . .*
*The preference of the 'wise and prudent'*
*for ontological religions represents*
*the mind's abhorrence of the incredibilities of history.*
*The Christian faith asserts about God*
*that He is a person and that He has taken historical action*
*to overcome the variance between Man and God.*[1]

At the end of his career as a writer, Niebuhr was still what he was in the first phase: a preacher of the Christian Gospel. Though some adjustments can be noted in the vocabulary he employs, it must be said that there is no alteration in the character of his commitment to that Gospel as the basic discloser of life's meaning. There is, however, a profound correction of the perspective in which that Gospel is seen. The basic drift of Niebuhr's work—beginning with *The Nature and Destiny of Man*, that product of "the Crisis"—is towards an understanding of the Gospel in the context of history. This progress can be traced in terms of an evolution in his use of the word "history." In his early works (that is, up to *The Nature and Destiny of Man*), the word "history" has the meaning of immediate background to existent individual life: it can be translated, "existential circumstance." It usually appears in tandem with the word "nature"—its opposite in Niebuhr's early vocabulary.

Significantly, it was during the early years of the war, when

Niebuhr was developing his views on post-war reconstruction—struggling, that is, to find some orientation towards the future—that Niebuhr began to use the word "history" in quite a different way. Careful attention to the articles of the early 1940s will bear this out. In this brief chapter in the Niebuhr canon there is significant reiteration of certain phrases—"the stubborn inertia of history," "the intractable forces of history"—that give a clue to what is to come when he will get around to a proper development of those ideas (in the books with which we shall shortly be dealing).[2]

Niebuhr's flirtation with Marxism owed a great deal to the promise in that creed of "some drastic judgment in history." But are there ever "*drastic* judgments" in history? The lesson of "the Crisis" was that our capacity to transcend the inertial effects of our "history" (in the correct, time-dimensional sense of the word) is much more limited than we had believed.

The one thing needful for the casting out of this delusion is a realistic view of history, one that takes account of both our capacities and our limitations in regard to the inertial effects of the past. What is needed is the Gospel. But then (as Mark Twain would say), we repeat ourselves. For the whole effect of the lesson Niebuhr had learned was that the Gospel of Christ is Good News about the meaning of history. This, I am persuaded, is the key to understanding the mature work of Reinhold Niebuhr.

The failure of the Christian Church to assess correctly the meaning of "the Crisis" was that it had abandoned its Gospel in favor of the prevailing secular view of man's circumstance—a view whose basic fault was its naive "historiography." (Here we use the word in the sense that Herbert Butterfield intends when he remarks that, "What was unique about the ancient Hebrews, was their historiography, rather than their history.")[3] The modern mind is biased by its contempt for the past. For the modern mind, man's meaning is discovered in the habit of looking forward: the *meaning* of the present is its coming vindication in the consequences of our strivings. The perfect expression of this modern faith was achieved in our formative age, the age of Enlightenment. Niebuhr cites Carl Becker's formulation of this Enlightenment faith: "For the love of God [the men of the Enlightenment] substituted love of humanity; for vicarious atonement the perfectibility of man through his own efforts, and for the hope of immortality in another world the hope of living in the memory of future generations.... The thought of posterity was apt to elicit from eighteenth century philosophers and revolutionary leaders a highly emotional and essentially religious response." (Carl L. Becker, *The Heavenly City of Eighteenth Century Philosophers*, p. 130.)[4] "The essentially religious character of this appeal to posterity," Niebuhr writes, "is perfectly expressed in the words of Diderot: 'O posterity, holy and sacred!' ... Posterity is for the philosopher what the other world is for the religious."[5] This bogus immorality, though it may have had some psycho-therapeutic efficacy in less hazardous times, has lost its power to persuade in the twentieth century. As a protest against the unqualified other-worldliness to which religion tempts many people, it is understandable—and perhaps (the ways of Providence being as mysterious as they are) it was a necessary corrective.[6] But it was doomed from the beginning as a satisfactory rival faith because of its contempt for the legitimate instinct for immortality which is in all of us.

> The plight of the individual in his relation to the whole process of history is derived from his two-fold relation to the historical process. His creativity is directed towards the establishment, perpetuation and perfection of historical communities. Therefore the meaning of his life is derived from his relation to the historical process. But the freedom which makes this creativity possible transcends all communal loyalties and even history itself. Each individual has a direct relation to eternity; for he seeks for the completion of the meaning of his life beyond the fragmentary realizations of meaning which can be discerned at any point in the process where an individual may happen to live and die. The end of an individual life is, for him, the end of history; and every individual is a Moses who perishes outside the promised land. But each individual also has an indirect relation to eternity. In so far as he takes historical responsibilities seriously he must view the problem of fulfillment from the standpoint of the ultimate and final "end."[7]

The problem of individual death and the problem of history's meaning are linked together in a paradoxical way:

> The fear of death springs from the capacity not only to anticipate death but to imagine and to be anxious about some dimension of reality on the other side of death. Both forms of fear prove man's transcendence over nature. His mind comprehends the point in nature at which his own existence in nature ends; and thereby proves that nature does not fully contain him. ... The fear of death is thus the clearest embryonic expression of man's capacity as a creator of history.
> Classical naturalism seeks to beguile man from this fear of death by attempting to persuade him that it is illusory and unwarranted. The argument contains two points. One is that there is nothing

in history which man need to fear, since there is in fact no history, but only natural sequence and natural recurrence. . . .

Thus Epicurus writes: "There is nothing terrible in living to a man who rightly comprehends that there is nothing terrible in ceasing to live; so that it was a silly man who said that he feared death not because it would grieve him when it was present but because it did grieve him when it was future. . . . The most formidable of all evils, death, is nothing to us, since, when we exist, death is not present to us and when death is present we have no existence. It is no concern then to either the living or the dead; since to the one it has no existence and the other class has no existence itself."

The fact that classical naturalism must seek to beguile men from the fear of death not only by reducing history to the dimension of natural sequence but also by denying the reality of any possible realm of life and meaning beyond history is doubly significant. *It proves that there can be no sense of history at all (as embodied embryonically in the fear of death) without a further sense of an eternity transcending history.*[8]

One grave consequence of modern philosophy's suppression of the dilemma of individual death is the temptation to substitute the community (the state, the tribe, the *volk*, the class) for history as the the ultimate frame of reference for individual meaning; thus, in modern political theories: "The breadth of the communal life and the majesty of its power supposedly complete and fulfill the partial interests and inadequate power of the individual. The relative immortality of the community is intended to compensate for the brevity of an individual's life."[9] Paradoxically, it is the persistent sense of individuality that finally brings mankind back to a reconsideration of history and its claims:

Each individual knows instinctively that he is so much more, even while he is so much less, than the community. His years are briefer than those of his community; but both his memories and anticipations have a longer range. The community knows only of its own beginnings but the individual knows of the rise and fall of civilizations before his own. The community looks forward to the victories, and fears the defeats of history; but the individual discerns a more final judgment. If the nations stand before that last judgment too, they do so in the conscience and mind of sensitive individuals. The brotherhood of the community is indeed the ground in which the individual is ethically realized. But the community is the frustration as well as the realization of individual life. Its collective egotism is an offense to his conscience; its institutional injustices negate the ideal of justice; and such brotherhood as it achieves is limited by ethnic and geographic boundaries. Historical communities are, in short, more deeply involved in nature and time than the individual who constantly faces an eternity above and at the end of the time process.[10]

Karl Barth was therefore right to this extent: recovering the Gospel means putting the consciousness of individual death back into the center of the picture. But, *defying Barth*, Niebuhr was able to argue that a vigorous examination of the dilemma of death drives us *paradoxically* towards a recovery of positive meaning for human history. This is, in my opinion, Niebuhr's greatest accomplishment as a theologian.[11]

Death. Individuality. History. These are the three vital and interconnected themes whose meaning is obscured by modern philosophy. While modern liberal culture rightly prides itself on achieving the blessings of freedom of enquiry, we cannot fail to notice (argues Niebuhr) that certain assumptions about human nature and human destiny have an undeserved immunity from critical examination by the modern mind. Though we have, as a culture, long since given up debating these assumptions, certain of them are quite false—and every culture but our own saw through them long ago. Their persistence into our age of reason demonstrates that if the present does stand upon the shoulders of the past, we may yet fail to see parts of the landscape which our ancestors saw and knew well.

The most dangerous of these false assumptions is our faith in progress. Our modern liberals were so incredibly optimistic about the future only because they were so careless in their approach to the past. Significantly, Niebuhr finds that working historians are, of all scholarly types, least given to optimistic judgments about man's present and future. But historians are not much listened-to by moderns, who prefer philosophers and other system-makers.

The grievous errors of Liberal-Humanism need not have been made, had liberal-humanists read more history. Instead, they had assumed, from their optimistic premises about human nature, that history was working towards ends which they devoutly wished. The historians, Niebuhr claims, could have shown them better, had humanists valued history sufficiently to have bothered to enquire.

The spirit of liberal optimism was first grievously shaken by the First World War. The unbroken series of international crises, culminating in the present season of nuclear terror, further tested that spirit, and has perhaps done it in for good: "The general movement of our day," Niebuhr writes, "is from complacency to despair."[12] A parable of our times is the life and sad end of H. G. Wells, the most full-blooded of all liberal optimists, whose gradual surrender to the drift of events can be traced through his *Shape of Things to Come* (1933) to his *The Mind at the End of its Tether* (1945): ("a frightful queerness has come into life.... The writer is convinced that there is no way out, or around, or through the impasse. It is the end.").[13]

Tragically, modern Christianity (or at least Protestant Christianity) seemed too much implicated in the decline of liberalism to lend a helping hand. For the fact is that it was a misinterpretation of Christian faith which got us into this fix. The idea of progress, Niebuhr argues, could only have been conceived within Christian culture, whose positive and dynamic attitude toward history is the feature which most radically distinguishes it from classical philosophy and eastern mysticism. Had the Western world continued to work the seams of thought known to the classical world, had Christianity not burst upon the Western world when it did, or had any of the other Eastern cults which were such promising rivals with Christianity for the attention of the Roman Empire in the third and fourth centuries in fact carried the Graeco-Roman world, the Western world would have lacked the materials out of which to shape its doctrine of progress. Only in our culture, which was borne out of a messianic expectation, is history "taken seriously."[14]

It is the basic premise of the Biblical concept of history that God does reach down into human affairs and does propel events one way or another. The process by which God reaches into history, supplying historical characters with motives and energies they could not otherwise have had, and thereby radically altering the factors in the human adventure—and thereby making history move—is called "revelation." The process is remarkable for its sporadic and somewhat arbitrary character. The Biblical account shows us a God who enters into the issues of history, at critical junctures, and chooses one side against another (Israel against Egypt) and encourages one man against another (Jacob against Esau). The most enlightened thinking of later ages has not always approved of the company which Jehovah keeps in these encounters. Even if the Hebrews and their various and sundry captains were no worse than other causes and other captains, the notion that God has actively intervened in the dynamics of history has about it what has been called "the scandal of particularity."[15]

We should therefore be perfectly honest about the implications of what we are saying when we say that history has *meaning*—any meaning at all, let alone the profound meaning that Niebuhr discovers in it. The contemporary philosopher Karl Popper speaks for most moderns when he discusses the possibility of our finding meaning in history in these words:

> *"History"* in the sense in which most people speak of it simply *does not exist.* . . . [People] speak about the *history of mankind,* but what they have learned about in school, is the *history of political power.* . . . A concrete history of mankind, if there were any, would have to be the history of all men. It would have to be the history of all human hopes, struggles, and sufferings. For there is no one man more important than any other. Clearly, this concrete history cannot be written. We must make abstractions, we must neglect, select. . . . The theory that God reveals Himself and His judgement in history is indistinguishable from the theory that worldly success is the ultimate judge and justification of our actions. . . . To maintain that God reveals Himself in what is usually called "history," in the history of international crime and of mass murder, is indeed blasphemy; for what really happens within the realm of human lives is hardly ever touched upon by this cruel and at the same time childish affair. The life of the forgotten, of the unknown individual man; his sorrows and his joys, his suffering and death, this is the real content of human experience down the ages. If that could be told by history, then I should certainly not say that it is blasphemy to see the finger of God in it. But such a history does not and cannot exist; and all the history which exists, our history of the Great and the Powerful, is at best a shallow comedy. . . . It is what one of our worst instincts, the idolatrous worship of power, of success, has led us to believe to be real. And in this not even man-made, but man-faked "history," some Christians dare to see the hand of God.[16]

This is precisely what Niebuhr *has dared* to do—not only in terms of a general theory of history (which occupies him in *Faith and History* and in sections of *The Nature and Destiny of Man*), but in an extended essay in applied historical theory, which is how we must describe his three books on the subject of the history of the United States: *The Irony of American History* (1954), *Pious and Secular America* (1958), and *A Nation So Conceived* (1963). In these works, Niebuhr boldly applies the Old Testament concept of *election* to American history, and on this analogical foundation has built a unique commentary.[17] Those (like Karl Popper) who flinch from the thought of there being *meaning* in history will part company immediately with historiography of the sort that Niebuhr offers. To spare them trouble, we offer the worst first: "Only those who have no sense of the profundities of history would deny that various nations and classes, various social groups and races are at various times placed in such a position that a special measure of the divine mission in history falls upon them. In that sense God has chosen America in this fateful period of world history."[18] But America's future, Niebuhr believed, was made perilous by the responsibilities placed upon her as the concomitant of her blessings. Because of the special good fortune of her situation as the possessor of a virgin continent, kept beyond the reach of Europe's troubles for the first two centuries of her existence by great distance—and (though this is little appreciated) by her insignificance as a power—she has had an inordinately easy time of it—relative, that is to the experience of other western nations. It is characteristic, Niebuhr argues, of all nations who enjoy over a long period of time a steady improvement of their material situation and a steady increase in their power and responsibilities, to succumb to the temptation of believing themselves to be a special people—a people who are exempt from the general laws of frustration and decay which accompany the history of other nations. Thus, it became unthinkable to citizens of Imperial Rome that Rome could ever die— for to say that Roman history would end was the same as to say that history itself would end. (St. Paul himself was not exempt from this view.) This is the myth of *exceptionalism*—that the history of our nation is an exception to the general history of nations. The hazards in this faith are many and serious. There is the hazard of pride, which blinds us to our national shortcomings, and renders us unpopular. (That is the least serious one.) There is the hazard of underrating the virtues of other nations, blinding us to our need to learn from them. Perhaps most serious of all, there is the hazard of despair when we confront situations that seem to be outside of our control. A nation "whose secret thought" (as the Psalmist put it) "is that they will live forever," is not equipped to deal with challenges to itself which cannot be dealt with swiftly by the bringing into play of its superior force. The second President of the United States, John Adams, understood this: "Power," he wrote, "always thinks it has a great soul and vast views beyond the comprehension of the weak, and that it is doing God's service when it is violating all His laws."[19]

The temptation to exceptionalism was implicit in the situation which created America. There was the happy circumstance of a new world of unlimited natural resources, tempting Americans to believe that God meant there to be no limits on America's expansive opportunities; there was also the absence of considerable rivals for possession of the continent. To heighten this conviction of special providence, there was all the evidence of failure and decay of the Old World. America was conceived as a great opportunity for repudiation of all that was evil in Europe; it was to be "a City set up on a hill," to serve as the faithful remnant in the time of general unfaithfulness.

By the time of the establishing of the new nation at the end of the eighteenth century, the estate of Europe had declined further in American eyes. Europeans had lost the mandate of heaven, as evidenced by their general retreat from religious faithfulness and their increasing resort to warfare among themselves. In the betrayal of republican freedoms by Napoleon, and then in the repressions of the Age of Metternich which followed, Americans were sure that they saw the beginning of the working-out of a death-wish. With each passing decade, the American sense of election was confirmed. The more it appeared that Europe was slipping from grace, the more obvious it was that the U.S. lived under special election. It was America's peculiar mission to uphold and to advance all of the positive ideals that Europe was plainly abandoning. While Europe was enslaved to a death-wish, America must affirm the *purposefulness* of history. It is this faith that gives American history its peculiar dynamism.

For most Americans, this faith was still being expressed in religious terms—the concept of the Covenant with God, of the City set on a hill. But the sense of ambiguity (or of irony, to use a term that Niebuhr prefers) is gone. The sense of election is no longer qualified by the original Puritan's guilt-feelings about his abandonment of Europe. This rapid "descent from Puritanism to Yankeeism"[20] represents a decline in the sensitiveness of the religious conscience of Americans.

Even where this faith in America is not expressed in explicitly religious terms, some secular equivalent is concocted to take its place. Jefferson's version stemmed from his faith in the superior virtue of the American yeoman farmer. Being a rationalist, he was not satisfied with supernatural explanations of America's special grace, but worked-out an elaborate theory whereby the circumstance of America's unlimited agricultural land—enough he was convinced in 1801 (two years before the Louisiana Purchase) to provide farms for every man "to the thousandth generation"—would guarantee that America would remain a land of independent yeomen farmers, while Europe would continue to sink into the iniquities of city life. This would guarantee that Americans would never have to create significant social differences among themselves—no man would ever have to bow to another—the habit of deference would never be learned by Americans. Americans could not help, therefore, but speak the truth —since the need to lie or to deceive is socially created, a by-product of the circumstance that in older societies men had had to earn their bread by kow-towing to other men.

"If all the sovereigns of Europe," Jefferson said, "were to set themselves to work to emancipate the minds of their subjects from their present ignorance and prejudice, and that as zealously as they now attempt the contrary, a thousand years would not place them on that high ground on which our common people are setting out."[21] The official Jeffersonian court-poet, Philip Freneau, put it this way:

Here [America] independent power shall hold sway,
And public virtue warm the patriot's breast.
No traces shall remain of tyranny,
And laws and patterns for the world beside
Be here enacted first.
A new Jerusalem sent down from heaven
Shall grace our happy earth.[22]

(These last two lines—"a new Jerusalem"—betray how poor a job rationalists had done of translating the religious concept of election into secular terms.)

Thus, Niebuhr writes:

It is remarkable that the two great religious-moral traditions which informed our early life—New England Calvinism and Virginian Deism and Jeffersonianism—arrived at remarkably similar conclusions about the meaning of national character and destiny—whether our nation interprets its spiritual heritage through Massachusetts or Virginia, we come into existence with the sense of being a "separated" nation, which God was using to make a new beginning for mankind. Whether, as in the case of the New England theocrats, our forefathers thought of our "experiment" as primarily the creation of a new and purer church, or, as in the case of Jefferson and his coterie, they thought primarily of a new political community, they believed in either case that we had been called out by God to create a new humanity. We were God's "American Israel."[23]

This American view of its historical role has thus two sides to it. On the one side, there is the conviction of America's *exceptional* nature. De Tocqueville comments on this as he discovered it in the days of Jackson:

> If I say to an American that the country he lives in is a fine one, aye, he replies and there is not its equal in the world. If I applaud the *freedom* its inhabitants enjoy, he answers, "Freedom is a fine thing, but few nations are worthy of it." If I remark on the purity of morals that distinguishes the United States, he declares, "I can imagine that a stranger who has witnessed the corruption which prevails in other nations would be astonished at the difference."
>
> At length I leave him to contemplation of himself. But he returns to the charge and does not desist until he has got me to repeat all I have been saying.
>
> It is impossible to conceive of a more troublesome and garrulous patriotism.[24]

On the other side of this coin is the sense of mission ("laws and patterns for the world beside," Freneau had sung, would be "here enacted first"). The U.S. was a disinterested force in international affairs, the bearer of virtues not current any longer elsewhere—virtues that were no longer recognizable to others. It is inseparable from the faith of American *exceptionalism*, therefore, that her mandate derives not from the recognition of other nations but from heaven.

What we have been talking about up to this point is a theory of history—of the forces that are directing human affairs forward from one condition to another—a theory of history which has been, however disguised, the theory cherished by the American consensus, from that time to this. The American consensus about America's historical role was grounded on a faith in the perfectibility of man—at least of *American* man. America moves in step with Providence—or (a secular version of the same thing) with Progress. This allows for a positive, affirmative, untrembling approach to history.

This consensus view, in one form or another, colors the philosophy of American secularists as well as those whose thought contains a religious component. It explains why, as late as the 1930s, American liberals were, virtually to a man, isolationists. Dewey, Charles Beard, Vernon Parrington, and that entire generation of liberal-intellectuals, argued that America must keep completely clear of Europe's affairs. It was like arguing that America must stand clear of history. But Pearl Harbor brought America, kicking and screaming, into the mainstream of history. The war itself left the U.S. sharing with the Soviet Union virtual hegemony (at least for a while) in world politics. Interestingly the Soviet Union is committed to her own version of the exceptionalist heresy—deriving, in her case, from Marxist-Leninist ideology. For both great powers, the period since about 1940 has provided a cruel education in the realities of history.

When we look back to the age of Dewey, therefore, we have to look back across the watershed represented by Pearl Harbor—to an age of innocence as to the crueler side of history, to an age when American thought was still largely insulated against the negative aspects of European thought and experience. It is almost (as Paul Tillich argues) as if America had skipped the nineteenth century! "[I was] astonished [on arriving in America in 1930] at how much more Americans are dependent on the eighteenth century than Europeans. The reason is very simple. America experienced very little of the romanticist reaction against the eighteenth century. I believe that the resistance of American students against taking history seriously is due in part to the fact the Romanticism has never had a profound influence in this country. This is not by chance. The Enlightenment feeling that a new beginning has been inaugurated is part of the American experience."[25]

There can be, in the canonical view of America's meaning, no ultimate incompatibility between the purposes of history and the purposes of America. The starting-point, *however disguised*, is an assumption not susceptible to rational scrutiny. It is an article of faith.

It seems self-evident, then, that since the problem was at root *theological*—a problem in the misapplication of supernatural faith—its cure must be effected by *theological* criticism. What is needed, Niebuhr argues, is the recovery of the legitimate Biblical view of history. The first step in this direction is an appreciation of the Biblical concept of *mystery*, and the paradoxical relationship which exists between mystery and meaning in history. The fact (if we accept it as a fact) of God's choosing Israel as the agent of His plan of redemption for men is the first of these "mysteries" with which we must deal. It is a mystery in that on no objective or reasonable grounds can one explain Israel's qualifications for its calling.[26] If it is a fact, it is known as such not to reason, but to faith. Once apprehended by faith, the mystery repays the investment of faith which we have made by illuminating areas of meaning that are otherwise closed to us. Yet if we try to patch over the gap between what we know by reason and what we know by faith, we become guilty of a presumption which will be charged against us. If Israel claims to have its blessings by dint of anything less than the inexplicable grace of God, it will fall into the sin of pride and will suffer the natural consequence of pride, which is destruction.[27]

Niebuhr is thus insistent that to have a philosophy of history which deals adequately with the perplexities of the human situation, we must admit an area of mystery into that philosophy: which is another way of saying that an adequate philosophy of history has in fact to be a theology of history. "Mystery does not annul meaning, but enriches it."[28] The surest way of losing our grasp on historical reality is to allow the category of meaning to swallow up the category of mystery—to swallow up theology in philosophy.

For all who are seeking a clue to the meaning of history, Niebuhr thus starkly sets, side by side, the alternative claims of faith and reason. This brings us back to a line of consideration touched upon some pages back—namely, the matter of the connection between the Christian faith and the idea of progress (which we had tentatively identified as a Christian heresy). We have suggested that it was the conviction, peculiar to Judaeo-Christian thought, that history is being drawn forward toward some completion prepared for it by God, and foreshadowed in His renewed Covenants with Israel, that accustomed our ancestors to think of history as therefore "going somewhere." Centuries of exposure to these religious assumptions have produced in us an apparently unshakable commitment to what Albert Schweitzer called "world-and-life-affirmation." We are committed to an active, positive attitude toward the challenges of environment. We are educated to believe that the circumstances of life really do change as the result of efforts we expend. So thoroughly ingrained is this habit of thought in us, that it never occurs to us to wonder whether another attitude toward life is possible. The opposite attitude is, however, not only possible, but the attitude of the majority of men—as we discover if we detach ourselves from Western intellectual preoccupations long enough to test the preoccupations of other civilizations. Yet, the corollary of the activist ethic which was peculiar to the Judaeo-Christian ethos—the thing which allowed the Biblical writers to have their conviction of meaning in history—was their conviction of the active intervention of God in history. The Biblical authors denied that sinful man alone had the resources to advance the circumstances of life an iota.

The gist of Niebuhr's quarrel with modern thought is, therefore, that it has abandoned the theological underpinnings of the intellectual tradition which made the idea of progress conceivable in the first place. Niebuhr argues that it is in separating the notion of the active God (the Redeemer) from the concept of historical advance that modern thought has exposed itself to the disillusion and despair which beset it. Modern thought, impatient with mysteries, has preferred to find the principle of advance within history itself.

Modern thought is plainly naive as well as optimistic. It is extremely hard on human "selfishness," because of its conviction that selfishness is something that is being overcome by the increasing sway of reason over men's affairs. It is this conviction, that self-concern *must* go and *will* go out of human reckoning, that explains the conspiracy of silence maintained in modern literature on the questions which all the great religions are designed to meet. The general verdict of modern thought is that religion is "an expression of impotence."[29] The individual salvation of which Christianity speaks is not, for the typical modern, a subject, or a prospect, worthy of our consideration. The interest in personal redemption is seen by moderns as a pathetic product of an age which lacked the grounds for believing in the redemption of the whole human adventure—that is, of History. The quest for personal redemption is unworthy, because it is selfish.

For Niebuhr, it is precisely the fact that religion speaks to the anxieties experienced by the self which marks it as a promising source of a philosophy of history. Modern thought, says Niebuhr, dismisses the legitimate claims of the self too brusquely, thus destroying any prospect of a satisfying philosophy of history. Niebuhr regards the notion, current since the Enlightenment of the eighteenth century, that the individual can transcend the claims of selfishness by an effort of reason, as foolish and dangerous. The cardinal error of modern humanism was to identify selfish man with natural man, holding out to us the prospect that we could achieve pure disinterestedness, and thus perfect peace within society, by the education of the reason. But the ambitions of the self grow precisely as reason grows, giving it new horizons. "The selfishness of men and of nations is a fixed datum of historical science."[30]

No philosophy of history will satisfy us unless it accounts for the permanence of human selfishness as a fact of history, and at the same time delivers us from the despair which assails us when we reckon with the fact of selfishness as an obstacle to pure progress and a bringer of possible chaos. An adequate philosophy of history must contain the promise of personal redemption from the consequences of selfishness. These are precisely the claims which Niebuhr makes for Christianity. Only the Christian faith, he argues, "recognizes the peril, as well as the creativity of human freedom."[31]

It is surely not necessary to show that secularists must reject Reinhold Niebuhr's view of history outright. The insights upon which it draws are non-rational and mythical. It should be clear that religious naturalists must reject him: religion that is not founded on revelation is clearly not religion at all for Niebuhr; and we have been emphasizing throughout Niebuhr's stand that without an adequate theology of history there is no philosophy of history. We have presented Niebuhr's theology of history up to this point as something created to meet the fact (as he sees it) that our liberal-humanist culture has no philosophy of history worth considering. There seems little point in going through to draw up a bill of particulars. Niebuhr parts company with all liberal-humanists at the very outset, in his appeal to revealed religion.

If one wishes to see Niebuhr's views attacked with genuine vigor, one has to move inside the Christian camp. The gist of the complaint against Niebuhr is that, having spent so much labor exposing the inadequacies of secular answers to problems of life and of history, he nonetheless persists in attributing too much of positive meaning to mere history. Here he parts company with the school which follows Karl Barth. Indeed, a good case could be made for the suggestion that the one area in which the views of Niebuhr and the "neo-orthodox" theologians are utterly irreconcilable is in the matter of their understanding of the meaning of history. And for our purposes, the shortest way to the heart of that problem is by way of a comparison of Niebuhr's views with those of the Barthian philosopher, Karl Löwith, whose *Meaning in History* (1957) has received a deserved celebrity among the philosophers of history.[32]

Löwith's approach has one considerable advantage over that of Niebuhr: its relative simplicity. Löwith shares with many Christian critics of Niebuhr the conviction that Niebuhr prefers the complex and the paradoxical to the simple out of sheer cussedness—or perhaps out of a desire to have best of all worlds. Löwith finds not the least difficulty in fixing the relationship between *Heilsgeschichte* and mere history: "The 'meaning' of the history of this world is fulfilled against itself because the story of salvation, as embodied in Jesus Christ, redeems and dismantles, as it were, the hopeless history of the world. . . . A 'Christian history' is [therefore] nonsense."[33] The most that Löwith is prepared to admit is that mere historical events might have some kind of loose "meaning" as parables, or shadowy illustrations of the basic religious fact that God stands over all of creation and intends to judge it: "Thus historical catastrophes can be interpreted as intimations of the last judgment, though the latter cannot be comprehended in terms of historical disasters."[34] So shadowy and elusive is this species of submeaning, that the chronological order in which mere historical events happen tells us nothing about them worth knowing: "The factual coincidence of Rome under Augustus with Christ does not exclude the possibility that God could have revealed himself a thousand years earlier or two thousand years later in Europe under Napoleon or in Russia under Stalin or in Germany under Hitler. And since the story of salvation does not refer to historical empires, nations, and civilizations but to each human soul, one cannot dismiss the thought that Christianity, that is, faith in Christ, is essentially indifferent over against world-historical differences, even over the difference between civilization and barbarism."[35] Thus, "To walk in the line of the history of salvation is to renounce the highways of general happenings, glorious and spectacular or common and miserable. . . . Man's historical experience is one of steady failure. . . . [A] Christian understanding of history can only be based on the fundamental antagonism between the Kingdom of God and the Kingdoms of man."[36]

It seems, indeed, that some such formulation as Löwith gives us is the only logical alternative for Christians who cannot come to terms with Niebuhr's formulation (or one essentially like it). Niebuhr offers us a way of dealing with history as interim, preserving the distinction between revelation and mere history, insisting upon the superior and overriding meaning of the former, but finding in the latter a real, though lesser, meaning illuminated by the former. As Niebuhr expresses it, in his reply to Löwith's strictures on himself: "I know that Christ is the 'light that shineth in darkness.' The question between us is how absolute the darkness is."[37]

Before we give Niebuhr the last word, however, it is necessary to warn that his solution is not simple. But it is essential to an understanding of any part of Niebuhr's work (and this applies to his political writings as well as to his theology) to recall that he regarded truth as essentially paradoxical. It is one of the most significant aspects of Niebuhr's work that the reader's reception of Niebuhr's message often seems to depend less on whether one shares his religious commitment than on whether one accepts paradoxical thinking with patience. To a certain type of mind, there is no excuse for paradoxical arguments. Some secular and religious-liberal critics of Niebuhr regard his use of dialectical arguments as a sham, evidence enough of the perverse effects of an orthodox religious training. Some Christian critics look upon his use of dialectical or paradoxical thinking as the predictable result of indiscriminate hobnobbing with atheists and cynics, who do not know the simplicity of the Gospel.

Niebuhr does find meaning in mere history, to the disgust of Löwith—and he finds it in a species of progress. But this is not to be confused with the liberal dogma of linear and cumulative progress. The completion of history remains beyond history. Thus, Christian optimism, which fixes on a completion of the incompleteness of life "beyond time" has nothing in common with secular optimism which strives for perfection "within time"; Niebuhr never compromises on this distinction:

Whenever history is understood as solving its own problems by the cumulation of knowledge and wisdom and the consequent increase of virtue; whenever the complexities of history's relation to eternity are not known to be characteristic of history on every level of its development, the Christian claim that God has been revealed in Christ cannot be taken seriously. This is why liberal Christianity can give no satisfactory answer to the question why Christ, rather than some other "good" character of history, should be revered as divine, or produce a higher form of "goodness" more worthy of our "highest devotion."[38]

In obvious contradiction to modern liberal interpretations of the power of love in history, Jesus discourages the hope that the preaching of the gospel will banish evil from history. . . . The love which enters history as suffering love, must remain suffering love in history. . . . And Jesus anticipates the growth of evil as well as the growth of good in history.[39]

Only one aspect of man can be seen as really developing within history and that is his freedom. As revelation is the story of man's salvation, mere history is the story of man's developing freedom.

Here Niebuhr is at his paradoxical best:

The question arises why the process of history should not gradually gather up the timeless values and eliminate the worthless. Why should not history be a winnowing process in which truth is separated from falsehood; and the falsehood burned as chaff while the wheat of truth is "gathered into the barn?" There is one sense in which this is true. . . . It is true in the sense that history is actually the story of man's developing freedom. Insofar as increasing freedom leads to harmonies of life with life within communities, in which the restraints and cohesions of nature are less determinative for the harmony than the initiative of man, a positive meaning must be assigned to growth in history. . . . [But] the perils of freedom rise with its promises, and the perils and promises are inextricably interwoven . . . [as in the] parable of the wheat and the tares. . . . There is, in other words, no possibility of a final judgment within history, but only at the end of history. The increase of human freedom over nature is like the advancing season which ripens both wheat and tares, which are inextricably intermingled. . . . [Thus we see] the significance of the symbol of Anti-Christ at the end of history, as indicative of the belief in the New Testament that history remains open to all possibilities of good and evil to the end.[40]

Applied to the case of America, the lesson is clear:

> We have grown from infancy to adolescence and from adolescence
> to maturity in quick and easy strides; and we were inclined to
> solve every problem, as young people do, by increasing our
> strength. Now we have suddenly come upon a mystery of life.
> It is that an infant in his cradle is in some respects more powerful
> than a man in his maturity. For the infant's every wish is fulfilled
> by some benevolent attendant; but the wishes of a mature man
> are subject to the hazards of many conflicting and competing
> desires. We were stronger as a nation when we rocked in the
> cradle of our continental security, than we are today when we
> "bestride this narrow world like a huge colossus." for the *patterns*
> of history have grown more rapidly than our strength.[41]

# CONCLUSION:

# MIDDLE AXIOMS

It was in Reinhold Niebuhr's third academic year at Union Theological Seminary (1930–31) that he encountered perhaps the most challenging (in every sense of the word) of all his students. This was Dietrich Bonhoeffer, then aged twenty-four. As a child, Bonhoeffer had listened to conversations in his living-room between his father, a leading German psychiatrist, and his father's colleagues at Berlin University, among them the theologian Adolf von Harnack, and the sociologist Alfred Weber. At Tübingen, he had studied theology under Karl Heim and Adolf Schletter; and at Berlin, under Harnack and his epigones. His doctorate behind him, he was now on leave from his lectureship at the University of Berlin while attending Union Theological Seminary on a Fellowship. He had scarcely got inside the front door before concluding that Union, reputedly the best of America's theological schools, was hopeless, and that they needed him more than he needed them.[1] Above all, what they needed was to have Karl Barth vouchsafed to them. Accordingly, he read them a seminar paper on "The Theology of Crisis":

> Coming to a man like K. Barth after half a year of consideration
> of the problem of relation between cosmology, philosophy, and
> theology [here, at Union Theological Seminary], I confess that
> I do not see any other possible way for you to get into real contact
> with his thinking than by forgetting at least for this one hour
> everything you have learned before concerning this problem. We
> have in Barth's theology not one of the countless variations of
> the solution to this problem from the Scholastics via Kant to
> Bergson or Dewey, but here we stand on an entirely different

and new point of departure to the whole problem. We stand in the tradition of Paul, Luther, Kierkegaard, in the tradition of genuine Christian thinking.[2]

Not everyone in that audience could have been thrilled to death by the proposition that everything that constituted the regular curriculum at Union Theological Seminary should stand aside while this twenty-four year old Visiting Fellow delivered "the tradition of genuine Christian thinking" to them. That he was not carried out bodily and lynched in nearby Central Park suggests that what this company may have lacked in Christian learning they made up for in Christian forebearance. Notwithstanding Bonhoeffer's arrogant assumption that he was casting his precious German seed on stony ground, the minds of at least some of that student body had been exposed, by Reinhold Niebuhr among others of their teachers, to the first products of the new dialectical theology, and the habit of deference to German scholarship was well established.

Bonhoeffer, however, never gave up, apparently, to the end, his conviction about the unfitness of American ground for genuine theology. In this, he was merely being faithful to certain preconceptions within the Barthian camp which would always make it impossible for the faithful to hope for anything good to come out of New York. He is an especially striking example of what Paul Tillich has called (with both irony and chagrin, since he believed himself to have been at one time especially guilty of it) the "intellectual provincialism of German scholarship."[3] What makes Bonhoeffer's example especially instructive is that he had such ample opportunities to unlearn his provincialism. He had visited America twice by the end of the decade, had lived in the homes of members of the Union faculty, and continued to correspond with several of them (including Niebuhr) to the end. Though his thoughts on the American religious scene became marginally less harsh by the end of the decade, this was at best a progress from blanket abuse to a general condemnation with a mild admixture of condescension. He evidently felt at the end of his life just about as he did at the beginning of his acquaintance with America, when he was recording for friends back in Germany his observations on "the threat which America signifies for us."[4]

In the present climate of enthusiasm for Bonhoeffer among American religious writers it may be well to remind ourselves of how totally hostile Bonhoeffer was to the most vital traditions of the American religious community. This especially needs doing in our present case, since it is an essential part of the argument of this book that what is best and most durable in the American Protestant tradition is represented in Reinhold Niebuhr—and that his contributions to American political and intellectual life were possible because of the continuing relevance of that tradition to secular political discussion. I can think of no better way of preparing the way for discovering what is most valuable in that tradition than to summarize here some of the observations of Dietrich Bonhoeffer, one of its most irreconcilable critics.

The gist of Bonhoeffer's indictment of American religious life was that it was hostile to the essential unity of the Church. The Church's complete "disintegration" in America manifests itself in denominationalism, the inevitable accompaniment of which is creedal disunity; the concomitant of that, in turn, is a downgrading of dogma, indeed of all theology. "They remind us from over there: you overrate thought, theology, dogma; it is only one of many expressions of the church, and not the most important at that. We reply: it is not a question of thought, but of the truth of the Word of God, by which we mean to live and die. It is a question of salvation. . . . Unity in thought is not superior to unity in work, but unity in faith, which is confession, breaks right through both and alone creates the preconditions for common thought and action."[5] It is of course this diversity of confession that is the pride of the American religious community. There is no doubt that Bonhoeffer had identified the ground of American religion's chief pride, and he was prepared to join issue upon it. He had nothing but contempt for the argument of Americans that diversity of creed and the tradition of liberty and toleration based upon it represents a spiritual accomplishment. Where Americans speak proudly of America's beginnings as a haven for the persecuted, Bonhoeffer prefers to see the early chapters of American religious history in terms of the flight of the weaker brethren from the struggle for Christian unity on the continent: "[The Christian fugitive to America] claimed for himself the right to forgo the final suffering in order to be able to serve God in quietness and peace. Now in the place of refuge, there is no more justification for a continuation of the struggle. . . . With his right to flee the Christian fugitive has forfeited the right to fight. . . . [T]he deep abhorrence which any confessional discrimination in American Christianity has always met with in the long run may be adequately explained from the Christian right to flee, from the character of America as a sanctuary."[6] The pride that Americans derive from their tradition of tolerance, Bonhoeffer argues, is misplaced—indeed, sinful. "The praise of freedom as the possibility for existence given by the world to the church can stem precisely from an agreement entered upon with this world in which the true freedom of the Word of God is surrendered."[7] Since it is the State which guarantees and underwrites this freedom (that is, in the constitutional protection of religious liberty), American

Christians are conditioned to believe that there can be and must be an accommodation between the demands of the Gospel and the requirements of citizenship. Thus American Christians exaggerate the benignity of the State, and "the dignity of the divine office of the sword 'to avenge the evil and reward the good' appears to be lost"[8] The authority for this judgment is Luther's "*doctrine of the two offices or the two realms*, which will remain ordained by God until the end of the world."[9] Failing to perceive the absolute distinction between the office of the church and the office of the State, "The [American] church claims for itself the right to speak and act in all matters of public life, for only so can the kingdom of God be built."[10]

Note how neatly Bonhoeffer draws the connections between (1) America's misguided faith in religious toleration, (2) her neglect of dogmatic theology, (3) her denominational confusion, (4) her confusion of the realms of public policy and church policy. Notice the absolutism of the whole argument: the Lutheran dogma of the two realms is God's final word on matters of public ethics. Americans live in ignorance or defiance of this dogma; *ergo*, true Christianity is doomed in America.

When Christianity succumbs finally in America it will be the fault, primarily, of the likes of Reinhold Niebuhr, thought Dietrich Bonhoeffer. "The theological education of this group [the social activists at Union Theological Seminary, under Reinhold Niebuhr's example] is virtually nil, and the self-assurance which lightly makes mock of any specifically theological question is unwarranted and naive. . . . [T]he theological atmosphere of Union Theological Seminary is accelerating the process of secularization of Christianity in America."[11] Between dogmatic theology (as rediscovered by Barth) and secular relativism, therefore, there is no middle ground.

In his little book, *Theology of Culture* (1959), Paul Tillich offers a thumbnail summary of German theology and philosophy through the nineteenth century and to the First World War, stressing (with some pride, since this is the tradition that shaped his own thinking) its scholarly seriousness, moral earnestness, its openness, and its thoroughness. "It was our feeling that only in Germany was the problem of how to unite Christianity and the modern mind taken absolutely seriously. . . . It was *Weltanschauung*, a vision of the world as a whole. And we despised every philosophy which was less than this. . . . And then it happened that at the end of the road of German philosophy and theology, the figure of Hitler appeared."[12] For all the scrupulousness and the integrity of German theological scholarship, even the greatest of the German theologians never succeeded in overcoming certain dogmatic assumptions of the continental Lutheran tradition—principally, Luther's dogma of the "two spheres." This is, Tillich claims, at the heart of the *total* failure of German theology to provide a social ethic adequate to deal with the demonic aspects of Nazism. The Lutheran notion that the obligation of obedience to the state is something imposed upon man as an unshakable curse, which it is blasphemy to reason about or to agonize over, delivered the leadership of the Churches into the snares of Adolf Hitler. "As humbly as I conduct myself when God sends me a sickness," wrote Luther, "so humbly should I conduct myself toward evil government." It was in this spirit that Bonhoeffer and the Confessing Church, the *opposition* wing of the Lutheran Church, met the challenge of, for example, the Aryan Clauses of 1933. Taking for his text a passage from Luther of 1546 ("We would still show them [the Jews] the Christian doctrine, and ask them to turn and accept the Lord whom they should by rights have honoured before we did. . . . Where they repent, leave their usury, and accept Christ, we would gladly regard them as brothers"), Bonhoeffer wrote in 1933:

> Without doubt, the Church of the Reformation has no right to
> address the state directly in its specifically political actions. It has
> neither to praise nor to censure the laws of the state, but must
> rather reaffirm the State to be God's order of preservation in a
> godless world. . . . History is made not by the church, but by the
> state. . . . Without doubt, the Jewish question is one of the
> historical problems which our state must deal with, and without
> doubt the state is justified in adopting new methods here. . . .
> The true Church of Christ, however, which lives solely from the
> Gospel and realizes the character of the State's actions, will never
> intervene in the state in such a way as to criticize its history-
> making actions, from the standpoint of some humanitarian ideal.[13]

And, sure enough, it did not!

Admirers of Bonhoeffer, captivated by the example of his martyrdom and by certain unfinished manuscripts smuggled from his prison and which *hint at some kind* of reconciliation between believers and secular society, have permitted themselves to believe that anything which we find unpleasant in the earlier writings can be simply discounted: everything was about to be radically revised, and brought in line with the best and most humane of contemporary thought and experience. Yet on this one vital matter—the matter of ethics—there is nothing in Bonhoeffer's last writings that gives even the merest hint that he had begun to think his way out of the hopeless Lutheran absolutism that had obliged him to believe to his dying day that questions of public policy—like the Final Solution to the Jewish question—were not proper subject-matter for the Church's attention. The whole of the opposition within the Churches to Hitler was directed towards removing the State's interference within the affairs of the Church. Provided that the Church was left autonomous within its own sphere, there could be no grounds for the Church's raising its voice in disapproval of the history-making decisions of the state.

Bonhoeffer talks of the state, the shaper of History, as being somehow obliged, within its own framework of values, to take into account in its actions certain "humanitarian principles," which are the product of secular (humanist) contemplation of the science of national and international statecraft. These humanitarian principles are products of secular thinking, and are rooted in secular thought. And with these, Christian ethics has nothing to do. The traditional American-Protestant response to the challenge of social ethics is utterly different. It assumes that, underlying the differences in the roles played by the Churches and the State, there are certain shared commitments. There is some common source from which all ethical propositions ultimately derive. The Kingdom of God, however defined, cannot be imagined as being divided against itself. And the Kingdom of God is the End of History. Where the continental tradition requires that the events of the past be segregated into the two watertight categories of *Geschichte* (mere history) and *Heilsgeschichte* (sacred history), American theologians have always seen History as one fabric.

In this connection, Paul Tillich speaks of "the predominantly vertical thinking in Europe" (referring here to secular as well as theological thinking). In European thought, "Life is a fight in the vertical direction between divine and demonic forces. It is not a struggle for the progressive actualization of human possibilities.... In Europe the problem of the Church is the problem of its ultimate foundation, and theology is supposed to explain this foundation in a completely balanced theological system."[14] In America, by contrast, theology partakes of the ubiquitous spirit of pragmatism, so that: "The whole history of America has turned the American mind in a horizontal direction.... In American Christianity, the Church is a social agent among others, which tries to surpass the others in attractiveness. Its foundations are more or less taken for granted, but the practical demands, following from its nature, are in the center of interest. Making man better, helping him to become a person, and making the social conditions better, helping them to become actualizations of the Kingdom of God on earth—this is the function of the Church."[15]

While warning his American readers of the hazards that there are in this pragmatic orientation to American theology, Tillich concludes —and in a moving bit of autobiography reveals that this has been a crucial lesson in his own intellectual life—that it is the pragmatic orientation which, when all is said and done, is "the glory of American theology." "The difficulties stressed by Continental theology, in applying the absolute principles of the Christian message to concrete political situations were met by American theological ethics in a rather ingenious way. One found that between the absolute principle of love and the ever-changing concrete situation, middle axioms exist which mediate the two. Such principles are democracy, the dignity of every man, equality before the law, etc."[16]

It is in this light that I have tried in this book to present the work of Reinhold Niebuhr. It is in no sense fortuitous that the most respected and powerful spokesman of the progressive impulses of the generation now passing was a Protestant preacher. The American Progressive spirit has its roots in the American version of Protestant thought. The secular principles in terms of which America has sought to explain its public actions to itself and to the outside world—the principles of democracy, liberty, equality—are the *middle axioms* between Christian theology and practical statesmanship.

Arthur Schlesinger, Jr., explains Niebuhr to us as "an instinctive empiricist."[17] Nothing could be further from the truth. While he spoke approvingly of the "pragmatic approaches to political issues," Niebuhr never thought of *pragmatism* as lovely for its own sake. "Pragmatism," he wrote, "as such has no particular virtue. There must be a proper framework of values in which pragmatic decisions are reached."[18] John C. Bennett, speaking of Niebuhr's arguments, in the latter months of the War, in favor of a non-punitive peace with Germany describes him as depending upon "[the] assumptions [which depend upon] the context of Christian faith."[19] These "assumptions" are the "middle axioms" that Tillich speaks of. Our political ideals are still dependent upon them.

I am convinced that the unmatched influence of Niebuhr's political philosophy upon his generation is testimony to the American liberal's continuing need for reference to the first principles, the transcendent, the *theological* principles which are the ground upon which American secular ethics stands. I am convinced with Morton White (whose observations on "the contemporary liberal's fascination with Niebuhr" we considered near the outset of this study) that it is a delusion to believe that one really stands on the same ground with Niebuhr in matters of political philosophy when one can deny the theological propositions which he claims to be the root of his own political faith. I have thus sought to make clear the primacy of his theological development throughout, and have insisted throughout that the "integrity" of his career, both on the reflective side and on the active side, has been secured by the religious seriousness of his commitments. It may be, as Morton White argues, that those of Niebuhr's admirers who believe that they can separate his political convictions from his theological ones owe us some explanation. Certainly Reinhold Niebuhr owes us none.

# NOTES

## NOTES TO PREFACE

1   "Niebuhr's re-interpretation of human nature and history helped to shift the basis of democratic faith from an optimistic rationalism to a tempered and skeptical pragmatism and thereby immeasurably strengthened that faith for the storms of mid-century." "Outstanding Books, 1931–1961," *American Scholar* (Fall 1961), 624.

2   "Niebuhr is the father of us all." Cited by June Bingham, *Courage to Change: An Introduction to the Life and Thought of Reinhold Niebuhr* (New York: Scribner's, 1961), p. 368.

3   "[RN] is probably the most influential single mind in the development of American attitudes which combine moral purpose with a sense of political reality." In A. M. Schlesinger, Jr. and Morton White, eds. *Paths of American Thought* (Boston: Houghton-Mifflin, 1963), pp. 293–308.

4   An address to a banquet in honor of the twenty-fifth year of Niebuhr's journal, *Christianity and Crisis* (February 25, 1966). Printed by the Office of the Vice-President, Washington, D.C., 1966.

5   Christopher Lasch, *The New Radicalism in America* (New York: Knopf, 1965), p. 290.

6   Morton White, *Social Thought in America: The Revolt Against Formalism* (Boston: Beacon Press, 1949); Revised paperback ed. (1957), pp. 258ff.

7   Ibid., pp. 257–59.

8   Hans Morgenthau, "The Influence of Reinhold Niebuhr in American Political Life and Thought," in H. R. Landon, ed., *Reinhold Niebuhr: A Prophetic Voice in Our Times* (Greenwich, Conn.: Seabury Press, 1962), p. 109.

9   Sidney Hook, "Prophet of Man's Glory and Tragedy;" a review of C. W. Kegley and R. W. Bretall, eds., *Reinhold Niebuhr: His Religious, Social and Political Thought* in the *New York Times* (Sunday, January 29, 1956), VI, 16–17.

## NOTES TO CHAPTER ONE

1   H. J. Behr to Editor, *Atlantic* (undated), Niebuhr Papers, Library of Congress.

2   "Failure of German-Americanism," *Atlantic Monthly* (July 1916), 13–18. This article is considered later, herein, pages 17–19.

3   Carl Wittke, *The German Language Press in America* (Louisville: University of Kentucky Press, 1957).

4   The details on Niebuhr's family background and childhood years derive principally from June Bingham, *Courage to Change*, chaps. 5 and 7. Mrs. Bingham's engaging account of these formative events is based upon extensive interviews and correspondence with members of the Niebuhr family, surviving in the later 1950s, but now all dead. Her records are on deposit in a separate companion collection to the Niebuhr Papers, at the Library of Congress.

5   "Intellectual Autobiography," in C. W. Kegley and R. W. Bretall, *Reinhold Niebuhr: His Religious, Social, and Political Thought* (New York: Macmillan, 1956), p.3.

6   Bingham, p. 51; "Intellectual Autobiography," p. 3.

7   Bingham, p. 55.

8   Ibid., pp. 79–82.

9   RN to S. D. Press, March 2, 1914; Bingham, p. 84.

10  RN to Press, March 2, 1914; Bingham, p. 83.

11  RN to Press, March 2, 1914; Bingham, p. 83.

12  RN to Press, July 1, 1915; Bingham, p. 86–87.

13  Bingham, p. 83.

14  "Intellectual Autobiography," p. 4.

15  RN to Press, July 1, 1915; Bingham, p. 87.

16  RN to Press, April 16, 1914; Bingham, p. 85.

17  Niebuhr's words, to Press, November 3, 1915; Bingham, p. 88.

18  Ibid.

19  Information for this and the following paragraph is drawn principally from an article in the denomination's paper, "The Church that Niebuhr Built," *Advance* (May, 1945).

20  Quoted in "The Church that Niebuhr Built."

21  RN to Dr. Robert E. Speer, March 4, 1921; Niebuhr Papers.

22  RN, *Leaves from the Notebooks of a Tamed Cynic* (Chicago: Willit, Clark and Colby, 1929); Meridian Living Age, ed., with a new preface by RN, 1957, pp. 19–21.

23  Bingham, chap. 9, "The Man of God" and chap. 11, "The Sin of Ford."

24  RN, *Leaves* (Meridian ed.), pp. 11–12.

25  R. G. Collingwood, *The Idea of History*, T. M. Knox, ed. (1946); (New York: Oxford University Press Galaxy ed., 1956), p. 304.

26  Bingham, p. 18.

27  See Allan Nevins, *The Gateway to History* (New York: Heath, 1938), Preface; and *Catalogue of the Oral History Collection of Columbia University* (New York: Columbia University, 1960), p. 7.

28  Bingham, chap. 9.

29  Paul Tillich, "Sin and Grace," in H. R. Landon, ed., *Reinhold Niebuhr: A Prophetic Voice in Our Time* (Greenwich, Conn.: Seabury Press, 1962), p. 39.

30  Bingham, p. 319.

NOTES TO CHAPTER TWO

1   June Bingham, *Courage to Change*, p. 114.
2   Ibid., p. 58.
3   Ibid., p. 85.
4   Ibid., p. 114.
5   Ibid. The article is "The Failure of German-Americanism," *Atlantic Monthly* (July, 1916), 13–18.
6   One qualification should be noted. Niebuhr's papers reveal that he offered an article on some aspect of "the German-American situation" to the *New Republic* in the Fall of 1918, but it was refused. Herbert Croly to RN, October 24, 1918, Niebuhr Papers.
7   "What the War Did to My Mind," *Christian Century* (September 27, 1928), 1161–63.
8   "The Nation's Crime Against the Individual," *Atlantic Monthly* (November, 1916), 609–14.
9   Herbert Croly to RN, October 24, 1918 and June 19, 1919; Shailer Mathews to RN, July 31, 1919, Niebuhr Papers.
10  Sherwood Eddy, *Eighty Adventurous Years: An Autobiography* (New York: Harper's, 1955), p. 9. From the Introduction written by Reinhold Niebuhr.
11  The point here is that Niebuhr was not an accredited chaplain, and thus not under the discipline or in the pay of the war machine. He was merely a civilian pastor on visit.
12  *Leaves* (Meridian ed. 1957), pp. 32–33. The emphasis is mine. The date of the entry is simply given as "1918."
13  See Niebuhr's testimony on this point before the Senate Committee considering Roosevelt's Lend-Lease proposal. U.S., Congress, Senate, Committee on Foreign Relations, *To Promote the Defense of the United States*, 77th Cong., 1st Sess., S 275, Parts 1–3.
14  *Leaves*, p. 32.
15  Ibid., p. 34.
16  "What the War Did to My Mind."
17  Supra, pp. 55ff.
18  *Leaves*, pp. 68–69.
19  "Can Christianity Survive?" (January 1925); "Germany and Modern Civilization" (June 1925); "Puritanism and Prosperity" (June 1926); "Critique of Pacifism" (May 1927); "The Unhappy Intellectuals" (June 1929); "Awkward Imperialists" (May 1930).
20  *Nation*, "Heroes and Hero-Worship" (February 23, 1921); *New Republic*, "Protestantism and Prohibition" (October 24, 1928).
21  For example: The Editors of *New Republic* to RN, August 11, 1921; Niebuhr Papers.
22  The following two paragraphs draw mainly upon J. T. Hefly, "The Christian Century in American Culture, 1920–1941" (Ph.D. dissertation, University of Minnesota, 1952, University Microfilms); and upon correspondence between C. C. Morrison and RN, Niebuhr Papers.
23  Morrison to RN, July 31, 1922; Niebuhr Papers.

24 Presumably he means the *Nation* (February 23, 1921)—or perhaps he is referring to Niebuhr's lengthy letter to the Editor, "Twilight of Liberalism," *New Republic* (June 14, 1919), 218.

25 Morrison to RN, September 1922, Niebuhr Papers.

26 Morrison to RN, February 23, 1923, Niebuhr Papers.

27 At the height of his celebrity, Niebuhr was always ready with uncompensated contributions to journals whose cause he shared—notably, the theological and church publications. But when an editor or publisher could pay, Niebuhr saw to it that he did. More than once, he had to take the gloves off with publishers who were slow with royalties.

28 *Does Civilization Need Religion? A Study in the Social Resources and Limitations of Religion in Modern Life* (New York: Macmillan, 1927); *Leaves* (1929); *The Contribution of Religion to Social Work* (New York: Columbia University, 1932).

29 *Christian Century*, "To Whom Shall We Go?"—Sermon (March 10, 1927), 299–301.

30 *Christian Century*, "Why I am not a Christian" (December 15, 1927), 1482–83.

31 *Survey*, "A Religion Worth Fighting For" (August 1, 1927), 444–46.

32 *Leaves*, pp. 146–47.

33 *Christian Century*, "Wanted: A Christian Morality" (February 15, 1923), 201–203.

34 "Wanted: A Christian Morality."

35 *Leaves* (dated 1928), pp. 193–94. For a public confession on the same lines, *see*, "Why I am not a Christian."

36 *Biblical World*, "The Church and the Industrial Crisis" (November 1920), 588–92.

37 *Does Civilization Need Religion?*, p. 46. The mature Niebuhr's view of the *uses* of religion is quite different from this. Perhaps the best source on this matter is his collection of sermons, *Beyond Tragedy* (1937).

38 "The Church and the Industrial Crisis."

39 Author's conversation with Niebuhr, 1962.

40 *Christian Century*, "Christianity and Contemporary Politics" (April 17, 1924), 498–501.

41 *New York Times* (December 31, 1925), 6:6.

42 *New York Times* (December 30, 1926), 40:2. (RN to National Student Conference, Milwaukee, Wisconsin.)

43 "Our Secularized Civilization," *Christian Century* (April 22, 1926), 508–10.

44 "Our Secularized Civilization."

45 See Niebuhr's review article, "Capitalism: Protestant Offspring," *Christian Century* (May 7, 1925), 600–601.

46 See R. H. Tawney, *Religion and the Rise of Capitalism* (1926); (New York; Mentor ed., 1947), pp. 261–62.

47 H. R. Niebuhr, *The Social Sources of Denominationalism* (1929); (New York: Meridian Living Age ed., 1957). See the author's preface, in which he acknowledges his brothers "constant interest" in the preparation of the book. See also S. E. Ahlstrom, "H. R. Niebuhr's Place in American Thought," *Christianity and Crisis* (November 25, 1963), 213–17.

48  See his "Walter Rauschenbusch in Historical Perspective," in Ronald H. Stone, ed., *Faith and Politics* (New York: Braziller, 1968), pp. 33–45.

49  "Heroes and Hero Worship," *Nation* (February 23, 1921), 393–94.

50  D. R. Davies, *Prophet from America* (London: J. Clark, 1945).

51  RN, "Intellectual Autobiography," 5.

52  For example, Bingham, p. 134.

53  For example, Bingham, pp. 137–38.

54  The circumstances are described in Donald Meyer, *The Protestant Search for Political Realism, 1919–1941* (Berkeley and Los Angeles: University of California, 1960), pp. 83–84, which draws principally upon the Federal Council of Churches' paper, *Information Service*. See also, *Report of the Forty-Sixth Annual Convention of the American Federation of Labor, Held at Detroit, Michigan, October 4 to 14, 1926* (Washington, D.C., 1926), especially pages 143–58; and Worth M. Tippy, "Why the Church Sympathizes with Labor," *American Federationist* (November 1926), 1308–10.

55  The entire piece from the *Detroiter* was read into the minutes of the A.F.L. Convention *Report*, 157–59.

56  Evidently, while seven A.F.L. speakers eventually spoke from six different pulpits during the course of Sunday, October 10, only two local clergymen associated themselves with the invitation to their own churches— namely, Augustus P. Record of the First Unitarian and Reinhold Niebuhr of Bethel Evangelical, *Nation* (October 20, 1926), editorial, page 387; *New York Times* (October 6, 1926), 1:3; (October 26), 5:3.

57  *Leaves*, pp. 132–33.

58  Wm. Leuchtenburg, *The Perils of Prosperity, 1914–1932* (Chicago: University of Chicago Press, 1958), pp. 186–87.

59  "How Philanthropic is Henry Ford?" *Christian Century* (December 9, 1926), 1516–17.

60  "How Philanthropic?" (December 9, 1926), 1516–17; "Ford's Five-day Week Shrinks" (June 9, 1927), 713–14. These are among the most effective of Niebuhr's early articles. He has done his homework for them carefully and offers much concrete documentation for his arguments about salaries, man-hours and the rest. I would be tempted to include portions of them here, but for the fact that they are readily available in D. B. Robertson, ed., *Love and Justice: Selections from the Shorter Writings of Reinhold Niebuhr* (Philadelphia: Westminster Press, 1957), pp. 98–108.

61  An extended examination of Ford's employee policies is in the semiofficial biography of Allan Nevins and Frank E. Hill, *Ford: Expansion and Challenge, 1915–1933*, II (New York: Scribner's, 1957), notably chaps. 13 and 20. Nevins and Hill feel that Ford's sterner critics (they mention Niebuhr among them, pages 528 and 665) have overstated their case. They admit only that Ford's reputation for enlightened labor policies was "inflated" (p. 526). See J. K. Galbraith's lively article on the Ford literature (including Nevins and Hill), "Was Ford a Fraud?" in his *The Liberal Hour* (Boston: Houghton-Mifflin, 1960).

62  "Ford's Five-day Week Shrinks."

63  See especially, "Religion's Limitations," *World Tomorrow* (March, 1920), 77–79; "The Church and the Industrial Crisis," *Biblical World* (November, 1920), 588–92; "The Church and the Middle Class," *Christian*

*Century* (December 7, 1922), 1513–15; "Wanted: A Christian Morality," *Christian Century* (February 15, 1923), 201–203; "The Paradox of Institutions," *World Tomorrow* (August, 1923), 231–32; "Christianity and Contemporary Politics," *Christian Century* (April 17, 1924), 498–501.

64 "The Church and the Industrial Crisis."
65 Ibid.
66 Ibid.
67 Ibid.
68 "The Church and the Middle Class."
69 Ibid.
70 "The Church and the Industrial Crisis."
71 Cited in Bingham, p. 65.
72 "Is Protestantism Self-Deceived?," *Christian Century* (December 25, 1924), 1661–62.
73 An instructive comparison can be made with the thought of Walter Lippmann in this period. See especially his *Public Opinion* (1922); *The Phantom Public* (1925); "Why Should the Majority Rule?" (1926), in C. Rossiter and J. Lare, eds., *The Essential Lippmann* (New York: Random House, 1965), 6–14; see also A. M. Schlesinger, Jr., *The Politics of Hope* (Boston: Houghton-Mifflin, 1962), chap. 10, "Walter Lippmann: The Intellectual vs. Politics," and frequent extended references to Lippmann in the 1920s in Schlesinger's *Crisis of the Old Order* (Boston: Houghton-Mifflin, 1957); also Charles Wellborn, *Twentieth Century Pilgrimage: Walter Lippmann and the Public Philosophy* (Baton Rouge: Louisiana State University Press, 1969), chaps. 2 and 3.

### NOTES TO CHAPTER THREE

1 From the jacket appreciation of Niebuhr's *Kingdom of God in America* (New York: Harper Torchbook ed., 1959).
2 Willem A. Visser't Hooft, *The Background of the Social Gospel in America* (1928); (St Louis, Mo.: Bethany Press Abbott Books ed., n.d. [1963?], pp. 20–21.
3 June Bingham, *Courage to Change*, p. 58.
4 Richard Hofstadter, *The Age of Reform* (New York: Vintage ed., 1960).
5 Hofstadter, *Age of Reform*, pp. 148–64.
6 Niebuhr's Columbia Oral History memoir, cited in Bingham, pp. 58–59.
7 Ibid.
8 Bingham, p. 55.
9 Hofstadter, *Age of Reform*, p. 151.
10 Ibid., p. 150.
11 Henry F. May, *Protestant Churches and Industrial America* (New York: Harper Torchbook ed., 1967), p. 91.
12 Hofstadter, *Age of Reform*, p. 149.
13 Richard Hofstadter, *The Progressive Movement 1900–1915* (Englewood Cliffs: Prentice-Hall Spectrum books, 1963), p. 8.
14 Interest in the Social Gospel as a major force in the shaping of American

liberalism is reflected in: A. M. Schlesinger, Jr., *The Crisis of the Old Order* (Boston: Houghton-Mifflin, 1957); Eric Goldman, *Rendezvous with Destiny* (New York: Knopf, 1952), Vintage books ed., 1956; Richard Hofstadter, *Age of Reform* (New York: Vintage Books, 1955); Richard Hofstadter, *Anti-Intellectualism in American Life* (New York: Knopf, 1963).

A basic bibliography on Social Gospel would include: H. Shelton Smith, R. T. Handy, and L. A. Loetscher, *American Christianity: An Historical Interpretation with Representative Documents* (New York: Scribner's, 1963), II, chaps. 19, 20; Charles H. Hopkins, *The Rise of the Social Gospel in American Protestantism, 1865–1915* (New Haven: Yale University Press, 1940); Robert M. Miller, *American Protestantism and Social Issues, 1919–1939* (Chapel Hill: University of North Carolina Press, 1958); Paul Carter, *The Decline and Revival of the Social Gospel* (Ithaca: Cornell University Press, 1954). Henry F. May, *Protestant Churches and Industrial America* (New York: Octagon, 1949); Aaron I. Abell, *The Urban Impact on American Protestantism, 1865–1900* (Cambridge: Harvard University Press, 1943); J. N. Hughley, *Trends in Protestant Social Idealism* (New York: King's Crown Press, 1948); F. H. Littell, *From State Church to Pluralism: A Protestant Interpretation of Religion in American History* (New York: Doubleday Anchor book, 1962), chaps. 3–5; H. R. Niebuhr, *The Kingdom of God in America* (1937); (New York: Harper Torchbook ed., 1959); Donald B. Meyer, *The Protestant Search for Political Realism, 1919–1941* (Berkeley and Los Angeles: University of California Press, 1960).

The reader wishing to sample Social Gospel writings of the period is referred to the extensive bibliographies given in the works already cited by Smith *et al.*, Hopkins, Carter, and Meyer. The first claims on the reader's attention belong to the works of Mathews, Gladden, Peabody, and Rauschenbusch.

15  Eric Goldman, *Rendezvous with Destiny*, pp. 82–84.

16  "The largest and hardest part of the work of Christianizing the social order has been done." Walter Rauschenbusch, *Christianizing the Social Order* (1913), p. 124. See also the address of Arthur C. McGiffert, "The Kingdom of God" (1909) reprinted in Smith *et al.*, *American Christianity*, II, 285–90.

17  *Biblical World* (January 1920). This journal was edited, according to its masthead, by Shailer Mathews "with the cooperation of the members of the Divinity Conference of the University of Chicago."

18  Francis G. Peabody, *Jesus Christ and the Social Question* (New York: Macmillan, 1901), pp. 324–26.

19  Ray Abrams, *Preachers Present Arms* (New York: Round Table Press, 1933); "War and the Christian Ethic," (Editorial), *New Republic* (January 11, 1922), 166–69; Granville Hicks, "The Parsons and the War," *American Mercury* (February 1927), 129–42; and John M. Mecklin, "The War and the Dilemma of the Christian Ethic," *American Journal of Theology* (1919), 14–40.

20  Abrams, *Preachers Present Arms*, chap. 4.

21  Smith *et al.*, *American Christianity*, chap. 22; Meyer, 8f.

22  James H. Timberlake, *Prohibition and the Progressive Movement, 1900–1920* (Cambridge: Harvard University Press, 1963).

23  Ibid., pp. 23–30.

24 Rauschenbusch, *Christianizing the Social Order* (1913), 209, 276.

25 "The Failure of German-Americanism," *Atlantic Monthly* (July 1916), 13–18.

26 The story of the Interchurch Movement is best got at in the files of the *New York Times*, which gave considerable news coverage to it, as well as extensive coverage in its editorial pages and magazine section. Donald Meyer gives several pages to the story, and offers a bibliography, pp. 9–10, 58–63, 420.

27 Major references on organization and purpose of Interchurch are, *New York Times* (Oct. 1, 1919), 2:6; (Oct. 3), 8:1; (Nov. 3), IV (magazine), 5; (Dec. 8), 2:3; (Feb. 24, 1920), 22:2; (March 14), VII, 7:1–3.

28 *New York Times* (February 24, 1920), 22:2.

29 *New York Times* (March 14, 1920), VII, 7:1–3.

30 Cited in Donald B. Meyer, *Protestant Search*, p. 9.

31 *New York Times* (October 1, 1919), 2:6; (November 30, 1919), IV, 5; (December 8), 2:3; also Meyer, 58–63.

32 Meyer, *Protestant Search*, p. 60.

33 On the Report, on the collapse of Interchurch, and on the possibilities of connection between the two, the principal references are: *New York Times* (June 30, 1920), 13:3; (May 19), 8:1; (June 13), VII (magazine) 3:1–8; (July 3), 14:8; (July 5, 1920), 8:7; (July 30, 8 (editorial); (Nov. 6), 12:8; (Dec. 14), 12:2 (Oct. 2, 1921), 2:6; (Oct. 3), 14:6; (Oct. 4), 6:1; (Oct. 5), 36:2. Meyer, pages cited. R. M. Miller, *American Protestantism and Social Issues*, pp. 211–16.

34 Meyer, *Protestant Search*, pp. 62, 420.

35 *Nation* (June 5, 1920), 746–47.

36 Meyer, *Protestant Search*, pp. 60ff.

37 F. H. Littell, *From State Church to Pluralism: A Protestant Interpretation of Religion in American History* (New York: Doubleday Anchor, 1962), p. 97.

38 André Siegfried, *America Comes of Age* (New York: Harcourt, Brace & World, 1927), p. 33; cited in H. R. Niebuhr, *Kingdom of God*, p. 17.

39 Cited in Winthrop S. Hudson, *American Protestantism* (Chicago: University of Chicago Press, 1961), p. 166.

40 Will Herberg, *Protestant—Catholic—Jew: An Essay in American Religious Sociology* (New York: Doubleday Anchor ed., 1960), chap. 5.

41 Ibid., p. 81.

42 Hofstadter, *Anti-Intellectualism*, p. 131.

43 A. M. Schlesinger, Jr., *The Age of Roosevelt (Crisis of the Old Order)*, (Boston: Houghton-Mifflin, 1937), I, 71–72.

44 Their principal sounding board during these years was the *World Tomorrow*, edited by Norman Thomas, and later on by a board of editors, including Reinhold Niebuhr. Published by the Fellowship of Reconciliation, it declared itself to be "a journal looking forward toward a Social Order Based on the Principles of Jesus" (from its masthead). The importance of this journal is considered later on.

45 "In the Progressive era the intellectuals had felt themselves to be essentially in harmony with the basic interests and aspirations of the people.

Now it was evident once more that this harmony was neither pre-established nor guaranteed." Hofstadter, *Anti-Intellectualism*, p. 131.

NOTES TO CHAPTER FOUR

1  June Bingham, *Courage to Change*, p. 276.

2  Conversation with Niebuhr, 1962.

3  "The Twilight of Liberalism" (letter to the editor) *New Republic* (June 14, 1919), 218.

4  For example: "The Church and the Industrial Crisis," *Biblical World* (November 1920), 588–92; "Christianity and Contemporary Politics," *Christian Century* (April 17, 1924), 498–501; "European Reform and American Reform: How They Differ," *Christian Century* (August 28, 1924), 1108–10; "Capitalism—Protestant Offspring," *Christian Century* (May 7, 1925), 600–601; "Germany and Modern Civilization," *Atlantic Monthly* (June 1925), 843–48; "Our Secularized Civilization," *Christian Century* (April 22, 1926), 508–10.

5  R. H. Tawney, *Religion and the Rise of Capitalism*, first published in 1926.

6  "Why We Need a New Economic Order," *World Tomorrow* (October 1928), 395–98. A few weeks after the stock market crash Niebuhr wrote an impressive article on "The Speculation Mania," which continues these arguments, *World Tomorrow* (January 1930), 25–27.

7  See "Intellectual Autobiography," in Kegley and Bretall, 7ff.

8  (Report of an address by RN), *New York Times* (January 28, 1929), 27:2

9  Murray Seidler, in his *Norman Thomas: Respectable Rebel* (Syracuse: Syracuse University Press, 1961), p. 105, includes Niebuhr in a list of "[Socialist] party members" who were active in the formation of the L.I.P.A. in the weeks immediately following the election of 1928, but he gives no hint of the evidence for Niebuhr's membership.

10 *New York Times* (Tuesday, November 6 [election day], 1928), 19:1.
   During a radio interview in 1960, Niebuhr recalled for Joseph P. Lyford that he had voted for Al Smith in 1928. Lyford, *The Agreeable Autocracies: A Series of Conversations on American Institutions* (New York: Oceana Publications, 1961), p. 138. Niebuhr's memory about how he has voted has failed him more than once, however. In a discussion with the present writer, he admitted that he had been under the impression that he had voted for Roosevelt in 1932 and again in 1936, until Arthur Schlesinger, Jr. convinced him, from the record, that he had voted for Norman Thomas on the first of those occasions (conversation with Niebuhr, 1962). In fact, the record shows (as we shall see) that he voted for Thomas in 1936 as well.

11 Seidler, *Norman Thomas*, pp. 73–74.

12 Ibid., pp. 73, 77, 145. David A. Shannon, *The Socialist Party of America: A History* (New York: Macmillan, 1955), pp. 54–57.

13 Daniel Bell, "The Background and Development of Marxian Socialism in the United States," in Donald Egbert and Stow Persons, eds., *Socialism in American Life* (Princeton: Princeton University Press, 1952), I, 369.

14 Seidler, *Norman Thomas*, p. 105; Meyer, *Protestant Search*, pp. 126, 179–80; Shannon, *Socialist Party of America*, p. 208; Bell, "Background and Development of Marxian Socialism in the United States," 370ff.; Schlesinger,

Crisis, p. 198; Morris Hillquit, *Loose Leaves from a Busy Life* (New York: Macmillan, 1934); Paul H. Douglas, *The Coming of the New Party* (New York: McGraw-Hill, 1932), esp. pp. 202ff.

15 Meyer, *Protestant Search*, p. 126.

16 Ibid., pp. 48–49; Miller, *American Protestantism*, p. 46.

17 Sherwood Eddy, *Eighty Adventurous Years*, 128ff.; Eddy, *Pilgrimage of Ideas* (New York: Farrar & Rhinehart, 1934), Chapter XI.

18 "Protestantism in Germany," *Christian Century* (October 4, 1923), 1258–1260; "Youth Movement of Germany," Ibid. (November 1, 1923), 1396–97; "Christianity and Contemporary Politics," Ibid. (April 17, 1924), 498–501; "European Reform and American Reform: How They Differ," Ibid. (August 28, 1924), 1108–10; "The German Klan," Ibid. (October 16, 1924), 1330–31; "Germany and Modern Civilization," *Atlantic Monthly* (June 1925), 843–48.

19 *Leaves*, pp. 67–68.

20 Letter in reply to an editorial on "War and Christian Ethics," *New Republic* (February 22, 1922), 272.

21 "Germany and Modern Civilization."

22 Ibid.

23 This theme is resumed and developed at length in a brilliant article of some years later: "English and German Mentality: A Study in National Traits," *Christendom* (Spring 1936), 465–76.

24 "Christianity and Contemporary Politics."

25 Ibid.

26 Ibid. See as well, "Labor's Story in England"; review of G. Elton, *England Arise!* in *World Tomorrow* (October 1931), 331.

27 "Germany and Modern Civilization."

28 "The German Klan."

29 "Germany and Modern Civilization."

30 "Christianity and Contemporary Politics."

31 Presumably the La Follette Progressive movement, or perhaps the Farmer-Labor Party of Minnesota (which was to give strong support to La Follette in 1924).

32 "Christianity and Contemporary Politics."

33 A reference to the first MacDonald government, January 22 to November 4, 1924. After the General Election of October, it was much less obvious that the British workingman was "gradually assuming ... power." This turn of events undoubtedly played some part (together with the unimpressive showing of La Follette in the American elections a few days later) in leading Niebuhr to revise his views about "enlisting" the middle-class by appeals to their "idealism."

34 "Christianity and Contemporary Politics."

35 *Leaves* (1923), p. 68.

36 "Christianity and Contemporary Politics."

NOTES TO CHAPTER FIVE

1 The circumstances of Niebuhr's call to Union Theological Seminary in 1928 are told in Bingham, *Courage to Change*, pp. 138–39, 154ff.; RN, "Intellectual Autobiography," 8.

2 "Intellectual Autobiography," 8–9.

3 "Intellectual Autobiography," 3.

4 See especially the observations of Dietrich Bonhoeffer, *No Rusty Swords: Letters, Lectures, and Notes, 1928–1936* (New York: Harper and Row, 1965), pp. 89–91, 116–17.

5 "De Tocqueville long since observed the strong pragmatic interest of American Christianity in comparison with European Christianity; and that distinction is still valid. I have been frequently challenged by the stricter sects of theologians in Europe to prove that my interests were theological rather than practical or 'apologetic,' but I have always refused to enter a defense, partly because I thought the point was well taken and partly because the distinction did not interest me." RN, "Intellectual Autobiography," 3.

6 Paul Tillich, "The Conquest of Intellectual Provincialism: Europe and America," *Theology of Culture* (New York: Oxford University Press, 1959), p. 165.

7 Tillich, *Theology of Culture*, p. 159.

8 "Intellectual Autobiography," 4.

9 Ibid.

10 Sidney Ahlstrom argues that there is something in the "national character" of Americans, "an underlying element of temperament that has made the German-American intellectual relationship so close ... [and] no explanation of the theological transformation of the last three or four decades can be adequate unless it takes account of this fact." Sidney E. Ahlstrom, "Continental Influence on American Christian Thought Since World War I," *Church History* (September 1958). A corollary to this thesis is that Americans of German background are specially equipped to give leadership in American intellectual life. I find this a very tempting lead, since it plays so well into my case for the significance of Reinhold Niebuhr as a leader in contemporary American thought. But the implications of this notion are so sweeping that I am reluctant to try to make anything of it in these pages. I offer it instead to some other bolder, and more qualified intellectual historian.

11 Kenneth S. Latourette, *Christianity in a Revolutionary Age*, V, *The Twentieth Century Outside Europe* (New York: Harper's 1962), pp. 506–507.

12 Paul Carter, *The Decline and Revival of the Social Gospel, 1920–1940* (Ithaca: Cornell University Press, 1954), pp. 117–18.

13 Ibid., p. 119.

14 A basic bibliography (in English) on the "Crisis theology" of the 1920s should be headed by Heinz Zahrnt, *The Question of God—Protestant Theology in the Twentieth Century* [translated from the German by R. A. Wilson, 1966] (New York: Harcourt Brace Jovanovich, Harvest ed., 1969); and William Nicholls, *Systematic and Philosophical Theology*, I, *The Pelican Guide to Modern Theology* (Penguin Books, 1969). In my

account of the impact of this movement upon American theology, I am particularly indebted to H. Shelton Smith, R. T. Handy, and L. A. Loetscher, *American Christianity: An Historical Interpretation with Representative Documents* (New York: Scribner's, 1963), II; Meyer; Harold E. Fey, ed., *How My Mind Has Changed* (New York: Meridian Living Age ed., 1961); Mary F. Thelan, *Man as Sinner in Contemporary American Realistic Theology* (New York: King's Crown Press, 1946); H. D. Lewis, *Morals and the New Theology* (London: Gollancz, 1947); George Hammar, *Christian Realism in Contemporary American Theology* (Uppsala, Sweden: Lundequistka Bokhandeln, 1940); Walter Lowrie, *Our Concern with the Theology of Crisis* (Boston: Meadow. 1932); Sidney E. Ahlstrom, "Continental Influence on American Christian Thought Since World War I," *Church History* (September, 1958). In my account of the impact of "crisis theology" upon the thought of Reinhold Niebuhr, I am particularly indebted to: Kegley and Bretall, eds.; Gordon Harland, *The Thought of Reinhold Niebuhr* (New York: Oxford, 1960); H. D. Odegard, *Sin and Conscience: Reinhold Niebuhr as Political Theologian* (Yellow Springs, Ohio: Antioch Press, 1956); Hans Hoffman, *The Theology of Reinhold Niebuhr* (New York: L. P. Smith, 1956); Edgar L. Allen, *Christianity and Society: A Guide to the Thought of Reinhold Niebuhr* (London: Hodder, Stoughton, 1950); D. L. Bloesch, "Reinhold Niebuhr's Re-evaluation of the Apologetic Task" (unpublished dissertation, University of Chicago, 1956); E. J. Carnell, *The Theology of Reinhold Niebuhr* (Grand Rapids, Michigan: Eerdmans, 1951); Georgette P. Vignaux, *La théologie de l'histoire chez Reinhold Niebuhr* (Paris: Délauchaux & Niestlé, 1957); Paul F. Battenhouse, "Theology in the Social Gospel, 1918–1946" (unpublished dissertation, Yale University, 1930).

15 Originally written in 1918, it was almost entirely rewritten for a second edition in 1922. It became available in English for the first time in 1933, in a translation by E. C. Hoskyns, published by the Oxford University Press. It is (at this writing) available in a paperback edition, Oxford University Press, 1968.

16 Karl Adam, cited in William Nicholls, *Systematic and Philosophical Theology*, p. 75.

17 Karl Barth, *Epistle to the Romans*, p. 10.

18 Barth testifies to the influence of Kierkegaard upon his thinking at the time of the composition of *Romans* in his essay, "A Thank-You and a Bow—Kierkegaard's Reveille," in *Fragments Grave and Gay*, edited by Martin Rumscheidt (London: Collins Fontana Books, 1971), pp. 97–98.

19 Barth, *Romans*, pp. 301, 303, 310.

20 A reference to the "Manifesto of the Intellectuals," drafted by the then undisputed leader of liberal theology, Adolf von Harnack, and signed by the leading German scholars, among them: Wilhelm Hermann, Wilhelm Windelband, Karl Lamprecht, Max Planck, and Max Reinhardt. Zahrnt, 15–16.

21 Karl Barth, *The Humanity of God* (London: Collins, 1961), p. 14.

22 This theme was later developed at length in his *Die Protestantische Theologie im 19. Jahrhundert* (1952) the larger portion of which appears in translation as *From Rousseau to Ritschl* (London: S.C.M. Press, 1959).

23 Barth, *Romans*, pp. 220–21.

24 Ibid., p. 9.

25  Ibid., p. 225.

26  Ibid., pp. 241–42, 243–44, 246, 253.

27  Karl Barth, *The Word of God and the Word of Man*, trans. Douglas Horton, 1928 (New York: Harper Torchbook ed., 1957). On Barth's initial impact on American theology, see Ahlstrom, "Continental Influence," 262ff.

28  "Barth—Apostle of the Absolute," *Christian Century* (December 13, 1928), 1523–24.

29  Emil Brunner, "Some Remarks on Reinhold Niebuhr's Work as a Christian Thinker," in Kegley and Bretall, *Niebuhr*, 28.

30  "Barth—Apostle of the Absolute."

31  Ibid.

32  Ibid.

33  "Barthianism and the Kingdom," *Christian Century* (July 15, 1931), 924–25.

34  "Barth—Apostle of the Absolute."

35  On the place of Marxist criticism in the indictment worked out by German theologians against *Kulturprotestantismus*, see Ahlstrom, "Continental Influence," 262–63.

36  Charles West, *Communism and the Theologians: Study of an Encounter* (London: S.C.M. Press, 1958), chap. 5, "Revelation and Ideology: Karl Barth"; and Paul Tillich, *The Religious Situation*, translated from the German by H. R. Niebuhr, 1932 (New York: Meridian Living Age ed., 1956), 196–97.

    Barth's own Social Democratic politics divided his congregation in Safenwill, in Switzerland, earning him a more-than-local reputation as the "Red Pastor." Edward B. Fiske, "Karl Barth Dies in Basel . . .," *New York Times* (December 11, 1968), 1:4–5, 42:1–6. See also, Nicholls, *Systematic and Philosophical Theology*, pp. 78–79.

37  Barth, *Romans*, pp. 478–80.

38  West, *Communism and the Theologians*, p. 179.

39  Will Herberg, "The Social Philosophy of Karl Barth," in Karl Barth, *Community, State, and Church: Three Essays*, (1960) (Gloucester, Mass.: Peter Smith, 1968), 23.

40  "Barth—Apostle of the Absolute."

41  Karl Barth, "A Thank-You and a Bow—Kierkegaard's Reveille," in *Fragments Grave and Gay* (London: Collins Fontana Library, 1971), 95–101.

42  "Barth—Apostle of the Absolute," *Christian Century* (December 13, 1928), 1523–24; "Church Currents in Germany," *Christian Century* (August 6, 1930), 959–60; "Barthianism and the Kingdom," *Christian Century* (July 15, 1931), 924–25; "Barthianism and Political Reaction," *Christian Century* (June 6, 1934), 757–59; "Marx, Barth, and Israel's Prophets," *Christian Century* (January 30, 1935), 138–40; "Karl Barth and Democracy," *Radical Religion* (Winter 1938); "Karl Barth on Politics," *Radical Religion* (Spring 1939).

43  "Barth—Apostle of the Absolute."

44  Ibid.

45  Ibid.

46 Ibid.

47 "Barthianism and Political Reaction."

48 See especially, "Church Currents in Germany," and "Barthianism and Political Reaction."

49 "Barthianism and Political Reaction."

50 H. S. Smith, R. T. Handy, L. A. Loetscher, *American Christianity: An Historical Interpretation* (New York: Scribner's, 1963), II, 432.

51 "Barth—Apostle of the Absolute."

52 William James, *The Will to Believe and Other Essays in Popular Philosophy* (1896) (New York: Dover edition, 1956), from the Preface, p. ix.
   The gist of James' whole argument is, it has always seemed to me, compacted into this brief and much-quoted passage: "For my own part, I do not know what the sweat and blood and tragedy of this life mean if they mean anything short of this. If this life be not a real fight, in which something is eternally gained for the universe by success, it is no better than a game of private theatricals from which one may withdraw at will. But it *feels* like a real fight,—as if there were something really wild in the universe which we, with all our idealities and faithfulnesses are needed to redeem." (Dover ed., p. 61.)

53 "I stand in the William James tradition. He was both an empiricist and a religious man, and his faith was both the consequence and the presupposition of his pragmatism." As cited in June Bingham, *Courage to Change*, p. 224.

54 "Barthianism and the Kingdom."

55 Ibid.

56 Ibid.

57 Karl Barth, "The Christian Community as the Civil Community," *Community, State and Church* (1946), 173.

58 On Tillich's religious socialism, the primary source in English is the series of articles he did in Niebuhr's journal, *Radical Religion*, from 1935 onward, among which are the following: "Marx and the Prophetic Tradition" (Fall 1935), 21–39; "Marxism and Christian Socialism" (Spring 1942), 13–18; "Man and Society in Religious Socialism" (Fall 1943), 10–21. See also Tillich's "Autobiographical Reflections," in C. W. Kegley and R. W. Bretall, eds., *The Theology of Paul Tillich* (New York: Macmillan, 1961); Paul Tillich, *Perspectives on Nineteenth and Twentieth Century Protestant Theology* (New York: Harper and Row, 1967), pp. 156–57; D. Mackenzie Brown, ed., *Ultimate Concern: Tillich in Dialogue* (New York: Harper and Row, 1965), pp. 30–31, 123–24.
   For Tillich's influence on Niebuhr, see Kegley and Bretall, *Niebuhr*, especially the chapter by J. C. Bennett; H. R. Landon, ed., *Reinhold Niebuhr: A Prophetic Voice in Our Time* (Greenwich, Conn.: Seabury Press, 1962); D. D. Egbert and Stow Persons, eds., *Socialism in American Life* (Princeton: Princeton University Press, 1952), II, 66ff. and 225ff. Finally, there are these articles by Niebuhr himself: "The Contribution of Paul Tillich," *Religion in Life* (Autumn 1937), 574–81; and "Biblical Faith and Socialism: A Critical Appraisal," in W. Leibrecht, *Religion and Culture: Essays in Honor of Paul Tillich* (New York: Harper's, 1959).

59 Tillich, *Religious Situation*, p. 50.

60 Ibid., p. 73.

61  Ibid., p. 217.

62  See especially, Donald B. Meyer, *The Protestant Search for Political Realism, 1919–1941* (Berkeley and Los Angeles: University of California Press, 1960), chap. 15.

63  Cited in Meyer, *Protestant Search,* p. 280.

64  Tillich, *Religious Situation,* 112–13.

65  Ibid., 113.

66  Ibid., 114ff.; Paul Tillich, *The Protestant Era* (Chicago: University of Chicago: Phoenix edition, 1957), xiiif, 49ff.

67  In the writing of this paragraph and the one that precedes it, I am much indebted to the late Professor Tillich, who replied to a request for criticism of an early draft of this section with some very considerable objections to the neglect in the first draft of the differences between his socialist analysis and that of secular Marxists. I have, in response to these criticisms, gone through this entire section, purging it of phrases like "vengeance" and "the proletarian cause" (to which he took particular exception), and have added the paragraphs just referred to. In the course of considering these criticisms, I have had to reread Tillich's writing of those years and have come away from this task with an increased appreciation for the exactness in the use of language which has always been the hallmark of Tillich's philosophical writing. (Paul Tillich to the writer, May, 1965.)

68  Tillich, *Religious Situation,* Part One, chap. 3.

69  Kegley and Bretall, *Tillich,* p. 315.

70  Tillich, *Protestant Era,* chap. II, "The Protestant Principle and the Proletarian Situation."

71  "The proletariat must deny the very reality by whose strength it fights the Bourgeois Principle, [namely] the Origin; and it must affirm the reality it wants to shatter, the Bourgeois Principle. This is the inner conflict of its situation." Cited from a work of the early 1920s, not available in English translation (and not precisely identified) in West, *Communism and the Theologians,* p. 97.

72  Tillich, *Protestant Era,* 49.

73  "Eternity and Our Time"; a review of Tillich, *The Religious Situation,* translated by H. R. Niebuhr, *World Tomorrow* (December 21, 1932), 596.

74  This seems to be the argument of A. M. Schlesinger, Jr., in his article, "Reinhold Niebuhr's Role in American Political Thought and Life," in Kegley and Bretall, *Niebuhr.* The same essay also appears in Schlesinger's own collection, *Politics of Hope* (Boston: Houghton-Mifflin, 1962).

75  Schlesinger, in Kegley and Bretall, 138.

76  A scholarly study of this subject is Charles West, *Communism and the Theologians.*

### NOTES TO CHAPTER SIX

1  For example, A. M. Schlesinger, Jr., *Crisis of the Old Order,* chap. 24.

2  A basic bibliography would include: Granville Hicks, *Where We Came Out* (New York: Viking, 1954); Murray Kempton, *Part of Our Time* (New York: Simon and Schuster, 1955); Daniel Aaron, *Writers on the Left*

(New York: Harcourt, Brace & World, 1961); Christopher Lasch, *The New Radicalism in America* (New York: Knopf, 1965); John Chamberlain, *Farewell to Reform* (New York: John Day, 1932).

3   In the literal sense, too, Niebuhr found a place for Tillich at Union Theological Seminary. Hearing of Tillich's removal by the Nazi government from the University of Frankfurt, Niebuhr persuaded the faculty of Union to have him brought to the Seminary from his place of exile in the Baltic in November of 1933. Tillich at that time did not speak English. Tillich, "Autobiographical Reflections," 16, and Tillich's contribution to Landon, ed., 29–30.

4   "Intellectual Autobiography," 9–10.

5   See especially, Morton White, *Social Thought in America: The Revolt Against Formalism* (Boston: Beacon Press, 1949); revised paperback edition, 1957), pp. 247–74; and W. H. Dray, *Philosophy of History* (Englewood Cliffs, N.J.: Prentice Hall, 1964), chap. 8. Professor White blames this "thunderous cannot" of Niebuhr's *Moral Man*, and "the dark theory of human nature which it has fostered" for doing irreparable damage to the whole attempt to establish a respectable political philosophy for Americans. Niebuhr (together with Walter Lippmann) in Morton's opinion has derailed the hopeful work of Dewey and his followers and led moral philosophy in America into its present "smoggier climate." The phrases in quotation marks are from the section cited and from the Preface, pp. x–xi.

6   Victor Gollancz, *My Dear Timothy* (London: Gollancz, 1952), pp. 242–43. Among the religious and theological critics of Niebuhr's "thunderous cannot," the reader is referred to: H. D. Lewis, *Morals and the New Theology* (London: Gollancz, 1947); D. G. Bloesch, "Reinhold Niebuhr's Re-evaluation of the Apologetic Task" (unpublished dissertation, University of Chicago, 1956); E. J. Carnell, *The Theology of Reinhold Niebuhr* (Grand Rapids, Michigan: Eerdmans, 1951); G. H. C. Macgregor, *The Relevance of an Impossible Ideal: An Answer to the Views of Reinhold Niebuhr* (1941); "Fellowship of Reconciliation," revised ed. (Nyack, New York: 1960).

7   Kegley and Bretall, *Niebuhr*, p. 301.

8   "Communism and the Clergy," *Christian Century* (August 19, 1953), 937.

9   RN, "Biblical Faith and Socialism: A Critical Appraisal," in Walter Leibrecht, ed., *Religion and Culture: Essays in Honor of Paul Tillich* (New York: Harper's, 1959).

10  *Reflections on the End of an Era* (New York: Scribner's, 1934).

11  *Beyond Tragedy* (1937) and *Discerning the Signs of the Times* (1946).

12  *Reflections*, 127–31.

13  "The Religion of Communism," *Atlantic Monthly* (April 1931), 462–70.

14  Ibid.

15  Ibid.

16  On this theme, see further, "Mr. Laski Proceeds," review of H. Laski, *The State in Theory and Practice* in *Nation* (March 20, 1935), 338–39; "The Pathos of Liberalism," *Nation* (September 11, 1935), 303–04; "The Blindness of Liberalism," *Radical Religion* (Autumn, 1936); "Jerome Frank's Way Out," A review of J. Frank, *Save America First* in *Nation* (July 9, 1938), 45–46.

17  "Russia Makes the Machine Its God" (September 10, 1930), 1080–81; "Russia's Tractor Revolution" (September 17, 1930), 1111–12; "The Church in Russia" (September 24, 1930), 1144–46; "Russian Efficiency" (October 1, 1930), 1178–80; "The Land of Extremes" (October 15, 1930), 1241–43.

18  "Russia Makes the Machine Its God."

19  "The Church in Russia."

20  Ibid.

21  "Our Romantic Radicals," *Christian Century* (April 10, 1935), 474–76. Niebuhr develops this critique of the hazards of Marxist dogmatism in subsequent articles in the *World Tomorrow*: "Radicalism and Religion" (October 1931), 324–27; "After Capitalism—What?" (March 1, 1933), 203–05; "A Reorientation of Radicalism" (July 1933), 443–44; "A New Strategy for Socialists" (August 31, 1933), 490–92; "Marxism and Religion" (March 15, 1933), 253–55; "Making Radicalism Effective" (December 21, 1933), 682–84. Some of Niebuhr's most effective writing on this theme is in his reviews of books on Soviet Russia and on Communism in the presses in those days: "The Life of Lenin," review of F. Ossendowski, *Lenin, God of the Godless*, and G. Vernadsky, *Lenin, Red Dictator*, in *World Tomorrow* (August 1931), 265–66; "Events and the Man," review of L. Trotsky, *The History of the Russian Revolution* in *World Tomorrow* (July 1932), 210; "Waldo Frank in Russia," review of W. Frank, *Dawn in Russia*, in *World Tomorrow* (September 14, 1932), 261–62; "A Communist Manifesto," review of W. Z. Foster, *Toward Communist America* in *World Tomorrow* (October 26, 1932), 404–05; "Still on Probation," review of S. Anderson, *Beyond Desire* in *World Tomorrow* (November 30, 525–26; "Trotsky's Classic," review of L. Trotsky, *History of the Russian Revolution*, in *World Tomorrow* (February 1, 1933), 116–17; "The Ablest Interpreter of Marx," review of S. Hook, *Towards the Understanding of Karl Marx* in *World Tomorrow* (August, 1933), 476.

22  "The Question of the United Front," *Radical Religion* (Winter 1935–36), 2.

23  RN, "Religion and Marxism," *Modern Monthly* (clipping, not dated, in Niebuhr Papers). Judging from a reference in the editor's introduction to Niebuhr as the author of *Reflections on the End of an Era*, the article is not earlier than 1935. As *Modern Monthly* was the theoretical journal of the Communist Party, U.S.A., this article (the only one, to my knowledge, that Niebuhr wrote for that journal) is evidence that he was not a man to alter his message to suit the bias of his congregation. (It is also evidence that the pages of American Marxist journals of those days of the Popular Front were open to a certain amount of deviant preaching, provided the preacher was a man of some stature outside the fold.)

24  *Reflections*, p. 253.

25  Ibid., p. 144.

26  Ibid., p. 254.

NOTES TO CHAPTER SEVEN

1  From a letter to the author, January 8, 1962.

2  "Socialism and Christianity," *Christian Century* (August 19, 1931), 1038–40.

3  Notably: "Radicalism and Religion," World Tomorow (October 1931), 324–27; "The Ethic of Jesus and the Social Problem," Religion in Life (Spring 1932), 198–209; "After Capitalism—What?" World Tomorrow (March 1, 1933), 203–205; "Marxism and Religion," World Tomorrow March 15, 1933), 253–55; "Why German Socialism Crashed," Christian Century (April 5, 1933) 451–53; "A New Strategy for Socialists," World Tomorrow (August 31, 1933), 490–92; "A Reorientation of Radicalism," World Tomorrow (July 1933), 443–44; "The Germans: Unhappy Philosophers in Politics," American Scholar (October 1933), 409–19; "Making Radicalism Effective," World Tomorrow (December 21, 1933), 682–84; "Religion as a Source of Radicalism," Christian Century (April 11, 1934), 491–94; "The Fellowship of Socialist Christians," World Tomorrow (June 14, 1934), 297–98; "The Church and Political Action," Christian Century (August 1, 1934), 992–94; "Marx, Barth, and Israel's Prophets," Christian Century (January 30, 1935), 138–40; "Mr. Laski Proceeds," a review of Harold Laski, The State in Theory and Practice, Nation (March 20, 1935), 338–39; "The Revival of Feudalism," Harper's (March, 1935), 483–88; "Is Religion Counter-Revolutionary?" Radical Religion (Fall 1935), 14–20; "Radical Religion," Radical Religion (Fall 1935), 3–5; "The Blindness of Liberalism," Radical Religion (Fall 1936); "Pawns for Fascism—Our Lower Middle Class," American Scholar (Spring 1937), 145–52; "Socialist Decision and the Christian Conscience," Radical Religion (Spring 1938), 1–2; "Anatomy of Power," review of Bertrand Russell, Power: A New Social Analysis, Nation (October 1, 1938), 326.

4  "Stakes in the Election," Christian Century (November 9, 1932), 1379–81.

5  New York Times (September 30, 1932), 13:3.

6  "After Capitalism—What?" World Tomorow (March 1, 1933).

7  "[Roosevelt seemed to me] a little shady—on the dishonest side. I remember talking to a lawyer friend of mine; and we decided that he and Lloyd George were just alike. They were both very shrewd, and they were both skating on the thin edge of dishonesty." Author's conversation with Niebuhr, 1962.

8  Reflections, pp. 56, 77–81. On this same theme of the inevitability of fascism in America, see: "After Capitalism—What?"; "A Re-orientation of Radicalism,"; "Making Radicalism Effective," "The Revival of Feudalism," Harper's (March 1935), 483–88; "Is Social Conflict Inevitable?" Scribner's (September 1935), 66–69; "The Blindness of Liberalism,"; "Pawns for Fascism: Our Lower Middle Classes"; "Jerome Frank's Way Out."

9  "When the Virtues are Vices," Christian Century (January 21, 1931), 114–15.

10  June Bingham, Courage to Change, p. 162.

11  From a letter to the author, January 8, 1962.

12  The story is told in Bingham, pp. 163–64. Niebuhr's name was raised during the Party's convention. Niebuhr, who was in Europe at the time his name was put forward, did not get his letter of declination back to New York in time to have his name removed from the primary ballot. He became the Socialist Candidate for Congress from the Upper West Side of New York—but a reluctant and inactive one.

13  "Thomas for President!" letter to the New Republic (August 17, 1932), 22. See also, "Thomas and Nelson Independent Committee," a circular

letter, dated July 16, 1936, which appears in photostat copy in Henry B. Joy, *Our Pro-Socialist Churches*, Detroit, 1937 (privately printed; available at the New York Public Library).

14  I have relied for background on the Socialist Party in these years primarily upon: D. D. Egbert and Stow Persons, eds., *Socialism in American Life* (Princeton: Princeton University Press, 1952), I, esp. chap. 6, "The Background and Development of Marxian Socialism in the United States," by Daniel Bell; David Shannon, *The Socialist Party of America* (New York: Macmillan, 1955); Murray B. Seidler, *Norman Thomas, Respectable Rebel* (Syracuse: Syracuse University Press, 1961), chaps. 4 and 5; Harry Fleischman, *Norman Thomas: A Biography* (New York: W. W. Norton, 1964).

15  Cited from Socialist Party correspondence by Bell, "Background and Development of Marxian Socialism in the United States," 375. This paragraph draws as well on a letter from Norman Thomas to the author, May 19, 1965.

16  Irving Howe and Lewis Coser, *The American Communist Party: A Critical History, 1919–1957* (Boston: Beacon Press, 1957), chap. 8.

17  Shannon, *Socialist Party of America*, pp. 239–40.

18  Ibid., p. 240.

19  Bell, "Background and Development of Marxian Socialism," pp. 376–77.

20  I do not know where a complete file of the *World Tomorrow* might be found—if anywhere. The most complete file, to my knowledge, is at the University of California, Berkeley; but it has gaps—some of them, unfortunately, occurring in these months of immediate interest.

21  *World Tomorrow* (April 12, 1934), 185–86.

22  See especially the issue of April 12, 1934, and Norman Thomas, "What Happened at Detroit" (June 28, 1934), 321.

23  R. L. Roy, *Communism and the Churches* (New York: Harcourt, Brace & World, 1960), pp. 17–18.

24  "The Revolutionary Moment," *American Socialist Quarterly* (June, 1935), 8–13.

25  Shannon, *Socialist Party of America*, p. 245.

26  Arthur M. Schlesinger, Jr., *The Age of Roosevelt* (Boston: Houghton-Mifflin, III, *The Politics of Upheaval*, 1960), 179.

27  "The Conflict in the Socialist Party" (Editorial) *Radical Religion* (Winter 1936).

28  Shannon, *Socialist Party of America*, p. 241; Seidler, *Norman Thomas*, chap. 6.

29  "There were a handful of men and women in the thirties, not members of the Communist Party, whose names on a letter-head constituted a kind of imprimatur for the board of a radical organization, the rally of protest, the appeal for justice, the petition for redress of grievances: Reinhold Niebuhr, Harry F. Ward, Roger Baldwin, Robert Morss Lovett— and J. B. Matthews." Walter Goodman, *The Committee: The Extraordinary Career of the House Committee on Un-American Activities* (New York: Farrar, Strauss and Giroux, 1968), p. 36.

30  J. B. Matthews, *Odyssey of a Fellow Traveller* (1938); reprinted as "American Opinion" pamphlet by Robert Welch (Belmont, Mass.: John Birch Society, 1961), 42.

31 Matthews, *Odyssey*, pp. 76 and 78; Elizabeth Dilling, *Red Network* (published by Elizabeth Dilling, Kenilworth, Illinois, 1934), p. 31.

32 R. L. Roy, *Communism and the Churches*, p. 107.

33 Miller, *American Protestantism*, p. 174.

34 *New York Times* (April 13, 1935), 1; James Wechsler; *Age of Suspicion* (New York: Random House, 1953), 69ff., 77; Bingham, 217; Matthews, 49. See also, Wechsler, *Revolt on the Campus* (New York: Covici and Friede, 1935).

35 Miller, *American Protestantism*, chap. 5. The comment of Kirby Page is in Miller, p. 64.

36 In addition to the works already cited, see Paul Carter, *The Decline and Revival of the Social Gospel, 1920–1940* (Ithaca: Cornell University Press, 1952).

37 "Communism and the Clergy," *Christian Century* (August 19, 1953), 936–37. This article is *à propos* of Bishop Bromley Oxnam's counter-attack upon J. B. Matthews for his attempt to convince the American people (by convincing the House Un-American Activities Committee) that the Protestant leadership was virtually an arm of the Stalinist conspiracy. One brief excerpt from Niebuhr's article of 1953 is worth having here: "The files of many of us who are targets of the vigilantes, although we have resisted the Communist illusion for two decades, contain evidence that we were once members of organizations which were subsequently dominated by the Communists. But they contain no record of our struggle to prevent this development, or of our withdrawal when it took place." For a taste of what Niebuhr means by being "a target of the vigilantes," see John Benedict, "What Religion??? Does Reinhold Niebuhr Peddle?/ It has More Communism than Christianity," *American Mercury* (October, 1959), 18–27.

38 *Daily Worker* (New York, Wednesday, April 17, 1935), 1.

39 "The Moscow Trials" (Editorial), *Radical Religion* (Spring 1937); review of *Traitors on Trial, Verbatim Report of the Moscow Trials, Radical Religion* (Summer 1938), 38–39.

40 Niebuhr's side of the story is told in his journal, *Radical Religion* (Summer 1939), and in Bingham, *Courage to Change*, pp. 214–15. The story of the struggle for control of the Union can be followed in the *New York Times*, which gave it copious coverage during 1939; the most important references are: (January 4), 23:5; (January 6), 8:5; (January 20), 1:4; (March 5), 2:2; (April 28), 1:3; (April 29), 19:8; (May 24), 25:5; (May 28), 4:4; and (December 15), 22:2.

41 Roy, *Communism and the Churches*, esp. chaps. 5, 8 and 9.

42 The story is told in Charles Garrett, *The La Guardia Years: Machine and Reform Politics in New York City* (New Brunswick, N.J.: Rutgers University Press, 1961), chap. 13, esp. pp. 270–71. Niebuhr's role is described in Bingham, pp. 215–17. As this is written (1969) Gerson is executive editor of the *Daily World*, the Communist Party's newspaper in New York.

43 "Socialists and Communists" (Editorial), *Radical Religion* (Summer 1937).

NOTES TO CHAPTER EIGHT

1  The Fellowship's statement of Principles went through several revisions over the decade. The quotations just given are from the provisional declaration of 1931, which is to be found in *The Churchman* (an independent journal representing liberal Episcopalians) (January 2, 1932). It is reproduced in part in Carter, *Decline and Revival of the Social Gospel*, pp. 155–56. Subsequent Declarations tend to be increasingly moderate, less Marxist, less "catastrophic" in tone [e.g., *Radical Religion* (Winter issue, 1936), Ibid. (Winter 1937).] See also Niebuhr's article, "The Fellowship of Socialist Christians," World Tomorrow (June 14, 1934), 297–98. RN's own appraisal of this history of F.S.C., is in an article, "Christian Faith and Social Action," in J. A. Hutchison, ed., *Christian Faith and Social Action* (New York: Scribner's, 1953).

2  Meyer, *Protestant Search*, p. 177.

3  Reports on both types of activities appeared in every issue of the Fellowship's quarterly paper, *Radical Religion*. My description of the Fellowship's activities is based upon a careful examination of that paper for the period under review.

4  See the "Oral Memoir" of H. L. Mitchell, in Oral Research Library, Columbia University, New York, 40–41.

5  Miller, *American Protestantism*, pp. 248ff.

6  The story is told in Sherwood Eddy's *Eighty Adventurous Years*, 155ff. See also, "The Delta Cooperative Farm" (Editorial), *Radical Religion* (Summer 1938), and "Meditations from Mississippi," *Christian Century* (February 19, 1937), 183–84. Niebuhr was President of Cooperative Farms, Inc. Evidence that Niebuhr's interest in the cooperative movement goes back to 1929 at least, and that he had studied the theory and practice of cooperativism with some care, is in RN Papers (especially, W. P. Hapgood to RN, February 4, 1929). A large file in these Papers contains abundant illustration of the many headaches that there were in this position for Niebuhr: the constant obligation of fund-raising, legal and other squabbles with hostile neighbors in the Delta, the badgering of trade-union ideologists about Cooperative Farm's wage policies, and so on. I suspect that Niebuhr's experience in this venture had something to do with tempering his enthusiasm for socialism as a practical solution to problems of economic justice (though I confess that Niebuhr himself, in our conversation of 1962, did not recall that it did). In any case, Cooperative Farms, Inc., eventually ran afoul of that other beneficiary of the F.S.C.'s goodwill and money, the Southern Tenant Farmers' Union, and lived as well under the cloud of local resentment for its defiance of racial segregation. It eventually had to be sold out to individual ownership. (An intriguing description of the continuing troubles of Delta Cooperative in the 1950s is in Murray Kempton, *America Comes of Middle Age* (Boston: Little, Brown, 1963), 137ff. Of course, the question whether cooperatives undertaken within a capitalist community provide significant evidence of the socialist potential in men is still a wide-open one among socialists. But it does seem that Niebuhr (whom Eddy describes as an "impatient" man in *Eighty Adventurous Years*, pp. 202–203) begins to betray the first unmistakable indications of his doubts about the practicability of socialism about the time that Cooperative Farms, Inc., was facing its own diffi-

culties—which is to say, the early 1940s. It is worth noting, in passing, that Sherwood Eddy, pp. 157–58, believed that the Delta experiment provided inspiration for several of the experiments in community rescue which Franklin Roosevelt undertook in the later years of the New Deal. There is some supportive evidence for this argument in J. Lash, *Eleanor and Franklin* (New York: Norton, 1972), pp. 459–60.

7 *New York Times* (May 6 and 9, 1932). See also, "Religion and the Class War in Kentucky," *Christian Century* (May 18, 1932), 637–38.

8 *New York Times* (December 19, 1932), 13:1.

9 For example: *New York Times* (April 18, 1933), 17:2; (April 20, 1933), 15:3; (May 9, 1934), 21:2.

10 "Niebuhr Questions the Vitality of Protestant Religion," *Newsweek* (April 29, 1933), 28.

11 The minor shifts in Niebuhr's political philosophy before the end of the decade can be followed through the following articles: "Is Religion Counter-Revolutionary?" (Autumn 1935); "The Idea of Progress and Socialism" (Spring 1936); "The Conflict in the Socialist Party" (Winter 1936); "Socialist Decision and the Christian Conscience" (Editorial: Spring 1938); "The Creed of Modern Christian Socialists" (Spring 1938).

12 "The Relief Situation" (Editorial: Summer 1937).

13 "A New Party?" (Editorial: Fall 1937).

14 "Roosevelt's Merry-Go-Round" (Editorial: Spring 1938).

15 "The Domestic Situation" (Editorial: Summer 1938).

16 "The Political Campaign" (Editorial), *Radical Religion* (Fall 1936).

17 "The National Election" (Editorial), *Radical Religion* (Winter 1936).

18 "The Supreme Court" (Editorial), *Radical Religion* (Spring 1937).

19 See, for example, "The Relief Situation" (Editorial: Summer 1937); "The Administration and the Depression" (Editorial: Winter 1937); "Roosevelt's Merry-Go-Round" (Editorial: Spring 1938).

20 "A New Party?" (Editorial: Fall 1937).

21 Ibid.

22 "The Socialist Party and the Labor Movement" (Editorial: Winter 1937).

23 Ibid.

24 "The Roosevelt Purge" (Editorial: Fall 1938).

25 "The Recent Election" (Editorial: Winter 1938).

26 Howe and Coser, *The American Communist Party*, chap. 8.

27 "The Socialist Party" (Editorial: Winter 1938).

NOTES TO CHAPTER NINE

1 *Reflections*, p. 28.

2 "Germany Wrestles with her Debts," *Christian Century* (July 30, 1930), 934–36; "Church Currents in Germany," *Christian Century* (August 6, 1930), 959–60; "The German Crisis," *Nation* (October 1, 1930), 358–60; "Germany—Prophecy of Western Civilization," *Christian Century* (March 2, 1932), 287–89; "Why German Socialism Crashed," *Christian Century* (April 5, 1933), 451–53; "Hitlerism—A Devil's Brew," *World Tomorrow* (April 19, 1933), 369–70; "The Opposition in Germany." *New Republic*

(June 28, 1933), 169–71; "Notes from a Berlin Diary," *Christian Century* (July 5, 1933), 872–73; "The Germans: Unhappy Philosophers in Politics," *American Scholar* (October, 1933), 409–19.

3  "Why German Socialism Crashed."

4  Ibid.

5  The events to which Niebuhr refers are well described in Lewis J. Edinger, *German Exile Politics: The Social Democratic Executive Committee in the Nazi Era* (Berkeley and Los Angeles: University of California, 1956), p. 241, and in Gerhard Ritter, *The German Resistance* (New York: Praeger, 1958), pp. 41ff.

6  "Why German Socialism Crashed." See also, *Reflections*, chap. 12.

7  "Why German Socialism Crashed." See also report of a public address by RN, *New York Times* (November 7, 1933), 15:3.

8  "Pawns for Fascism—Our Lower Middle Class," *American Scholar* (Spring 1937), 145–52.

9  Which Way, Great Britain?—Will it be France or Germany? War or Peace?" *Current History* (November, 1936), 35–39. See also, "English and German Mentality—A Study in National Traits," *Christendom* (Spring 1936), 465–76.

10  Conversation with Niebuhr, 1962.

11  "Christianity and Contemporary Politics," *Christian Century* (April 17, 1924), 498–501.

12  "Crisis in British Socialism," *Christian Century* (September 30, 1931), 1202–04.

13  See further, *Reflections*, pp. 51, 68, 72.

14  "Awkward Imperialists," *Atlantic Monthly* (May 1930), 670–75.

15  This proposition can be tested by reference to the pages of the *New Republic* or the *Nation* of those years; or, as a short-cut approach, to Selig Adler, *The Isolationist Impulse* (1957) (New York: Macmillan, Free Press edition, 1967).

16  "Awkward Imperialists."

17  "Perils of American Power," *Atlantic Monthly* (January 1932), 90–96.

18  From a report of a speech by Niebuhr to the Community Church in New York, *New York Times* (March 11, 1929), 28:1.

19  "Perils of American Power."

20  Ibid.

21  Ibid.

22  Ibid.

23  "Economic Perils to World Peace," *World Tomorrow* (May 1931), 154–56.

24  Ibid.

25  Ibid. See also a report of a speech by Niebuhr before the Foreign Policy Association, in *New York Times* (December 21, 1930), II, 6:5; and, on the same speech, *New Republic* (December 31, 1930), 175–76.

26  On this theme, see especially: "A Critique of Pacifism," *Atlantic Monthly* (May 1927), 637–641; "Pacifism and the Use of Force," *World Tomorrow* (May 1928), 218–20; "Christian Pacifism," review of L. Richards, *The Christian's Alternative to War*, *World Tomorrow* (May 1929), 234–35; "The Ethic of Jesus and the Social Problem," *Religion in Life* (Spring 1932), 198–209; "Must We Do Nothing?" *Christian Century* (March 30,

1932), 415–17: "Moralists and Politics," *Christian Century* (July 6, 1932), 857–59.

27 "Why I am Not a Christian," *Christian Century* (December 15, 1927), 1482–83.

28 Letter to the *New Republic* (February 22, 1922), 372.

29 "What Chance Has Gandhi?" *Christian Century* (October 14, 1931), 1274–76; *Moral Man*, 242ff.
    Interestingly, Niebuhr used similar arguments in a prophetic anticipation of the relevance that the Gandhian technique would have in the struggle for civil rights which lay ahead of the American Negro. (*Moral Man*, 252ff: "The emancipation of the Negro race in America probably waits upon the adequate development of this kind of social and political strategy.")

30 *Moral Man*, esp. chaps. 8 and 9.

31 This is the language of Niebuhr's most careful presentation of his views on Christian ethics, *An Interpretation of Christian Ethics* (1935). The most effective theological retort to Niebuhr's ethical formulation is, in my opinion, G. H. C. Macgregor, *The Relevance of an Impossible Ideal* (1941); also worth reading are: H. D. Lewis, *Morals and the New Theology* (1947); and John H. Yoder, "Reinhold Niebuhr and Christian Pacifism" (pamphlet published by "Concern," Scottdale, Pennsylvania, 1961).

32 "When Will Christians Stop Fooling Themselves?" *Christian Century* (May 16, 1934), 658–60.

33 The F.O.R. had absorbed the Fellowship for a Christian Social Order, in 1928.

34 On the F.O.R. split of 1933–34, see John K. Nelson, *The Peace Prophets: American Pacifist Thought, 1919–1941* (Chapel Hill: University of North Carolina Press, 1967), 73–79; Joseph B. Matthews, *Odyssey of a Fellow Traveller* (1938), reprinted as "American Opinion" pamphlet by Robert Welch (Belmont, Mass.: John Birch Society, 1961); Meyer, *Protestant Search*, chap. 12; Roy, *Communism and the Churches*, pp. 87ff.; and the following articles: "A Regrettable Rupture," *Christian Century* (January 10, 1934); E. B. Chaffee, "Pacifism at the Crosroads," *Christian Century* (November 15, 1933); A. L. Swift, "Fellowship Reverberations," *World Tomorrow* (January 18, 1934); E. B. Chaffee, "Why I Stay in the F.O.R.," *Christian Century* (January 3, 1934); J. C. Bennett, "That Fellowship Questionnaire," *World Tomorrow* (December 21, 1933); Kirby Page, "The Future of the Fellowship," *World Tomorrow* (January 4, 1934); Francis Henson, "A Dialectical Marxist Interpretation," *World Tomorrow* (January 4, 1934); RN, "Why I Leave the F.O.R.," *Christian Century* (January 3, 1934); J. B. Matthews, "An Open Letter to Kirby Page," *World Tomorrow* (January 18, 1934).

35 Meyer, *Protestant Search*, chap. 12; Roy, *Communism and the Churches*, pp. 87ff.

36 *New York Times* (December 23, 1933), 7:2.

37 "Why I Leave the F.O.R.," *Christian Century* (January 3, 1934), 17–19; and reply to correspondence, January 31, 1934, 155; "When Will Christians Stop Fooling Themselves?" "An Editorial Conversation," (July 26, 1933), 950–51 and further continued August 9, 1006–08.

38 "Why I Leave the F.O.R."

39 Ibid.

American Activities Committee), *Special Report on Subversive Activities Aimed at Destroying our Representative Form of Government* (Washington, D.C. 1942).

35  The first of these appeared as a Supplement to the *New Republic*, "A Congress to Win the War" (May 18, 1942): Goodman, *The Committee*, 134; Clymer, *Union for Democratic Action*, pp. 36ff.

36  Ironically, these same techniques have been successfully imitated in recent years by the conservative wing, notably by the organization called Americans for Constitutional Action, and the Conservative Party (of New York State).

37  Clymer, *Union for Democratic Action*, pp. 46ff.; U.D.A. Press Releases: August 9, 1942 and October 9, 1942; *New York Times* (August 9, 1942), 30:2; (October 7, 1942), 17:1; *et passim*.

38  Clymer, *Union for Democratic Action*, pp. 75ff.; *New York Times* (May 1, 1944), 34:4; (May 21, 1944), 1:3, 38; (July 28, 1944), 10:6–7.

39  The most useful source on the Liberal Party at this writing is an unpublished Ph.D. dissertation by Irvin H. Flournoy, "The Liberal Party in New York State" (Princeton University, 1956) (University Microfilms: Ann Arbor, Michigan, Doctoral Dissertation Series, no. 20, 115). Valuable discussions on the origin of the Liberal Party and its relations with both U.D.A. and A.L.P. are in Charles Garrett, *The LaGuardia Years*, esp. pp. 292ff.; Danish, *Dubinsky*, pp. 139–42, *et passim*.

40  A letter to the author, January 10, 1962.

41  Clymer, *Union for Democratic Action*, pp. 79ff. On A.D.A., the best source is Clifton Brock, *Americans for Democratic Action* (Washington, D.C.: Public Affairs Press, 1962). Brock discusses the relationship between U.D.A. and A.D.A. 49ff. See also, Robert Bendiner, "The Revolt of the Middle," *Nation* (January 18, 1947); James Wechsler, *Age of Suspicion*, pp. 211ff.; A. M. Schlesinger, Jr., *The Vital Center* (Boston: Houghton-Mifflin, 1949); RN, "The A.D.A. and the Liberal-Democratic Movement in the Past Decade," unpublished manuscript, Niebuhr Papers (Box I, "A.D.A." and related papers).

42  *New York Times* (January 5, 1947), 5:1–2; and Brock, *Americans for Democratic Action*, p. 51.

43  This list of Niebuhr's affiliations during the forties is by no means exhaustive. It is pieced together from news items appearing during these years in the *New York Times*, from the Niebuhr Papers and with some assistance from Bingham, *Courage to Change*, chaps. 17–22.

44  Author's conversation with Niebuhr, 1962; Bingham, *Courage to Change* chaps. 17–22; contributions of Schlesinger and Bennett to Kegley and Bretall, *Niebuhr*.

45  General sources include: Laura Fermi, *Illustrious Immigrants: 1930–41* (Chicago: University of Chicago Press, 1968); David S. Wyman, *Paper Walls: America and the Refugee Crisis* (Amherst: University of Massachusetts Press, 1969); Lewis J. Edinger, *German Exile Politics; the Social Democratic Executive Committee in the Nazi Era* (Berkeley and Los Angeles: University of California Press, 1956).

46  Fermi, *Illustrious Immigrants*, p. 26.

47  Bingham, *Courage to Change*, p. 169; James Wechsler, *Age of Suspicion*, pp. 113ff.

48  Edinger, *German Exile Politics*, pp. 24ff.; Gerhard Ritter, *The German Resistance* (New York: Praeger, 1958), 41ff.

49  Fermi, *Illustrious Immigrants*, pp. 63ff.

50  *New York Times* (August 15, 1940).

51  This is the subject of Edinger, *German Exile Politics.*

52  Melvyn Douglas to RN, February 13, 1940; RN to Douglas, February 20, 1940; RN to Mrs Louis J. Reizenstein, May 6, 1940; same, May 14, 1940; Anna Caples to RN, May 13, 1940; RN to George L. Warren, President's Advisory Committee on Refugees, November 6, 1940; Paul Hagen to RN, March 14, 1941; Erika Mann to RN, December 1, 1941; RN to Erika Mann, December 19, 1941; Paul Hagen to RN, October 5, 1943; RN to Wm. Bohn (Editor of the *New Leader*), October 6, 1943; Stanley M. Rinehart, Jr. to RN, February 28, 1944; RN to Rinehart, February 29, 1944. Also, *New Leader* (February 10, 1943) and (September 11, 1943); and *Daily Worker* (August 12, 1943).

53  Emil Brunner, "Some Remarks on Reinhold Niebuhr's Work as a Christian Thinker," in Kegley and Bretall, *Niebuhr*, 28.

54  *The Nature and Destiny of Man: A Christian Interpretation*, I, 1941; II, 1943 (New York: Scribner's).

55  Bingham, *Courage to Change*, p. 25; Kenneth Thompson," The Political Philosophy of R.N.," in Kegley and Bretall, *Niebuhr*, 163.

56  Bingham, *Courage to Change*, p. 277.

57  Niebuhr Papers, Box 22.

58  The books of Niebuhr's old age are, it seems to me, efforts to re-work more deliberately some of the sub-themes of the *Nature and Destiny of Man*. In the meanwhile, however, he had taken from him the great reserves of physical strength that had made possible the writing of *Nature and Destiny*. Unlike his only peers in the field of twentieth-century Protestant thought (Barth, Brunner, Bultmann, Tillich) he was not to have a third creative phase for harvesting the fruits of the scholarship of his creative youth and middle years.

59  *Inter alia*: D. G. Bloetsch, "R.N.'s Re-evaluation of the Apologetic Task" (unpublished Ph.D. dissertation, University of Chicago, 1956). Kenneth Hamilton, "R.N.'s Doctrine of Man" (unpublished Ph.D. dissertation, University of Toronto, 1965). Hans Hoffmann, *The Theology of R.N.*, translated by L. P. Smith (New York: Scribner's, 1956). Theodore Minnema, "The Social Ethics of R.N." (Grand Rapids: Eerdmans, 1959). M. F. Thelan, *Man as Sinner in Contemporary Theology* (New York: King's Crown Press, 1946), pp. 75–81; and the following essays from the volume edited by Kegley and Bretall: Emil Brunner, "Some Remarks on R.N.'s Work as a Christian Thinker;" Paul Tillich, "R.N.'s Doctrine of Knowledge;" John C. Bennett, "R.N.'s Social Ethics;" Paul Ramsay, "Love and Law;" Alan Richardson, "R.N. as Apologist;" William J. Wolf, "R.N.'s Doctrine of Man;" Paul Lehmann, "The Christology of R.N.;" Henry N. Weiman, "A Religious Naturalist Looks at R.N.;" E. A. Burt, "Some Questions about Niebuhr's Theology;" Gustave Weigel, "Authority in Theology."

60  Brunner, "Some Remarks on R.N.'s work," 29.

61  "Niebuhr has convinced himself and many others that his theology is basically kerygmatic and not ontological whereas only its language is kerygmatic. His theology is none the less ontological for not being con-

# Notes to Chapter Twelve

Man," 361.

62  Bloesch, "R.N.'s Re-evaluation," esp. 12ff; Minnema, "Social Ethics of
R.N.," esp. 112ff.

63  Emil Brunner to RN, March 23, 1938.

64  Heinz Zahrnt, The Question of God: Protestant Theology in the Twentieth Century, chap. 2; William Nicholls, Systematic and Philosophical Theology, pp. 109–116, 139ff.; Gerhard Ritter, The German Resistance, pp. 49–53; Will Herberg, "The Social Philosophy of Karl Barth," in K. Barth, Community, State and Church, 1960 (Gloucester, Mass.: Peter Smith, 1968), 38–55; Eberhard Bethge, Dietrich Bonhoeffer (New York: Harper and Row, 1970), esp. chaps. 7–9.

65  Quoted in Nicholls, Systematic and Philosophical Theology, p. 111.

66  Gerhard Ritter (himself an active "Confessing Christian" from the beginning) writes: "To stand up against secular authority was a new experience for German Lutheranism and one in contradiction of all its traditions." German Resistance, 50.

67  Quoted by Herberg, "Social Philosophy of Karl Barth," 38.

68  Nicholls, Systematic and Philosophical Theology, 113–14; K. Barth, "An Outing to Bruderholz," in Fragments Grave and Gay, 71–94.

69  Cited in Nicholls, Systematic and Philosophical Theology, p. 113.

70  Ibid.

71  Ibid., p. 114.

72  Ibid., pp. 114–16, 139ff.; Zahrnt, The Question of God, pp. 60–68.

73  Ibid. (quoting Barth), p. 56.

74  Ibid., p. 56.

75  Edward B. Fiske, "Karl Barth Dies in Basel," New York Times (December 11, 1968).

76  Dietrich Bonhoeffer, No Rusty Swords: Letters, Lectures and Notes 1928–36, edited by Edwin H. Robertson (New York: Harper and Row, 1965), 222–23.

77  There is, incidentally, a rather cruel slander on the loose in some quarters (hinted at, for instance, in a footnote in Sarvapali Radhakrishnan, Recovery of Faith [New York: Harper and Row, 1955, 71n]) to the effect that Barth was himself indifferent to the Nazis' anti-semitism. On the contrary, he spoke out against anti-semitism from the beginning. But it does not seem that it was until 1938 that he had moved the "Jewish question" over from the category of those issues that are properly outside of theological concern (being a part of "the National-Socialist ordering of state and society") to become (by 1938) a matter of "sin against the Holy Spirit" (cited by Herberg, "Social Philosophy of Karl Barth," 40). The point I have tried to make as regards Bonhoeffer is that Barth's theological formulation provides no basis for treating the "Jewish question" as other than a question in the rightful purview of the state—a mere political question. Nor, on its own premises, could it.

78  Ibid., 223, emphasis added.

79  Quoted by RN in "Karl Barth and Democracy," Radical Religion (Winter 1938).

80  Herberg, "Social Philosophy of Karl Barth," 47–50.

81  Ibid., 48.

82  Karl Barth, 'A Letter to American Christians," as quoted by Herberg, "Social Philosophy of Karl Barth," 50–53.

83  "Karl Barth and Democracy."

84  Herberg, "Social Philosophy of Karl Barth," 46–47.

85  "Karl Barth on Politics."

86  Herberg, "Social Philosophy of Karl Barth," 13, emphasis added.

87  As quoted by Herberg, "Social Philosophy of Karl Barth," 23.

88  RN, "Reply to Interpretations and Criticism," in Kegley and Bretall, *Niebuhr*, 439.

89  "He is basically a Biblicist, not in the bad sense [i.e., presumably of being a literalist], but in the sense that all his writings continuously refer to the Biblical foundations of Christian faith, and especially of the doctrine of man. He has a rather low evaluation of the non-Biblical literature." Paul Tillich, "Sin and Grace in the Theology of RN," in Harold R. Landon (ed.), *RN: A Prophetic Voice in our Time* (Greenwich, Conn.: Seabury, 1962), 33.

90  "[In Niebuhr], the immediate source of knowledge regarding human nature is not scripture, but the assumed ability in man to make himself his own object of study." Theodore Minnema, *The Social Ethics of Reinhold Niebuhr*, p. 113.

91  Brunner, "Some Remarks on R.N.'s Work," 29.

92  Hamilton, R.N.'s Doctrine of Man," 328, 331.


NOTES TO CHAPTER THIRTEEN

1  RN to Wm. F. Cochran, March 6, 1942.

2  *Nature and Destiny of Man*, II, 307n–308n.

3  *The Children of Light and The Children of Darkness: A Vindication of Democracy and a Critique of its Traditional Defense* (New York: Scribner's, 1944).

4  Clymer, *Union for Democratic Action*, p. 136.

5  A convenient sample of Niebuhr's writings on these themes, down to 1960, is provided in chap. 17 ("The Problem of Economic Power") of Harry Davis and Robert C. Good, eds., *Reinhold Niebuhr on Politics* (New York: Scribner's, 1960). Among his most developed essays on economic policy are: "Plutocracy and World Responsibility," *Christianity and Society* (Fall 1949); "Halfway to What?—An Answer to Critics of the Welfare State," *Nation* (January 14, 1950); "The Christian Faith and the Economic Life of Liberal Society," in A. Dudley Ward, ed., *Goals of Economic Life* (New York: Harper's, 1953); "The Fate of European Socialism," *New Leader* (June 20, 1955); "Neither Adam Smith Nor Karl Marx," *New Leader* (December 23, 1957).

6  "Fourth Term for Roosevelt," *New Statesman and Nation* (May 15, 1943); "Roosevelt's Chances," *Spectator* (August 25, 1944).

7  "My Choice for President" (Letter to the Editor), *New Republic* (February 21, 1944), 245.

8  James M. Burns, *The Deadlock of Democracy: Four Party Politics in America* (Englewood Cliffs: Prentice-Hall, 1963), pp. 173–76.

9   "Roosevelt's Chances," *Spectator* (August 25, 1944).

10  Ibid.

11  *The Call* (September 8, 1944). Thomas's letter and Niebuhr's reply are reproduced in full in Seidler, *Norman Thomas*, pp. 220–24.

12  R.N. and Alan Heimert, *A Nation So Conceived* (1963), pp. 112–13, 115–116. Compare this judgment with the tone of his obituary article on Roosevelt: "The Death of a President," *Christianity and Crisis* (April 30, 1945).

13  For Niebuhr's assessment of the A.D.A.'s place on the political scene at the time of its formation, see "American Scene," *Spectator* (February 14, 1947); and "The Organization of the Liberal Movement," *Christianity and Crisis* (Spring 1947).

14  Brock, *Americans for Democratic Action* (Washington, D.C.: Public Affairs Press, 1962), chap. 7.

15  Ibid., chap. 8.

16  "Halfway to What?"

17  "The Teamsters and Labor's Future," *New Leader* (August 26, 1957). The argument is further developed in "The Meaning of Labor Unity," *New Leader* (March 28, 1955) and in R.N. and Heimert, *A Nation So Conceived*, pp. 118–22.

18  "Halfway to What?"

19  "The Fate of European Socialism," *New Leader* (June 20, 1945).

20  Author's conversation with Niebuhr, 1962.

21  "Frontier Fellowship," *Christianity and Society* (Fall 1948).

22  John Kenneth Galbraith, "Who Needs the Democrats?" *Harper's* (July 1970).

### NOTES TO CHAPTER FOURTEEN

1   "The Possibility of a Durable Peace," *Christianity and Society* (Summer 1943).

2   *Inter alia*: "The Bombing of Germany," *Christianity and Society* (Summer 1943); "Vansittart's Obsession"; a review of Ld. Vansittart's, *Lessons of My Life* in *Nation* (January 1, 1944); "Is the Bombing Necessary?" *Christianity and Crisis* (April 3, 1944); "The German Question," review in *Nation* (November 4, 1944).

3   "The German Problem," *Christianity and Crisis* (January 10, 1944).

4   Edwin H. Robertson, ed., *No Rusty Swords*, p. 22; Bethge, *Bonhoeffer*, pp. 552–66.

5   Gerhard Leibholz to RN, September 24, 1943; H. S. Leiper to RN, September 20, 1945; G. Leibholz to RN, November 4, 1945.

6   For example: Niebuhr felt obliged to defend the record of Pastor Niemöller before the American public, in the aftermath of Mrs. Franklin D. Roosevelt's public statements (Letter to the Editor, *Nation*, April 5, 1947; Letter to the Editor, *New York Times*, October 10, 1947, 24:6).

7   Most of the published (and, for that matter the unpublished) studies of Niebuhr's political thought concentrate on the work of the post-war years—and on the theme of international relations during this period. Readers wanting greater commentary than we give here regarding

Niebuhr's positions on specific issues are referred to: Harry R. Davis, "The Political Philosophy of RN," (unpublished Ph.D. dissertation, Yale University, 1956); Ronald H. Stone, RN: Prophet to Politicians (Nashville: Abingdon, 1972).

8 "Plans for World Reorganization," Christianity and Crisis (October 19, 1942).

9 "American Power and World Responsibility," Christianity and Crisis (April 5, 1943).

10 "The Possibility of a Durable Peace."

11 "Plans for World Reorganization."

12 "The Possibility of a Durable Peace."

13 "American Power and World Responsibility."

14 These views were being put forward in the Senate by Taft as early as 1943, and were gathered together in a book intended to assist Taft's campaign for the Presidency in 1952: Robert A. Taft, A Foreign Policy for Americans (New York: Garden City-Doubleday, 1951).

15 "American Power and World Responsibility."

16 "The Possibility of a Durable Peace."

17 "Anglo-Saxon Destiny and Responsibility," Christianity and Crisis (October 4, 1943).

18 "Plans for World Reorganization."

19 Christian Realism and Political Problems (New York: Scribner's, 1953), pp. 58–59; see also, "The Limits of Military Power," New Leader (May 30, 1955).

20 "The Democratic Elite and American Foreign Policy," in Marquis Childs and James Reston, eds., Walter Lippmann and His Times (New York: Harcourt, Brace & World, 1959).

21 "American Hegemony and the Prospects for Peace," Annals of the American Academy of Political and Social Science (1962).

22 "The Limits of Military Power."

23 Author's conversation with Niebuhr, 1962.

24 "England Teaches Its Soldiers." Nation (August 21, 1943).

25 Paul Hagen to RN, July 3, 1946; Joseph Kaskell to RN, August 15, 1946; RN to Helmut Kuhn, August 15, 1946.

26 RN to Major Klous, War Department, October 7, 1946; RN to Miss Christensen, War Department, October 14, 1946, Wm. Benton (Assistant Secretary of State) to RN, October 15, 1946; also file on "Commission on the Occupied Areas, 1948–1950."

27 Jos. J. Greene (Infantry Journal) to RN, September 5, 1947; RN to W. L. Savage (Scribner's), September 25, 1947; Charles Carroll (Office of Military Government for Bavaria) to RN, November 7, 1947.

28 W. L. Savage to RN, October 7, 1946; RN to Charles P. Arnot (Department of State, U.S.I.A.), October 23, 1952; Sol Hirsch (U.S.I.A.) to RN, February 18, 1955.

29 Author's conversation with Niebuhr, 1962.

30 "Fight for Germany," Life (October 21, 1946): "For Peace We Must Risk War," Life (September 20, 1948).

31 Whittaker Chambers, Witness (New York: Random House, 1952), pp. 86–88, 502–508.

32  Walter LaFeber, *America, Russia, and the Cold War, 1945–1967* (New York: Wiley, 1967), p. 258.

33  A good account of the circumstances is in Theodore H. White, *Fire in the Ashes* (New York: Sloan, 1953), pp. 27–32; see also James F. Byrnes, *Speaking Frankly* (New York: Harper, 1947), chap. 10.

34  Karl M. Schmidt, *Henry Wallace: Quixotic Crusade, 1948* (Syracuse: Syracuse University Press, 1960), 16ff.

35  "Fight for Germany."

36  LaFeber, *America, Russia, and the Cold War*, p. 132.

37  Ibid.

38  "Power and Ideology in National and International Affairs."

39  "A Christian View of the Future," *Harper's* (December 1960).

40  "American Hegemony and the Prospects for Peace."

41  "Revolution in an Open Society," *New Leader* (May 27, 1963).

42  "Well-Tempered Evangelism," *New Republic* (June 26, 1961).

43  Ibid.

44  "A Tentative Assessment: Royalty and Politics," *New Leader* (December 9, 1963).

45  "Have We Gone Soft?" *New Republic* (February 15, 1960).

46  "Berlin and Prestige in Europe," *New Republic* (September 18, 1961).

47  "Cuba: Avoiding the Holocaust" (Editorial), *Christianity and Crisis* (November 26, 1962).

48  RN, *Irony of American History*, p. 21.

49  "Russia and the West," *Nation* (January 16 and January 23, 1943).

50  Ibid.

51  Ibid.

52  'An Essay for our Times," a review of H. S. Hughes, *An Essay for our Times*, *Nation* (March 1, 1950).

53  "Russia and the West," *Nation* (January 16, 1943).

54  J. C. Bennett, "RN's Contribution to Christian Social Ethics," in H. R. Landon, ed., *RN: A Prophetic Voice in Our Time*, 76–77.

55  Author's conversation with Niebuhr, January 23, 1962.

56  RN and Paul E. Sigmund, *The Democratic Experience* (New York: Praeger, 1969), pp. 146–48 and R. H. Stone, *RN: Prophet to Politicians*, pp. 218–19

NOTES TO CHAPTER FIFTEEN

1  Chap. 23 of Bingham's biography provides an extended account of the illness that struck Niebuhr in 1952, and of its effects upon his personal life. It draws on personal acquaintance with Niebuhr, his family, and his friends.

2  RN to S. D. Press, April 26, 1940.

3  Nola Meade (RN's secretary) to Waldo Frank, February 26, 1952; Nola Meade to C. W. Kegley, March 17, 1952.

4  RN to H. P. Van Dusen, May 28, 1953; RN to J. W. Pacey, January 12, 1954.

5   Notably, R. H. Stone, RN: Prophet to Politicians.

6   Faith and History (1949) was reviewed by (among others) Albert Guerard, Perry Miller, Northrop Frye; Irony of American History (1954) by Morton White, Peter Viereck, Crane Brinton, Anthony West, Francis Biddle, Max Beloff, Hebert Agar; The Self and the Dramas of History (1955) by Will Herberg, Charles Frankel; Structure of Nations and Empires (1959) by Robert Strausz-Hupé, Dexter Perkins, Arnold Toynbee, Hans Kohn, Arnold Wolfers; A Nation So Conceived (1963) by J. W. Ward, David Potter, George Lichtheim.

7   "The Religious Traditions of Our Nation," Saturday Evening Post (July 23, 1960); 'America the Smug," Saturday Evening Post (November 16, 1963); "Despair Can be a Source of Danger," Vogue (January 1, 1962). My conviction that he did fail in these articles is based upon impressionistic evidence only: namely, the reactions of those of my relatives who were subscribers, and who attempted to read them out of kindness to me.

8   Louis Minsky (Managing Editor, "Religions News Services") to RN, November 29, 1945; same, March 15, 1946; same, November 20, 1946; same May 15, 1947. RN to Louis Minsky, May 19, 1947; Lee Rosenthal (Editorial Department, RNS) to Nola Meade, January 23, 1948; Louis Minsky to RN, September 30, 1948.

9   Christianity and Crisis (March 7, 1966), 38.

10  "Exit from the Nation," Time (May 21, 1951); RN to Freda Kirchwey, April 26, 1951.

11  Dwight J. Bradley to RN, March 22, 1948.

12  Author's conversation with Niebuhr, January 23, 1962.

13  Morton White, Social Thought in America: The Revolt Against Formalism (Boston: Beacon Press, 1957), p. xi.

14  Victor Lasky, J. F. K.: The Man and the Myth (New York: Macmillan, 1963), p. 277.

15  Richard Rovere, The American Establishment (New York: Harcourt, Brace & World, 1962), p. 13.

16  Address by Honorable Hubert H. Humphrey, Vice-President of the United States, February 25, 1966. Pamphlet, n.d., provided by Office of Vice-President Humphrey, 1966.

17  "Christianity and Crisis," New York Times (February 20, 1966), Section E, 10.

18  Rowland Evans and Robert Novak, Lyndon B. Johnson: The Exercise of Power (New York: New American Library, 1966), pp. 468-69.

19  Bertram Wolfe to RN (including attachments), July 6, 1953, Niebuhr Papers.

20  LaFeber, America, Russia, and the Cold War, p. 258.

21  Ibid., p. 43.

22  Ibid., pp. 132-34.

NOTES TO CHAPTER SIXTEEN

1   RN, "Intellectual Autobiography," in Kegley and Bretall, Niebuhr, 19.

2   There is a considerable number of reviews of books on philosophy of history dating from this period, attesting to some part of the spadework he was doing in the literature. These include: A. Toynbee, A Study of History, IV, V, VI), in Christianity Today (Winter 1939); E. Wilson, To the Finland Station in Nation (September 14, 1940); B. Croce, History as the Story of Liberty in Nation (June 14, 1941); P. A. Sorokin, The Crisis of Our Age in Nation (December 20, 1941); J. Nehru, Glimpses of World History in Nation (August 8, 1942); H. Laski, Faith and Civilization: An Essay in Historical Analysis in Nation (June 17, 1944).

3   Herbert Butterfield, Christianity and History (New York: Scribner's, 1950; Fontana edition, 1957), 98.

4   Cited by RN, Nature and Destiny of Man, II, 310n.

5   Nature and Destiny of Man, II, 310n.

6   Ibid., p. 309.

7   Ibid., p. 308.

8   Ibid., pp. 8–9.

9   Ibid., p. 309.

10  Ibid., pp. 309–10.

11  For Niebuhr's philosophy of history, the principal sources are The Nature and Destiny of Man, especially volume II, chaps. 1–4 and 10; and Faith and History (1949).

12  Faith and History, p. 163.

13  H. G. Wells, as cited by RN, Faith and History, pp. 162–63.

14  Faith and History, chap. 2; The Nature and Destiny of Man, II, 16.

15  Faith and History, p. 105.

16  Karl Popper, The Open Society and Its Enemies, 2nd ed., 1950 (New York: Harper Torchback edition, 1963), II, 269–72.

17  In the following paragraphs, I have attempted a synopsis of Niebuhr's interpretation of American history as it is developed in Pious and Secular America (1958), The Irony of American History (1954), and A Nation So Conceived (1963), and in occasional articles on the theme during the 1950s and 1960s. There are, as well, some sections of Faith and History which deal with American history. I have used footnotes only to acknowledge specific quotations.

18  "Anglo-Saxon Destiny and Responsibility," Christianity and Crisis (October 4, 1943).

19  Irony of American History, p. 21.

20  Ibid., p. 52.

21  Ibid., p. 26.

22  Ibid., p. 27.

23  Ibid., p. 24.

24  Ibid., p. 28.

25  Paul Tillich, Perspectives on Nineteenth and Twentieth Century Protestant Theology (New York: Harper and Row, 1967), p. 3.

26  *Faith and History*, pp. 103–105.

27  Ibid., 104n.

28  Ibid., p. 103.

29  Ibid., p. 85.

30  Ibid., p. 94.

31  Ibid., p. 15.

32  Karl Löwith, *Meaning in History* (Chicago: University of Chicago Press, 1949), and Löwith, "History and Christianity," in Kegley and Bretall, *Niebuhr*.

33  Löwith in Kegley and Bretall, *Niebuhr*, 283–84 (emphasis mine).

34  Ibid., 289.

35  Ibid.

36  Löwith, *Meaning in History*, pp. 191, 144.

37  RN, in Kegley and Bretall, 439.

38  *The Nature and Destiny of Man*, II, 54.

39  Ibid., 49.

40  *Faith and History*, 231–35 (emphasis mine).

41  "The Moral Implications of Loyalty to the United Nations," *Hazen Pamphlet No. 29* (New Haven, 1952), 11–12.

NOTES TO CONCLUSION

1  William Kuhns, *In Pursuit of Dietrich Bonhoeffer* (New York: Doubleday, 1967; Image books ed., 1969), chaps. 1 and 4.

2  E. H. Robertson, ed., *No Rusty Swords: Letters, Lectures and Notes, 1928–36 from the Collected Works of Dietrich Bonhoeffer*, I (New York: Harper and Row, 1965), p. 362.

3  Paul Tillich, *Theology of Culture* (Oxford University Press, 1959), chap. 12.

4  Bonhoeffer, *No Rusty Swords*, I, 91.

5  Ibid., 99.

6  Ibid., 103.

7  Ibid., 104.

8  Ibid., 107.

9  Ibid. (Emphasis in the original.)

10  Ibid., 108.

11  Ibid., 89, 91.

12  Tillich, *Theology of Culture*, pp. 161–63.

13  Bonhoeffer, *No Rusty Swords*, I: 222–23.

14  Tillich, *Theology of Culture*, pp. 167–68.

15  Ibid., p. 168.

16  Ibid.

17  Kegley and Bretall, *Niebuhr*, p. 131.

18  "Halfway to What?" *Nation* (January 14, 1950).

19  Kegley and Bretall, *Niebuhr*, p. 71.

# BIBLIOGRAPHY

1 The Published Works of Reinhold Niebuhr

(a) Books:

*Does Civilization Need Religion? A Study in the Social Resources and Limitations of Religion in Modern Life.* New York: Macmillan, 1927.

*Leaves from the Notebooks of a Tamed Cynic* (Chicago, 1929). New York: Meridian Living Age ed., 1957.

*The Contribution of Religion to Social Work.* New York: Columbia University Press, 1932.

*Moral Man and Immoral Society: A Study in Ethics and Politics* (New York, 1932). New York: Scribner's paperback ed., 1960.

*Reflections on the End of an Era.* New York: Scribner's, 1934.

*An Interpretation of Christian Ethics* (New York, 1935). New York: Meridian Living Age ed., 1956.

\* *Beyond Tragedy: Essays on the Christian Interpretation of History* (New York, 1937). New York: Scribner's paperback ed., 1961.

\* *Christianity and Power Politics.* New York: Scribner's, 1940.

*The Nature and Destiny of Man: A Christian Interpretation,* 2 vols. New York: Scribner's, 1943.

*The Children of Light and the Children of Darkness: A Vindication of Democracy and a Critique of its Traditional Defense* (New York, 1944). New York: Scribner's paperback ed., 1960.

\* *Discerning the Signs of the Times: Sermons for Today and Tomorrow.* New York: Scribner's, 1946.

*Faith and History: A Comparison of Christian and Modern Views of History.* New York: Scribner's, 1949.

*The Irony of American History* (New York, 1952), New York: Scribner's paperback ed., 1961.

\* *Christian Realism and Political Problems.* New York: Scribner's, 1953.

*The Self and the Dramas of History.* New York: Scribner's, 1955.

\* *Pious and Secular America.* New York: Scribner's, 1958.

*The Structure of Nations and Empires.* New York: Scribner's, 1959.

*A Nation So Conceived: Reflections on the History of America from its Early Visions to its Present Power* (with Alan Heimert). New York: Scribner's, 1963.

\* A selection of shorter pieces published earlier.

*Man's Nature and His Communities*. New York: Scribner's, 1965.

*The Democratic Experience: Past and Prospects* (with Paul E. Sigmund). New York: Praeger, 1969.

(b) Collections of Niebuhr's Essays, Assembled by Other Hands

D. B. Robertson, ed. *Love and Justice: Selections from the Shorter Writings of RN*. Philadelphia: Westminster Press, 1957.

—. *Essays in Applied Christianity*. New York: Meridian Living Age ed., 1959.

R. H. Stone, ed. *Faith and Politics: A Commentary on Religious, Social and Political Thought in a Technological Age by RN*. New York: Braziller. 1968.

(c) Essays, Book Reviews, Pamphlets

A truly complete catalogue of Niebuhr's published work would be welcome to scholars, and the present author hopes some day to be able to provide the same in a separate publication. It would be totally impractical to include such a bibliography as an annex to this present work. Some notion of the scope of such a project can be gained from study of the "Bibliography of the Writings of RN to 1956," which was compiled by D. B. Robertson and is appended to C. W. Kegley, R. W. Bretall; *RN: His Religious, Social and Political Thought*. While it runs to twenty-three pages and lists four hundred and sixty-six shorter items for the period 1916 to 1956, it is nowhere near complete. It excludes editorials from three journals (*Radical Religion, Christianity and Society* and *Christian Century*), all of his book reviews, his columns for "Religion News Services," several of his pamphlets, and several of his essays which were published in volumes edited by others. I reckon some 676 shorter items for the same period, and over his entire career some 860. The Robertson bibliography does, however, serve to illustrate the range of themes and of the journals in which Niebuhr published over his fifty-five years, beginning with the "Failure of German-Americanism," in 1916.

II Studies of the Work of Reinhold Niebuhr

(a) Books, Dissertations, Pamphlets

Allen, Edgar L. *Christianity and Society: A Guide to the Thought of RN*. London: Hodder, Stoughton, 1950.

Bingham, June. *Courage to Change: An Introduction to the Life and Thought of RN*. New York: Scribner's, 1961.

Bloesch, D. G. "RN's Re-evaluation of the Apologetic Task," unpublished doctoral dissertation, University of Chicago, 1956.

Carnell, E. J. *Theology of RN*. Grand Rapids, Michigan: Eerdmans, 1951.

David, W. E. "Comparative Study of the Social Ethics of Walter Rauschenbusch and RN," unpublished doctoral dissertation. Vanderbilt University, 1958.

Davies, D. R. *RN: Prophet from America*. London: J. Clark, Co., 1945.

Davis, H. R. "The Political Philosophy of RN," unpublished Ph.D. dissertation. University of Chicago, 1951.

—, and Good, R. C. *RN on Politics*. New York: Scribner's 1960.

Bibliography 275

Gaede, E. A. "RN and the Relationship of Politics and Ethics," unpublished doctoral dissertation. University of Michigan, 1960.

Good, R. C. "The Contribution of RN to the Theory of International Relations," unpublished doctoral dissertation. Yale University, 1956.

Hamilton, Kenneth. "RN's Doctrine of Man," unpublished doctoral dissertation. University of Toronto, 1965.

Hammar, George. Christian Realism in Contemporary American Theology: A Study of RN, W. M. Horton, and H. P. Van Dusen. Uppsala, Sweden: Lundequistska Bokhandeln, 1940.

Harland, Gordon. The Thought of RN. New York: Oxford, 1960.

Hoffman, Hans. The Theology of RN. New York: Scribner's, 1956.

Kegley, C. W. and Bretall, R. W., eds. RN: His Religious, Social and Political Thought. New York: Macmillan, 1956.

Landon, H. R., ed. RN: A Prophetic Voice in Our Time. Greenwich, Conn.: Seabury Press, 1962.

Macgregor, G. H. C. The Relevance of an Impossible Ideal: An Answer to the Views of RN, 1941; Fellowship paperback ed. (revised), 1960, bound together with the same author's New Testament Basis of Pacifism. Nyack, N.Y.: Fellowship of Reconciliation, 1960.

Maier, V. E. "Ideology and Utopia in International Politics: A Critique of the Ethics of International Politics of RN and E. H. Carr," unpublished doctoral dissertation. University of Chicago, 1963.

Minnema, Theodore. The Social .Ethics of RN. Grand Rapids, Michigan: Eerdmans, n.d., probably 1959.

Odegard, H. P. Sin and Science: RN as Political Theologian. Yellow Springs, Ohio: Antioch Press, 1956.

Scott, Nathan A., Jr. RN (in series, "Pamphlets on American Writers," Minneapolis: University of Minnesota Press, 1963).

Stone, Ronald H. RN: Prophet to Politicians. Nashville: Abingdon, 1972.

Thelan, Mary F. Man As Sinner in Contemporary American Realistic Theology. New York: King's Crown Press, 1946.

Vignaux, Georgette. La théologie de l'histoire chez RN. Paris: Délachaux et Niestlé, 1957.

Yoder, John H. RN and Christian Pacifism. A pamphlet published as a "Concern" reprint, by the Church Peace Mission, New York, n.d., c. 1962.

(b) A Selection of Articles and Reviews of Niebuhr's Books (Arranged Chronologically):

Lovett, Robert Morss. "Politics and Ethics," review of Moral Man, New Republic, January 18, 1933.

Chamberlain, John. "Violence and Reform," review of Moral Man, Nation, February 15, 1933.

Lovett, Robert Morss. "The Christian Realist," review of Reflections, New Republic, April 18, 1934.

Burnham, James. "Religion and Pessimism," review of Reflections, Nation, July 11, 1934.

[Chambers, Whittaker.] "Sin Rediscovered," review of *Nature and Destiny of Man*, I, *Time*, March 24, 1941.

—. "Justification of Justice," review of *Nature and Destiny of Man*, II, *Time*, March 1, 1943.

—. "Niebuhr vs. Sin," review of *Discerning the Signs*, *Time*, April 29, 1946.

Schlesinger, A. M., Jr. "Niebuhr's Vision of Our Time," review of *Discerning the Signs*, *Nation*, June 22, 1946.

Sperry, W. L. "The Nature of Time," review of *Faith and History*, *Saturday Review*, June 11, 1949.

Miller, Perry. "The Great Method," review of *Faith and History*, *Nation*, August 6, 1949.

White, Morton. "Of Moral Predicaments," review of *Irony of American History*, *New Republic*, April 5, 1952.

Viereck, Peter. "Freedom is a Matter of Spirit," review of *Irony*, *New York Times*, April 6, 1952.

Smith, T. V. "Of Human Life and Destiny," review of *Christian Realism*, *New York Times*, October 25, 1953.

Miller, W. L. "The Irony of RN," *Reporter*, January 13, 1955.

Herberg, Will. "The Three Dialogues of Man," review of *The Self*, *New Republic*, May 16, 1955.

Thompson, K. W. "Beyond National Interest: A Critical Evaluation of RN's Theory of International Politics," *Review of Politics*, April, 1955.

Hook, Sidney. "Prophet of Man's Glory and Tragedy," review of Kegley and Bretall, *RN*, *New York Times*, January 29, 1956.

Schall, J. V. "The Political Theory of RN," *Thought*, Spring, 1958.

Ramsey, Paul. "A Prophet with Honor in his Own Time and Country," review of Harland, *Thought of RN*, and Davis and Good, eds., *RN on Politics*, *New York Times*, June 19, 1960.

Herberg, Will. "N's Three Phrases," review of Harland, *Thought of RN*, *Christian Century*, August 10, 1960.

Good, R. C. "National Interest and Political Realism: N's 'Debate' with Morgenthau and Kennan," *Journal of Politics*, November 1960.

Herberg, Will. "RN: Burkean Conservative," *National Review*, December 2, 1961.

Marty, Martin. "Thinker and Doer," review of J. Bingham, *Courage to Change*, *New York Times*, December 17, 1961.

McWilliams, W. C. "RN: New Orthodoxy for Old Liberalism," *American Political Science Review*, December 1962.

Scott, Nathan A., Jr. "Always a Ranging and a Robust Mind," review of *Man's Nature and His Communities*, *New York Times Book Review*, November 7, 1965.

(c) A Selection of Obituary Items

"RN, Protestant Theologian Dies," *New York Times*, June 3, 1971.

Novak, Michael. "Niebuhr: Where Men of Courage Might Stand," *New York Times*, June 6, 1971.

MacKaye, Wm. R. "Theologian RN," *Washington Post*, June 3, 1971.

Woodward, Kenneth L. "RN: 1892–1971," *Newsweek*, June 14, 1971.

"Death of a Christian Realist," *Time*, June 14, 1971.

Gordon, J. King. "Portrait of a Christian Realist," *Ottawa Journal*, June 21 and 22, 1971.

III Unpublished Materials

Reinhold Niebuhr Papers, Library of Congress.

Author's conversation with Reinhold Niebuhr, at Harvard University, January 23, 1962. (A transcript from tape recording, in author's possession.)

Author's correspondence with RN. Author's possession.

Author's correspondence with Adolf Berle (January 1962); Norman Thomas (January 1962, and May 1965); Paul Tillich (May 1965); Herbert Lehman (April 1962); Eleanor Roosevelt (April 1962); Hubert Humphrey (January 1962); Ben Davidson (April 1962). Author's possession.

Union for Democratic Action. Scrapbook of U.D.A. press releases. Possession of New York Public Library.

# INDEX